Land Fever

Dispossession and the Frontier Myth

JAMES M. MARSHALL

THE UNIVERSITY PRESS OF KENTUCKY

Publication of this book was made possible by a grant from the University of Rhode Island

Scholarly publisher for the Commonwealth,
serving Bellarmine College, Berea College, Centre College of Kentucky, Eastern Kentucky University, The Filson Club, Georgetown College, Kentucky Historical Society, Kentucky State University, Morehead State University, Murray State University, Northern Kentucky University, Transylvania University, University of Kentucky, University of Louisville, and Western Kentucky University.

Editorial and Sales Offices: Lexington, Kentucky 40506-0024

Library of Congress Cataloging-in-Publication Data

Marshall, James M., 1924-
Land fever.

Bibliography: p.
Includes index.
1. Morse, Omar, 1824-1901. 2. Pioneers—Wisconsin—Biography. 3. Pioneers—Minnesota—Biography. 4. Land tenure—Wisconsin—History—19th century. 5. Land tenure—Minnesota—History—19th century. 6. Wisconsin—Rural conditions. 7. Minnesota—Rural conditions. 8. Frontier and pioneer life—Wisconsin. 9. Frontier and pioneer life—Minnesota. I. Title.
F586.M78M37 1986 977.5'04'0924 [B] 86-4030
ISBN 0-8131-1568-X

Contents

Acknowledgments vii

Part One

Introduction 3

The Autobiography of Omar H. Morse 23

Part Two

1. The Dispossession of the Morse Family 93
2. The Morse Narrative and a Countermyth of Dispossession 124
3. The Repossession: A Creative Recovery of Community 176

Appendix A. Letters to Manly and Anna Morse 189

Appendix B. Morse's Essay on the Philippine Islands 208

Appendix C. Family Record of O.H. Morse 209

Notes 211

Works Consulted 221

Index 229

“ . . . and when arrived at this Heaven in idea what do they find? a goodly land I will allow but to them forbiden land. exhausted and worn down with distress and disappointment they are at last obliged to become Hewers of Wood and Drawers of water.”

Moses Austen, pioneer,
The Western Country in 1793,
ed. Marion Firsling and Godfrey Davis

Acknowledgments

No writer truly works alone, although he may persuade himself that he does. My first debt is to Omar Morse and his family; they significantly increased my understanding of the historical frontier and in so doing introduced me to a community of values, shrouded in hardships and a turbulent economy, which remains our cultural heritage. Our significant literature reflects the critical years of western settlement and its impact on our society in reflecting this transitional culture. In paying this tribute to the Morse family, I acknowledge a great debt to pioneers in all endeavors but especially those homesteaders who created a society of values which such American writers as Mark Twain and William Faulkner were able to introduce into the great tradition of literature.

I wish to acknowledge thanks to Evelyn Morse Peterson for finding and saving her grandfather Omar Morse's autobiography and letters, for establishing proof of his residence in Oswego County, New York, and for permission to publish this unique document in its entirety and edited portions of his letters. I wish also to thank her son, Jerry Peterson, for the use of enlarged copies of Morse photographs. Without Mrs. Peterson's unusual knowledge of Morse family genealogy, his early life and family references would have been lost. My debt to her can never be fully paid; I can only hope that this book will be an acknowledgement of my deepest gratitude.

My debt is also to the University of Rhode Island Research Committee for help that enabled my research in pioneer narratives and in the land records of counties where the Morse family had homesteaded. William Ferrante, Vice-President of Academic Affairs, made a subvention for publication possible through the university Alumni Fund.

Professor David D. Anderson, editor of *MidAmerica* and chairman of the Society for the Study of Midwestern Literature and Culture, has consistently encouraged my work and published articles later incorporated in this book. Without such encouragement and stimulus, there is never a true light at the end of the tunnel.

Without the scholarship of Henry Nash Smith and Paul Gates, I would have abandoned this project as futile; their scholarship pointed the direction that I (and hundreds of others) have followed. Countless research librarians in the several libraries I visited have facilitated my access to the resource materials I sought or, in many instances, would otherwise have wrongly neglected. The friendly staffs of county recorders' offices in obscure midwestern counties remain for me an image of tireless patience; they are the careful guardians of a yet unknown history.

I wish to thank the Newberry Library, Chicago, for permission to publish quotations from their typescript of Joseph Kirkland's letters, and the Minnesota Historical Research Library, St. Paul, for permission to quote from their holdings of Ignatius Donnelly materials. I also wish to acknowledge David D. Anderson, editor, for permission to quote from my articles in *MidAmerica* 9 and 10; and John Dickinson, editor, for permission to quote from an article in *The Old Northwest* (Winter 1980-81).

To friends at the University of Rhode Island I here give my special thanks for years of support even when a serious illness threatened to eliminate all hope of eventual publication. These friends, indeed all who encouraged this book, impressed on me an awareness that a book is never the work of a single hand; one person merely receives credit or blame. It is a collective expression.

PART ONE

Introduction

Land Fever is an analytical study of the relation between the autobiography of a dispossessed homesteader and a pioneer culture's resistance to the loss of the frontier promise of Jeffersonian democracy in the harsh natural and economic wilderness of the expanding West.

The plan of the book further suggests its purpose. Following this introduction, Part One contains the unique, vivid narrative of Omar Morse (1824-1901), a yeoman farmer in frontier Wisconsin and Minnesota, with memories of his youth in a backwoods region of north central New York. The three chapters of part Two offer, first, an objective study of the economic, demographic, and geographic conditions that contributed to the growing Morse family's dispossession from several homesteads; an analysis of the relation of Morse's witness to an evolving theme of dispossession in folk song, literature, and politics; and a summary essay indicating the values of the frontier society, which, with the notable exception of the economically secure few, had become a transient, often dispossessed culture by the 1890s, when Morse wrote his narrative, and which even yet remains shrouded in its own code of stoic ethical silences. The Appendices contain important supplemental material: excerpts from Omar Morse's letters to his son (1895-1900), his essay on the Philippines, and his family genealogy. These reveal an additional depth of character, especially his frontier independence and rebellious view of a gilded age of speculation and corrupt government. These values well served this toughened survivor of economic and social change in his senior years.

Land Fever thus offers a historical and cultural perspective on frontier life through Morse's unique, vivid witness. Like Huckleberry Finn, Morse and the frontier society that he and his family represent searched for the promised freedom of the country, which their daily lives often refuted. Because the myth of the garden of the West had promised them a new life as pioneers of a forthcoming egalitarian civilization, they felt themselves its heroes and heroines, but circumstances denied the passionate hopes that had been encouraged by the myth. Folklorists, frontier scholars, critics of American literature and culture, historians, and the general reader will find here a study revealing the cultural significance of frontier life usually concealed by that persistent guardian of common error—illusion. The purpose of the book is to reveal the unique strength in suffering and loss of a courageous people whose dispossession from homesteads bequeathed a heritage of strength and imaginative strategies of critical awareness in a nineteenth-century United States politically and socially adrift.

The historical context of the Morse narrative further illustrates the conditions of his experience. Thomas Jefferson's confident aspirations for an emergent aristocracy of merit from among the independent western homesteaders underwent sharp reversal with the rise of an aristocracy of wealth from farm, town, and village as well as among established investors, both eastern and western. Omar Morse was soon to experience the effect of this reversal, but when he first set foot on a broad expanse of prairie west of Sheboygan, Wisconsin, he saw a poor farmer's grassland paradise such as compelled his belief in the reality of the frontier myth. The myth of the West, as Henry Nash Smith has described it in *Virgin Land: The American West as Symbol and Myth*, was a garden of the world to be made manifest in the farms of a geographically vague region, its eponymous hero a plowman. On a popular level, it was all things become possible for all people.

For homesteaders like the Morses, it became an article of faith, serving him even when circumstances demanded the surrender of yet another farm to keep alive the promise of the independence a new homestead elsewhere would bring. There is a touch of religious awe, a mythic wonder, in his autobiographer's memory as he recalls the "everlasting grainfield" of the promising prairie. As Morse's consistent affirmation of his freedom on the homestead implies, the myth had not disappeared by midcentury, as Smith believes, but remained a framing perspective that encouraged a dispossessed people to retain their aspirations while protesting the serious economic threat of "land fever" in their loss. The government, then rich in land but poor in pocket, offered land at low prices, but many homesteaders remained burdened by mortgages and other loans. "Free" land, the dynamic of western expansion, concealed economic and climatic pitfalls that the average homestead family found difficult when not in fact disastrous. Life on the western prairie proved to hold less than the reward that even the most experienced farmers had expected, and Omar had no experience of prairie farming. Morse and his family, courageous in their hopes for freedom on the land, are representative voices in a frontier silence that may continue to mislead scholars of the nineteenth-century United States and its social turbulence.

The young rebel from upstate New York was happily unaware of the dangers the awesome open prairie held for his aspiration of owning a section of the appealing garden. Later, wiser and more mature, married to Delia Mason of Green County, Wisconsin, he struggled against debt on three homesteads where he and his growing family (three girls and two boys) were the first to till the land. He lived out his last years after Delia's death on his twenty acres of independence—a subsistence farm near the crossroads village of Roscoe, Minnesota—with his youngest son, Omar, Jr. His letters to his oldest son, Manly—who found life more remunerative as a skilled railroad blacksmith—warn of the dangers of being an employee who is not free to determine his own economic destiny.

The wrenching change from a frontier agrarian society to an interdependent urban industrial society in one generation had left this wry free spirit stranded at age seventy in a pine forest, which he and his son were tenaciously converting into a subsistence farm. In Morse's lost farms and his quixotic and stubborn resistance lies a history that remains clouded by the yet unresolved issue of the western homestead and its actual economic viability.

For many families, the demon of the frontier was the land speculator or moneylender with his usurious mortgage and seed loans. Even a willing neighbor or friend could play this role if he encountered hard times and payment was due—such were the conditions of the fronter; indeed, the ultimate entrapment became the friend or neighbor forced by circumstance to foreclose a mortgage and expose a family to destitution. This, in short, was the reality Omar Morse suggests in his narrative of farming in the mythical wilderness garden of the world.

Frontier scholars have not yet recognized that a generation of pioneers presented western novelists with the gift of a heritage of resistance. Such works as Johnson Hooper's *Adventures of Captain Simon Suggs: Late of the Lollapoosa Volunteers* illustrate the frontier spirit with its ironic humor. Two of Hooper's adventures are satires of land speculators' manipulative practices which the magical cleverness of Suggs, a frontier rogue as successful as the Duke and Dauphin in *Huckleberry Finn*, artfully demonstrates. (Hooper's genius lies in the creation of a rascal whose capacity for sly games exposes the flaws in a conceptually ideal frontier society of open opportunities and fair competition, which had yet to find the democratic cultural checks and balances needed to correct unlicensed freedom.) Although historians remain uncertain about the opportunities offered, many settlers and their political and intellectual leadership were acutely conscious of losing their values and becoming dispossessed from both their farms and their ideals. Many a pioneer feared he or she was merely to be another "peasant among peasants," to use Hamlin Garland's telling phrase, not a freehold western farmer.

On his death, Omar Morse left his autobiography and twenty acres of independence, as it were, to his son, Omar, Jr. The autobiography is an invaluable document, among our national treasures as a witness to the frontier during the years of greatest westward expansion, 1840-80. The son of Stephan and Polly Morse, themselves dispossessed pioneer homesteaders in Oswego County, New York, Omar became a homesteader farther west, first in Fond du Lac County, Wisconsin, and then in Goodhue and Dodge counties, Minnesota, following the promise of a myth on which a potentially viable new culture had been predicated. Although Morse's narrative has the familiar themes of other homestead narratives (hardship, survival, endurance, courage, rugged individualism, and of course family perpetuity on the land), his cultural significance—perhaps his universality—lies in his theme of the quest, a failed quest, for home and permanence. The hero of the frontier myth was the ordinary person, but too often only the successful have found print, seldom the ordinary family forced by taxes, farm costs, and—most painful of all—mortgages and loans, to leave land on which they had first broken ground and on which they had expended years of labor in an effort to become the owners, free and clear. The Morse witness illuminates the transitory frontier culture from the tragic perspective of the dispossessed family who suffered disillusionment as well as lost labor with each move to a new home in the West. The Morses moved four times, once into a village, each time hoping to realize the elusive promise of the garden.

A productive farm owned free and clear of debt, of course, was the tangible garden sought by the Morses and other homestead families. But many dreams were lost in the dust of fruitless years. The silent anger of these families eventually found a clear voice in the 1870s to early 1890s, taking political shape in the People's Party, or Populists, who deeply involved such idealists as Ignatius Donnelly, novelist and U.S. senator, and, for a time, the novelist Hamlin Garland, whose dark austerities of homestead life spoke for the silent farmers who had lived the history of the West. Although frontier studies have left the issue of economic viability unresolved, the threat and fact of poverty and dispossession from farms was a reality that many western settlers could never dismiss. Walt Whitman's "divine average" (in *Song of Myself*), the ordinary citizen and model of Jeffersonian democracy, was in dire straits, often with an income substantially lower than that of a European peasant. Thus, stranded by the loss of farms on which they had expended years of labor, with little cash reserve and less incentive to risk another failure, they became lost people, seeking to stay alive morally and spiritually while finding such employment as they could.

The serpent in the promised garden, Morse discovered, was riddling debt, a mythical beast—part land speculator, part mortgage and interest, part loan shark. The Morses' dispossession from three homesteads represents the dispossession of thousands of pioneer families who never rose to the position of landowners—a seriously neglected aspect of western frontier settlement. Strangely, few pioneer farmer-authors relate the story of lost homesteads. But whatever codes dictated such omissions, Morse's autobiography, intended only for his immediate family, candidly tells of his three lost farms and suggests his paradoxical strength in alienation from society. His defenses against loss were various, but the most significant are the verbal strategies of irony and critical attack, at times upon his own foolish mistakes. His narrative, moreover, illuminates an emerging grassroots liberalism. After long years of prairie silence, the western settlers wanted to expose the depredations of land speculators' greed behind the glittering illusions of the garden myth—or, more accurately, of the inflated nineteenth century variant that accommodated all fantasies of wealth and ease as well as the earnest hopes of ordinary people seeking the promise of the land. A style of irony, often unskilled, which conceals a dark, mordant laughter, indicates the cord of relation between the traditional (or folk) materials and the works of Mark Twain and other western writers. Because western settlers delighted in ironic inversions—the folk song "Starving to Death on a Government Claim" offers illustration—I have described their resistance to cultural and material loss as the theme of the "unweeded garden." It is a theme of dispossession that left an invaluable heritage of dissident protest useful to nineteenth-century novelists and certainly to such twentieth-century writers as Sinclair Lewis, Sherwood Anderson, Edgar Lee Masters, and William Faulkner.

The unweeded garden of homestead protest—or the cultural theme of dispossession—may be compared to a coin, a metaphoric Jeffersonian silver dollar: on one side, a Ceres of the Frontier, the ever-smiling goddess in the paradoxical wilderness garden of social mobility and democratic new hope; on the other, the helpless gardener among the rank weeds of debt where lurk the land speculator and moneylender, avatars of corporate bigness. It was the ironist's coin; it was minted of good metal and base, of faith and will, and of illusion where reality had been anticipated. However naive as art it may seem, it contained within it the tragic irony of death and loss on a government claim threatened by the mortgage and seed loans. Such ironies structure the dark perspective of the unweeded garden, a frontier society's inversion of the popular myth of settlement in the West—the last defense against the killing forces of societal indifference or worse, critical attack as lazy and shiftless citizens.

The cruel absurdities of the homestead farm have varied and ample illustration in the literature of the westward migrations. A speculator's advertisement that appeared in *Land: Buyers', Homesteaders', and Locators' Guide to Minnesota* by Walter Horton (Minneapolis: Swinburne Printing Co., 1894, p. 56) indicates the rank commercialism that undermined the aspirations of an expanding nation implied by the garden myth.

> Do you intend to enter free Homestead Land in Minnesota, Dakota, or even the Pacific Coast?
>
> Do you desire information of Indian reservations, recently opened for settlers, in the near future?
>
> Would you buy the first class hardwood timber lands, 1 to 2 miles from the railroad at $2.00 per acre, and upwards on easy terms of payment?
>
> Would you take time to investigate fertile and productive prairie land at $3.00 per acre and upwards, located in well-advanced and prosperous settlement?
>
> Do you want a cheap land-seeker or excursion ticket

> when going out to locate a new home, either on Government or Railroad lands?
>
> In either case, apply to A. E. Johnson, Land and Immigration Agents, 195 E. 3rd Street, St. Paul, Minn.[1]

By definition, a myth supports cultural values through a narrative action and an ethical hero. Only the anonymous plowman of the garden myth gives hint of an action; the setting is pioneer homesteading in a wilderness. This pseudo-action, lacking structure, fades quickly into the most abstract and vague of symbols. It was easily interpreted to suit the purposes of the interpreter, whether reformer, farmer, or land speculator. Notice that the land speculator in the quotation above blandly advertises the usual "free" or government land with the same unctuous smile as he advertises land for sale once deeded by the government to the Indians, that with the same unblinking purpose he offers to sell land near growing towns, his services, or railroad tickets. (Sinclair Lewis's Gopher Prairie [*Main Street*, 1920] was built on a foundation of such grotesque entrepreneurial absurdity.) A common fatuous assurance masks a laissez-faire attitude toward inflated land prices (here double the government price) as well as the implied deracination of Indian societies caused by their removal from land that had been central to their culture.

The smiling face of the counterfeit coin, the popular coin of great expectation, can be illustrated by much of the sentimental doggerel that puffed the potential beauty and adventure of western homesteading into monstrous artificiality. In the following poem a youth not unlike the young Omar leaves for an adventurous fulfillment of his dreams. Although he is torn by love for his mother (and the static civilization she represents), he will realize his ambitious plans for success in a vague fluid geography of false emotion.

The Emigrant's Farewell

Away to the Prairies! the hour is at hand,
My steed bounds with joy toward Missouri's far shore.

My dreams are of mountains, of river and plain.
Will they bring me my home and my mother again?

The complete poem appeared in the November 4, 1835, *Chicago Democrat* under the initials J.H.S. of Sheshequin, Pennsylvania, and was first published earlier by the *New Yorker* (not the prototype of the modern magazine). The democratic independence it might have defined stretched toward fathomless horizons, vague and unrealistic. The poem in any age is obviously too silly to consider analytically, but it illustrates the popular version of the smiling goddess on the coin of the West and suggests the naive optimism of early nineteenth-century aspirations for settlement. The fault, as we know, lay in a naive myth, too unsophisticated to hold ethical substance.

Frederick Jackson Turner's vision of the frontier in *The United States* seems somehow to remain a scholar's "magic" wilderness (with just enough savagery to excite the civilized sensibility) where the unfortunate worker, urban or rural, found opportunity for a new life and the promised freedom of a democracy in which to realize that life. For Turner, the rugged virtue of farm and forest was the seedbed of democracy's renewal. The historical frontier is less easily defined. I have already indicated the bias of this study toward an issue that apparently has no true resolution, only sharply antithetical viewpoints: the economic viability of the advancing frontier. The opposing views require brief clarification.

On the one hand, Paul Gates's *Landlords and Tenants on the Prairie Frontier* and Fred Shannon's *The Farmer's Last Frontier, 1860-1897* recognize the victimization of homestead families, pointing to the several dangers of ineffectual reformers and their abortive reforms of land policies, poorly stated or inadequate usury laws, corrupt officials at all levels of government, and shrewd, unethical speculators and mortgagers. But neither of these authoritative frontier histories estimates national dispossession rates; the authors confine their exhaustive studies to a region, yet their evidence, as well as my own study of deed and mortgage records in the counties where

Morse lived, offers forceful evidence of 30 to 40 percent loss. A definitive cultural study of the period supplements the findings of these liberal historians. Henry Nash Smith's *Virgin Land* demonstrates the erosion of the ambient myth of the garden during the post-Civil War gilded age and suggests an emerging disillusion caused by an economy that failed to encourage the growth of the western homestead as promised by the myth. Richard Hofstader's excellent *The Age of Reform: From Bryant to FDR* analyzes an emerging liberal vision in the concluding decades of the century, although his intellectual analysis finds the Populists to have retained the patriotic conservatism of farm owners in their revival of Jeffersonian agrarianism.

In resolute opposition, however, is Professor Alan Bogue, whose *From Prairie to Corn Belt* and *Money at Interest* command wide respect. He finds that land companies and mortgage houses did in fact "foot the bill"; they furnished capital for the homestead and its necessary technology—the grist mills, roads, blacksmith shops, stores, and other basic needs of the wilderness community—with the courage and flexibility of the pioneers themselves. This was intensified by the advancing mechanization of the farm and the need for capital to buy the new reaper and fencing so that cash crops could be efficiently produced. A new era of machines, however, eliminated the struggling pioneer who like Morse clung to his land in spite of poverty. The problem, essentially, remains unsolved.

Yet the homestead imagination perceived the land speculator and mortgager as the demonic tempter in the garden. "Land fever," as I have described it, seemed to overcome otherwise healthy (or rational) settlers, and of course there were speculators who fed the obsession, especially such large landowners as the railroads, timber companies, and mineral trusts who could and did control settlement in areas where their holdings were extensive. In addition, both eastern and western mortgage houses, advocates and practitioners of laissez-faire business, contributed to the exploitation of ordinary people—in fact and in the homestead mind. Only the extent of homestead dispossession and its significance for a nation undergoing growth too rapid for its own full awareness remain challenging issues for frontier scholars. In attempting to clarify the frontier mind and its cultural heritage of independence, often in severe distress, my research verifies that of Paul Gates and Fred Shannon. However, the concern of this book is less with fact than with the perception of the fact by an elusive frontier culture. The mood of a nation, even of a determined minority within its borders, often proves more critical in creating the imaginative shape of events than fact itself.

Morse's autobiography indirectly reflects that mood. It is not a somber mood, such as we might expect of a grim and angry homesteader; indeed, it is seldom even bitter. At first Morse is nostalgic for his youth and family in New York. He then protests; he laments loss and mistakes; but there is no verbal clenched fist. There is rather satire and amused distance from the pretenses of speculators peddling whole villages in areas where settlement was unlikely to be rewarding; there are the remembered details of his struggle to survive on land he had been the first to plow, of family illness and death, of moving west again with hope, only to confront dispossession from yet another home and fields that had required years of muscle-wrenching labor. But readers will find the resolved anger of earlier frustration in such moments as his condemnation of a land speculator who proved himself a "dishonest cuss." His memories reflect the fear that comes with a remembered injustice. In such remembrance we recognize his need to fit the pieces of his fragmented life together in a connected whole; his "chain of events," as he calls it, is a struggle to raise himself from virtual fieldhand on his debt-ridden land to true owner and farmer, but we see it become a chain that bound him and his family to the economic liability of acreage still to be plowed or fenced, yet taxed and mortgaged beyond his means. The Morse narrative is distinguished by its puzzled focus on the curious turns of fortune that made a few of his neighbors prosperous and happy while the rest, like Hamlin Garland's parents, were spiritually and physically emptied by exhausting labor. The Morse document thus provides a representative voice candidly stating the conditions of dispossession in the historical context of an apparent conspiracy of silence, at least until the Populists, a dissident minority, began to protest economic outrage.

An individual researcher cannot read all the extant homesteaders' narratives, even those in a single geographic region, but of the estimated two hundred I have read, only a few—and these indirectly—reveal the economic conditions that Paul Gates suggests undermined stable settlements.[2] "The Narrative of Noah Harris Letts" in *The Narrative of Noah Harris Letts*, Levi Countryman's unpublished diaries (Minnesota Historical Society Research Center, St. Paul), and Phoebe Goodall Judson's *A Pioneer's Search for an Ideal Home* all merely suggest, without exact references, that mortgages led to loss or near loss of homesteads in the West; none tells the full story of dispossession.[3]

But Morse candidly recounts the facts of dispossession by threat of immediate foreclosure and sheriff's sale, accepts the responsibility, vows to avoid future errors in management, and emigrates with his wife Delia and their increasing family to farm a homestead on another quarter-section, his previous years of labor virtually wasted. His narrative thus appears to be the most explicit, if not the *unique*, witness of dispossession from homesteads in midwestern and western pioneer settlements. Gates's studies of prairie homesteading are dramatically illustrated by this pioneer family's struggle for independence on the land. In addition, the Morse narrative is a mirror of the homestead farm conditions that were conducive to a widespread, vague, and growing populist agrarian resistance to land speculation and inadequate laws. If Morse does not protest the failure of government or suggest his loss of confidence in western economic mobility, his growing alienation is indicated by a letter to his son (see Appendix A) advising him to vote for the Populist candidate; neither Republican nor Democratic parties seemd to him capable of vigorous leadership. This disillusioned pioneer idealist thus suggests the native roots of discontent that gave birth to the liberal sentiment of the prairier homesteaders, some of them as frequently dispossessed from farms as he. He had emerged from what he felt to have been a mythically coherent past into a fragmented reality of puzzling economic dynamics beyond his comprehension. The difference between dispossessed father and dispossessed son was the enchanting, compelling materialism of an evolving garden myth.

The original manuscript of Morse's narrative appears in a bound oblong journal with multicolored hard covers. The handwriting is usually legible but undergoes a marked change from a flowing Spencerian script to the penmanship of the later nineteenth century, similar to contemporary handwriting. The main body of the manuscript is seventy-six pages long, with several additional pages given to the genealogy of his immediate family and to a short essay on the United States in the Philippines. The pages measure 7½ by 12¼ inches, with the journal cover a quarter-inch larger. On the inside of the front cover is a photograph of Morse; no date is given, but he appears to be in middle age. Wearing the coat, vest, and mutton-chop whiskers of the entrepreneur, he might seem to be an affluent man. On closer scrutiny, however, one sees that his coat and vest are of heavy and serviceable wool, as is his checked shirt with its two decorative white buttons replacing the usual tie—apparently the "Sunday best" of a family man in this area. The photo shows Morse as a balding, wide-shouldered man with the look of his Yankee ancestors; his slightly forbidding appearance seems both dignified and kindly, as seems often the case in nineteenth-century portraits and photographs. In old age, however, as the photograph included with his narrative shows, Morse's face reveals the memory of an ideal lost in the puzzling mazes of his experience on the land. His wife Delia's face seems to reflect the austere history of the frontier woman.

Under Morse's photograph in his journal is a white card on which a printer set in an elegant script type the lengthy title: "Some of the Things that Happened When I was a Lad and later on Through a Period of Seventy-Five Years," to which he added the author's name. Since Morse died at seventy-seven in 1901, he probably pasted his photograph and the printed title inside the front cover at least two years before his death, then continued to add a few comments to his narrative in the remaining years of his life.

After Morse's death his autobiography passed into the hands of his second son, Omar Morse, Jr., who sold his father's twenty-acre "homestead" and bought a larger farm near Warroad in northern Minnesota. When he died, his wife, Lulu, kept it in her possession; upon Lulu's death, the manuscript was saved from almost certain loss by Evelyn Morse Peterson, the granddaughter of Omar, Sr. It was Mrs. Peterson who discovered that Stephan D. Morse, Omar's father, is mentioned by Elizabeth Simpson in her history of Oswego County, New York, *Mexico, Mother of Towns*.[4] Stephan joined his father-in-law, the Rev. Gamaliel Barnes, in pioneering Parish Township, and later Stephan was employed to clear other homesteaders' land in the town. Barnes, a chaplain in the American Army during the Revolution, became known for his backwoods ministry; he was an almost legendary figure before his death, having baptized, married, and buried three generations. Although blind after the age of ninety, he continued his pastoral duties, led by a daughter, until his death at ninety-six and burial in the Colosse, New York, cemetery. Morse's parents, Stephan and Polly, married in Oswego County around 1800, according to his "Family Records" (see Appendix C), and in their old age moved to Fond du Lac County next to Omar, the youngest of their nine children. County deed records show their ownership of ten acres. The published Morse genealogy by J. Howard Morse and Emily Leavitt gives several Stephan D. Morses of his generation, one of whom was born in the Connecticut Valley, but no direct relation to any of these can be established, nor is there any established link to Anthony Morse, the progenitor of the line that produced Samuel F.B. Morse and his father, Jedidiah, the great Yale geographer.

In editing Omar Morse's autobiography, I have silently corrected Morse's errors when the intention of his sentence or paragraph was unclear. I have, however, kept correction to a minimum in order that the pioneer idiom and American colloquial flavor of Morse's language be retained. Idiosyncratic spellings, various unique locutions, and metaphors have been retained. When an awkward word, phrase, or mistake seemed problematic, I have suggested an alternative and this only when it was imperative. Wherever I have made an interpolation, or where a word or phrase is illegible, I have editorially bracketed it in the customary way. As Morse's narrative is somewhat repetitious in its later pages, some deletions have been made and a summary inserted to retain continuity. The editing of Morse's letters to his son and daughter-in-law also follows this method, but the process of excerpting necessarily requires more ample editorial comment than I would like. My aim whenever possible is to allow Mr. Morse to speak through the authenticity of his original manuscript.

The authenticity of the original manuscript has been verified by checking U.S. census records in Wisconsin and Minnesota for his years of residence and by following references to deeds and mortgages in the county courthouses in Fond du Lac, Wisconsin, and Mantorville and Red Wing, Minnesota. Although such research was needless, objective verification was obviously needed. From childhood, I had heard tales of a legendary ancestor who had written an autobiography of his youth and young manhood as a pioneer. Thanks to the inventive stories of my maternal grandmother, Anna Morse, my imagination was quickened to the hardships of his days as a homesteader. Thanks to my aunt, Mrs. Evelyn Morse Peterson, I have been given the opportunity to know the person who inspired my grandmother's stories: my maternal great-grandfather, Omar Morse. Research has proved fascinating and tedious in turn; it has taken me to New York, Wisconsin, Minnesota, and the research libraries of Chicago, New Haven, and New York; to the dullest statistics imaginable (county census figures, for example) and into the surprising revelations, among rigidly patterned narrative sequences, of obscure pioneer narratives. The latter were put aside as the prerogatives of other students; my interest has remained with Morse (who died only twenty-four years before my birth) because he was candid in his story of dispossession, and because his struggle struck me as the ordinary man's struggle in any age.

Moreover, the narrative provides an unusual view of

American society as an organic process of development, an evolution that forms a twentieth-century legacy. Dispossession from the pioneer farms that were nineteenth-century models of American independence and freedom was obviously the harshest of realities underlying the beautiful illusion of the western garden. If the extent of dispossession from farms during the progress of settlement remains contestable, Morse's narrative illuminates the effect of such a loss after years of labor, which many homesteaders suffered but seldom mentioned. For him the result was a retreat to the barrier of frontier idealism, with its potent belief in the freedom and independence of the individual, on his small homestead in Roscoe Township. His experience of the land as a farmer and builder—more accurately, his *story* of homesteading—becomes the representative voice of the silent homesteaders who lived and passively suffered western history, although the myth of settlement had told them they were to be the heroes and heroines who made history.

To be certain, one voice, however significant, is not a groundswell of real public opinion; Morse obviously could not speak for Indians or black people, for the great ethnic variety of immigrants, for the fortunate of the opulent gilded age, or for the desperate poor of the new raw towns—Poker Flat or populous Minneapolis. But Morse's groping for causes suggests cultural erosion. The myth of the garden is in fact the root metaphor of the American Dream. F. Scott Fitzgerald recognizes this in Gatsby's spontaneous birth on Dan Cody's yacht: Cody is the type of the western unethical man of fabulous wealth. It was the Codys, as Morse and western Populists guessed, whose greed suppressed the aspirations of homesteaders; to be more precise, who deliberately misled a folk culture, a vital society whose democratic values had been tested by adversity and who yet continued to believe in the hope represented by the land. The folk art of resistance is evident in their songs and humor and eventually in the dissident political resistance of the Farmers' Alliance and later the Populists. Morse, like many American novelists, found himself an observer of changes he felt powerless to alter. His suffering and his historic context offer the configuration of a nation's tragic destiny.

The nineteenth-century pioneer writers of journals, diaries, autobiographies, and similar narratives seldom defied the western code of stoic silence: the myth demanded a gambler's acceptance of all risk without complaint. In addition, an unofficial censorship obscures the real values of the unique society in which the Morse family lived. Omar's sketchy portrayal of Delia, his wife, for example, may reflect Victorian taboos toward verbal expression of love and sex common through the country and certainly in pioneer narratives. In women's narratives as in men's, euphemisms are common in discussions of pregnancy, childbirth, and death. Morse's portrayal of his relationship to his wife may simply reflect the common decency of an age and a society given to constraint. Although he may seem indifferent to Delia's chronic illness (the Morses continued to have children in spite of her medical history), he was limited by the blindness of a dominantly masculine society. Such excellent studies as Joanna L. Stratton's *Pioneer Women: Voices from the Kansas Frontier*, with its selection of memoirs from Lila Day Monroe's collection of eight hundred women's narratives; Lillian Schlissel's study of women's western journey narratives, *Women's Diaries of the Westward Journey*, with its spectra of authors; Julie Roy Jeffrey's *Frontier Women: The Transmississippi West, 1840-1880*, with its provocative cultural analysis of frontier women and their values, all illuminate an otherwise unexplainable silence. In sum, a pioneer society was culturally bound to a code of silence—which Morse illuminates in his portrayal of his wife, although not in his candor in writing of his failures, of death and gossip.

Morse's memories of his wife begin with their courtship and marriage in 1848 and extend until her death in 1876. After their wedding, however, in his infrequent mention she appears as a person burdened by chronic illness who deserves understanding and sympathy, but would seem not to receive it from a husband who fails to mention his joy in the birth of another child. Contemporary perceptions of such apparent indifference would find Morse criminal in his neglect. Yet the attraction of a young laborer on the stone foundation of a gristmill near Fairwater, Wisconsin, to a cook in the boardinghouse where he lived became an enduring love. Later that winter he visited Delia at her parents' home near the present town of Ripon. He found the Mason family "very social and good company" and recalls that "western fever had led them from place to place" since leaving Pennsylvania. (Morse did not mention first names; research into this restless homestead family has thus proved fruitless.) After the wedding, he recalls, the couple went visiting in a nearby county, enjoying the companionship of friends and relatives. Such social gatherings were among the pleasures of the homestead community, serving to establish the solidarity of communal friendships and creating an enjoyable diversion from the isolation and monotony of farm life and labor. Delia's death was a day of grief vividly remembered; indeed, her loss seemed almost to disable Morse psychologically: his family and their struggle to own and operate a homestead farm gradually disintegrated thereafter. Delia had been the keystone of Omar's arch; on her death his dream lay in rubble at his feet. He never again attempted to farm as his main source of income, resourcefully becoming hired hand, laborer, stonemason, and house builder, thus reflecting the acceptance of her death expected of men. What his economic losses could not accomplish, his personal loss did.

The photograph of Delia Mason Morse that appears in these pages, lent me by Evelyn Morse Peterson, suggests the tragic forces of homestead life almost as powerfully as Omar's unusual narrative. It shows a beautiful woman; close observation reveals dark eyes, hair wrapped severely in a bun, a sad downcurved mouth, thin face, and slender neck. Hers is a face of suffering, not elegant suffering such as we associate with romance—the Gothic lady mysteriously haunted by some ancestral crime or oppressed by a cruel husband or lover—but an anguish and pain masked by the stoic acceptance and endurance of frontier women. Pioneer women have written of the awesome loneliness of the prairie, especially when their husbands were away and a double responsibility fell on their shoulders; of their hard, unending labor in the house and fields; of their deep longing for relief in female companionship, for social gatherings, for distant family and friends. Delia's face seems an image of the suffering that families learned to accept as pioneers of a new land. Like Ole Rölvaag's Hilda in *Giants in the Earth*, she appears to be the type of the frontier lost lady whose sacrifices to farm and settlement brought into being a society from the dread immensity of western space in spite of shrewd land speculators.

If Morse is insensitive in his portrayal of Delia, he can be best understood as a man of an age and its culture. But clearly he is a person whose frankness speaks in liberal views uncommon among the writers of early narratives. The autobiography, which he began to write in 1882 and completed shortly before he died in 1901, shows his unusual democratic attitudes: he points out the gross disparity between men's and women's wages (he also recalls the low pay of "boys" who he felt could hoe their row as well as their male parents), the dishonesty of a land speculator, the unfairness of employers, the cruelty of gossiping neighbors, the inconsiderate inflation of medical bills (he recalls borrowing at 25 percent interest to pay a pharmacist's bill). A unique personality—often ironic, unafraid to voice complaint, remorseful, and at times self-pitying and despairing—he breaks the western code of silence with his seldom heard discouraging words. Yet, as I have indicated, his fist is not raised in anger at the gods or government; time had yielded some perspective. The candor of his observations suggests an American ironist, compassionate and honest, whose everyday idealism reflects the homestead theme of the unweeded garden.

Significantly, Morse writes to his son Manly, telling him of an allegiance to the Populists. The frontier culture that Morse typifies, stranded by time and a now urban West, sought expression of its ideals and passions in the strident speeches and inflammatory songs of this angry organization of family farmers. When the stoic code of silence was relinquished, it released a burst of thunderous protest. But, though leaving its helpful legacy, the frontier culture with its Populist voice dissolved into the white-frame-house society of Victorian respectability. Because Morse held a mirror to the legacy of this protest, his narrative points to the significance of an indigenous popular revolt.

Ignatius Donnelly, U.S. senator and Populist leader in Minnesota (who campaigned in Dodge County, where the Morses lived), gave expression to the disillusioning poverty of a nineteenth-century laboring class, both urban and rural, in his novel *Caesar's Column*: "Take a child a few years old; let a blacksmith weld around his waist an iron band. At first it causes him little inconvenience. He plays. As he grows older it becomes tight; it causes him pain; he scarcely knows what ails him. He still grows. All his internal organs are cramped and displaced. He still grows larger; he has the head, shoulders and limbs of a man and the waist of a child. He is a monstrosity. He dies."[5] Donnelly's allegory suggests the major purpose of *Land Fever*, intended for the general reader as well as scholars in history, sociology, and that broadly humanistic discipline, American studies. It is intended to give shape to the vague figure of the homestead pioneer and his several strategies of defense against a society indifferent to his plight.

The Autobiography of Omar H. Morse

"Some of the Things That Happened When I Was a Lad and Later On through a Period of Seventy-Five Years"

Chapter 1st

I was born November 12, 1824 in the Town of Hastings, Oswego County, State of New York.[1] My Parents were in very limited circumstances financially yet blessed with a large family of children which is a poor man's capital though capital of this kind is not considered very available in case of financial Depression.

I was set down on the List as the last adventure in the family and classed No—9—[2] I have a very faint recollection of things which took place for about Six years although I can very distinctly remember a few circumstances which transpired at an Earlier date as I believe all children have some impressions made upon the memory at a very early stage of life which are never erased from their minds though they may live their three score and ten!

1. The exact location of Morse's birthplace is unknown. The recorded deed for the property of his father, Stephan D. Morse, was destroyed by a fire in the schoolhouse in Central Square where the Hastings Township deeds had been stored. Morse's description of the "town line farm" suggests two possibilities. The first is on the north township line west of the village of Hastings (the present Markowitz

At the age of six years in company with four or five older than myself I was allowed to commence my Alphabetical experience which to me was surely an important event as it was to all children. From that time on till I was 18 year of age I kept regularly at school Summer and Winter.

In that latitude the winters were very severe long and tedious—there were deep snows through which it was many times almost impossible to get to and from school—

The country was very thinly settled at that time and it was with difficulty that the few settlers could keep the roads open sufficient to keep the schools in running order, provide themselves with fuel, attend to the little stock they possessed which generally consisted of one or two cows, a yoke of oxen and a few sheep—which by the way was considerable indispensible in any family. A little piece of ground was sown to Flax. This with the wool from a few sheep constituted the groundwork of all the wearing apparel of Each family—corn cake, maple sugar and Bacon was the principle diet from January to New Years of the year around.[3]

And right here let me speak of the little Brook which had its rise in what was termed the Sulphur Spring—these large springs were situated near each other at the Head of what was

---

Road) about three miles from the U.S. 11 intersection. Morse later describes a trout stream, a five-mile journey to the mill (the hamlet of Carley's Mill, once the location of the nearest mill, is approximately this distance), and the "old school with the tall Elm tree" in the village, then walking distance away. In addition, Morse's brother Sanford's recorded deed locates *his* farm in the northwest quadrant of this section west of the village on the town line (Oswego County Deeds, Book P, p. 282), suggesting the likelihood of this location, where father and son could conveniently exchange labor and other necessities. A second but less likely possibility is on the town-line road that separates Hastings and Parish, to the east. The distance to Carley's Mill and the school are about the same. Stephan had owned land near Cooperstown before emigrating to Oswego County with Gamaliel Barnes, his father-in-law and a former Revolutionary chaplain.

2. See Appendix C for Morse genealogy.

3. Simpson, *Mexico, Mother of Towns*, gives an interesting history of Hastings and nearby townships.

called Beaver Meadow and running through the timber some four miles before emptying into what was called Little Salmon River.[4]

This little stream was alive with the real Speckled Trout, the best variety of fish in the known world, and why I speak of this here is because at this period of my life I spent some of the happiest days of my boyhood wandering up and down the banks of this little Brook with the implements necessary for the capture of the finny tribe! A few hours was sufficient to catch a nice string— Those fish have some peculiar habits which it was necessary to thoroughly understand in order to be sure of success and any noise or hasty movements on the Banks was sure to disperse and drive them to parts unknown! A cloudy yet hot day with an occasional sprinkle of rain was the most favorable and anything but a novice was sure of a good days sport and well filled Haversack.

When I was yet quite a small lad I was learned to ride Horseback but my experience in this branch of business was in the Cornfield principally among stumps and roots on newly cleared land and many a time did old Grey bring up against some snags with such force as to send me headlong to the ground! I can remember very distinctly some of these sendoffs to the present day—Another pleasant task was to be sent off to the Mill[5] with two bags full of grain on horseback and I perched up top to carry the reins and balance the Load—

I very often demurred against such sports but I was told that it was just as necessary to understand all these little tactics as it was to read and spell: perhaps it was but I never could see it in that light!

We left the town line farm as it was called—the Old school near the tall Elm tree and many objects of interest to me which

---

4. Neither maps nor field research in northern Hastings Township located Sulphur Springs or Beaver Meadow, although the Little Salmon, or South Branch of the Salmon River, as it is now called, is still in evidence, flowing west and northwest across New York State Highway 69A to Parish Village.

5. This may be the grain mill which was in Carley's Mill, about five miles east of Hastings village.

are still fresh in my memory and moved to an adjoining town which then seemed to be a long way as I had never been more than a dozen miles from home. Here we settled on ten acres of land which my father Bought for Five hundred Dollars of a man named Ansel Barnes, a distant relative.[6] As far as the soil was concerned it was unmistakably poor but the buildings were considered a bargain and consisted of quite a large square Building, a huge fire place and chimney in the center, a wood shed, Hog House, Hay Barn and cowshed all attached together and all in unfinished condition. What little available property my Father possessed was turned over towards this unfinished and almost shapeless structure which was in future to be termed Home.

This move was made Sept 1st[7] a few months before my 14th birthday.

I was let out to do fall work—digging potatoes, husking corn [and other chores] for 25 cents per day which was considered a fair remuneration for my services in as much as I was fed when I worked. With the proceeds I was allowed to buy what clothing I was obliged to have as far as it would go, furnish myself with Books for the winter school which opened about the first of December in a new schoolhouse at the corner about a mile away and was conducted by E. Erskine.

This was the first storecloth Homemade clothes that I ever had on my back—you may well think I was proud of my success—a Rugar's arithmetic, a new slate, English Reader, coat, pants and a pair of New Boots—a straw Hat which I wore all winter as my funds run out before I completed my outfit but it was all the same to me. I was tough and hearty and bound to learn to cipher as studying figures was termed in them days.

I was pretty soon called an expert in my studies and more so in outdoor sports as running, jumping, and Scuffling was an

---

6. The adjoining town (or township) would be either Mexico or Parish. It was most likely the latter as it was the area to which Stephan Morse first emigrated. Ansel Barnes may have been related to the family through Omar's mother, Polly Barnes Morse.

7. Presumably, 1838, since Omar was born in 1824.

Every day sport practiced by all the school, the teachers not Excepted.

When the school closed I was presented with a pass from my teacher marked—Studious and Obedient, good in figures, a fair reader, a No 1 speller and in outdoor sports No 1.[8]

I began to consider myself of some importance and on the road to fame and glory.

The next summer [1839] I worked at odd jobs such as I could get to do in a farm neighborhood for very small wages. As I was yet a new lad and not strong enough to do heavy work, I hoed corn for many a day for 25 cts keeping up my roe but I was a boy and must work for 1/2 price. I never could see why a boy should not receive as much pay as a man for the same labor Equally well done—and I never could see any Justice or Equality in girls working for One Dollar pr Week and doing the cooking, Baking, Washing, Ironing for a family of Ten and then pear apples till Ten O'clock at night but girls and boys of today or Ladies and Gentlemen as they are now termed know but little of the times forty or fifty years ago, but of this more here after.

The next term of school that I attended Opened Nov 1st—a few days before my fifteenth Birthday—I was all rigged, clothed and Equipped—as I thought—for Business.

---

8. Although the one-room district school remains a cultural model of discipline and learning, it is well to keep in mind that many residents of New York and other states did not believe in its educational worth. See George F. Miller, *The Academy System of the State of New York*, 34. Miller points out early nineteenth century protests against the inequality of educational opportunity between the one-room school and the academy (roughly equivalent to a private middle and high school), where only the relatively well-to-do could afford to send their children. Mexico Academy (established 1826) was a few miles north of Morse's home, but the lot of farm children was the district one-room school. Miller quotes from a New York State Assembly Document of 1831: "Our beloved country ought not to be behind in the pleasing employment of giving facilities to the poor and industrious young men of our State, thereby enabling them to obtain situations in life which they otherwise could not do" (p. 35). Not until 1853, however, did New York establish a more equitable school system in which rural and urban students from poor families had adequately trained teachers.

This term the school consisted of over forty scholars, quite a number of them ranging from 16 to 20 years of age. Some of them were fine fellows and their acquaintance was very pleasant and they are remembered to the present day although I have not seen or heard of them for over thirty years—how many of this number have passed over the river I have no means of knowing.

In the spring following [1840], the remaining payment was due on the Homestead but the funds were nowhere and we were obliged to seek a new home—[9]

At this time Six of my Brothers and Sisters were married yet all living not a great distance from us except One. My sister Lydia she was always my pet and is still although she is now 66 years of age—at this present time [probably around 1882, as Morse later states] she is now at Colosse, Mexico, New York—a Brother and Sister unmarried were away from home—and I, my Father and Mother were all that were left of a once numberous household. This time we moved to a little town on the Watertown and Syracuse road 23 miles north of Syracuse and called Hunts Corners.[10] This town then consisted of a Hotel and Store combined, a Blacksmith shop, a little Building formerly used as a grocery and dwelling and was at present used as the village schoolhouse and one or two farmhouses on the opposite corners. The country here was pretty well settled and supported a good school. In this place we lived one year and the next spring which was in 1840 [1841] we moved in with my Br Ansel a short distance from our present location.[11] My Br Myron bought One acre of land off from Ansels farm lying on the stage road and about a half mile south from Hunts corners.[12]

---

9. Foreclosure was one of the hidden problems of the American land system. See Gates, *Landlords and Tenants*.

10. Hunt's Corners is not given in atlases available in the Historical Archives of the New York State Education Library in Albany. Morse's description suggests that his family had moved to Hastings Center, a hamlet three miles south of Hastings village. Morse may be in error, or the name may have been changed.

11. By "present location," Morse means his previous location in Hunt's Corners (Hastings Center).

12. According to several early maps, the stage road roughly approx-

This acre of land was intended for a Home for Father and Mother and I was told if I would be a good boy and work through the summer, help to build, etc. I should in time own the place in common with him when Father and Mother were done with it. This was all right and suited me well—while this place was being improved and a house Built I worked like a sailor at anything and everything that I was able to do.

This was the summer of 1840, the memorable year that Harrison was elected president of the United States—

Political meetings—Speeches, Log Cabins and everything pertaining to a presidential campaign was uppermost in the minds of men, women and children.

The 4th of July 1840 was a day such as has never had its Equal. A Liberty Pole was erected and a Log Cabin at the Corners. The Political parties at that time were styled Whig and Democrat or Locofoco. The Presidential Election in Nov was held in Each township and lasted three days—The third day was needed for Drunks—Fights—Races, etc.[13]

Harrison and Van Buren were the Candidates—Harrison was elected by a large majority.

As I have said I was only 16 years of age in November following but I was put right into harness in good earnest.

My Brother Myron had induced me to enter in to this Job of Building, Digging stone—chopping and securing timber and all manner of hard work with a promise of a division of the property when Everything was completed—but I found in time this was all a hoax. Well I had a good time and enjoyed myself well. A few of the young people in the neighborhood [and] I had become acquainted and when I had Leisure I spent some very

---

imated the present U.S. 11. Myron's farm on the stage road south of Hunt's Corners further verifies the supposition that this village was a still tiny Hastings Center, which is located just south of the small village of Hastings on U.S. 11.

13. Morse refers to the Liberty Pole, symbol of the American Revolution, and the log cabin, symbol of the westering pioneer (as well as of Harrison's campaign). Both symbols represent the free and independent farmer, democracy's common man in the eighteenth and nineteenth centuries, when the United States was a predominantly frontier and agricultural nation.

pleasant hours with them in sports and rambles of various kinds which served to pass the time very pleasantly

Our House that we undertook we got so far along that in August we moved into it. The inside finishing was put over till some future time.

I still continued to work where ever I was directed, my Brother assuming the post of Overseer. The following winter I attended school which I think was taught by [a man by] the name of D Carey, a farmer and neighbor. He was an excellent teacher and I made good progress in my studies which consisted of Arithmetic, Geography, Reading, Writing although pensmans[hip] never to my knowledge has been taught in District schools with any sucess— Still all were required to be supplied with Paper and Goose quills as this was the standard pen in them days. And I doubt their being far behind what is used at the present day. Well I continued to work through summer seasons for 2 or 3 years attending school at the winter term.

In July 1843 my Father and a brother in law started out with me to get work in haying. There were two or three large Hay farms near Syracuse where we intended to stop for work. We arrived at the first about 4 oclock P.M., I well remember, tired and footsore, it being very hot and a distance of twenty miles— They were well begun with their haying and we were told they had plenty of hands—

We traveled and call[ed] at the other places where we expected to get work but with the same success.

We arrived at Syracuse about sundown, stopped at a one horse grocery—got some crackers and cheese which we devoured with a will. We went aboard of a Canal Boat for the City of Rochester distant about one hundred miles from Syracuse.

We had just funds enough to take us through and the second day at noon we arrived in the city with 15 cents among us.

This we invested in a dry lunch and then started south through as rich a country as ever lay out of doors—

Everybody was in the midst of cutting and securing hay and we were told that we were too late to get work. We halted at a number of farm houses and asked for work but hands were plenty and begging for work— This surplus of help kept wages down. Good hands could only get 75 cents [per day] for mowing and pitching and many were glad to work for less—

At Five oclock, the hour for supper, the dinner horns set up a chorus that still rings in my Ears, knowing that we were far from home, Penniless and hungry—

The aristocratic farmers of Western New York had about as much real humanity and feeling for a poor laboring man as nigger drivers had [for slaves] in them days in the south.[14]

I believe I went three days without a morsel of food before I would ask one of them for a meal without the means to pay for it—

Not so however with my partners. They had sense enough (I called it cheek) when meal time come to continue some way of appeasing their appetites while I like a fool as I see it now would set by the road side and wait while they filled their shirts.

About sundown a farmer overtook us on horse Back wanting help the next day, offering us three Two dollars, adding if we would get through to his farm six miles [away] before he got to bed we could get supper and Lodging and be ready to start in at sunrise the next morning. This additional six miles on an empty stomach was a sore one for me but I nerved myself up to the scratch and we arrived soon after he did, not daring to let him get far lest we might be too late.

We got what is called a good square meal and laid down for the night sore and weary.

At ½ past 4 the next morning the horn Sounded as a signal for every man fit for duty to report! Little did I feel like turning out to swing a scythe 14 hours through the heat but It was do or die.

We were in the field before six and if ever the sun stood still in Joshua's day it did that day—

---

14. Morse is unique among pioneer homesteader-authors for his liberal and egalitarian statements. He may reflect the class conflict between the homestead farmer and the "broadcloth" professional and educated upper-class person common in the settlements. See Moore, *The Frontier Mind.*

But it is said that there is an end to all things and on this day also the sun went down and if any three poor mortals earned their money I think we did— The next morning we three were up by [be?] times and after partaking of a good substantial breakfast we were once more on the highway begging work. A little before noon that day we were lucky enough to run across a Daniel Morse, a distant relative which we none of us had ever seen but it was all the same. He offered us good quarters. It being saturday we stayed with him over sunday and Monday morning—we left him on his farm situated some 18 miles south of Brockport and if I am not mistaken near the northern boundary of Genesee County.

We stopped at a little town for Dinner named Holley between [near?] the village of Albion[15] and at five P.M. pulled up at the farm of a man named Allen who it was said had something to do with the Destruction of [?].[16]

On we went and at night found our Old Neighbor George Storer. Here we halted for a few days to rest and reconoiter—

We again started out and on the following evening arrived at Brockport where we engaged passage on a Boat for Syracuse—where we arrived after a two days sail on the Erie Canal—

Not being satisfied to give it up as a bad job and go home without any money my Brother in law and myself made for the country while my Father was content to steer for Home.

We made a circuit of 25 miles which brought us round to Syracuse. We then lit out for Hastings and Home—

We walked about 12 miles and it began to rain and we pitched our tent in a hay barn where we staid till toward morning and then walked the remaining 10 miles and was home to Breakfast. All this and much more was in the summer of 43.[17]

---

15. Holley remains a village due west of Brockport on N.Y. 31. Albion is also a village, about fifteen miles west of Holley on N.Y. 31. These three towns are all linked by the Erie Canal.

16. Word illegible: possibly "Morgan," but research yields no clues to such a person.

17. Part II, Chapter 2 of this book discusses the significance of

This trip not withstanding the poor success we had in getting work just put me in a mood for another raid. Some time in October I started out again back to Monroe County north of Brockport where I staid through the Winter— My brother and I bought a contract for a piece of land containing about 70 acres, all heavy timber. We put up a small shanty and in two days time took possession and and went to keeping Batch.

We made ashes, sold Hemlock, sawlogs, made shingle and had fine times generally. We had plenty of fruit and Eatables during the winter which was a long tedious one, the weather being intense cold and deep snow as was the custom in that Latitude. In march I took a notion to go Home as I had an opportunity to ride with little Expense, intending to remain at home a few weeks and then return and work for some farmer in what was called western New York. Some time in April I started out for my new home[18] in company with C.B. Loveridge[19] and his family. [We] Were three days on the road, the roads being terrible muddy and heavily loaded and a balky team in the bargain.

When I arrived at my new quarters I found my Brother with whom I had gone into this land operation had sold out our chance, receiving $50 and pocketed the money and gone into what was called a Fourier association. It is useless for me to explain the workings of this Association; it will benefit no one in particular and be a tedious task.[20]

Morse's "summer of 43" as an unusual protest from a farm laborer against oppressive working conditions as well as his initiation into socioeconomic realities.

18. The reference is to the Monroe County logging operation in partnership with his brother Myron: in short, the "shanty" where, like Huck and Jim on the raft, they had "fine times."

19. See Appendix C. Loveridge, who was Omar Morse's brother-in-law (married to his sister Louisa) accompanied Omar and Stephan in the summer of this year.

20. Wisconsin archive records indicate that Myron E. Morse was a member of the Fourierist Phalanx at Ceresco (now Ripon). He was a teacher and also a secretary of the organization. The Phalanx began in 1844 and disbanded in 1850, selling their productive farm land at a handsome profit. The community adhered to the principles of humanitarian ethics and Fourierist communal rather than family

I was rather taken aback by this move yet let the thing slide and after a few days consideration I took it into my head to go to Michigan to see my brother Sanford who had been in that state since 1833—some Eleven years.[21]

I had never took a trip of this magnitude and it seemed a big thing unexperienced as I was (times has changed since them days) to made such a journey [he was twenty]. The tenth day of May 1844 I took passage on Board of a regular Line Boat on the Erie Canal at Brockport, Monroe County, for Buffalo where I arrived on the morning of the 18th. I well remember how I felt when we cited the City and its surroundings. There were quite a number of Steamers and Sail Vessels and several within a few hours sail of the City coming and going! Lake Erie looked larger than the Pacific and as I watched the tiny crafts rising and falling with the waves which were running high, there being a heavy breeze—my courage almost failed me as I considered the chances of ever reaching the opposite Shore—almost doubtful—but the thing had to be done—and—on reaching the harbor I made for the first steamer in reach to secure a ticket for Detroit.[22]

---

living, although some families ate and lived together by preference. They also practiced a strict equality of the sexes and were dedicated to the advancement of culture and the arts. Lack of skilled craftsmen—blacksmiths, millers, wheelwrights, potters, and so forth—led to the decision to disband. The still prevalent notion that the Fourierists resembled the Shakers in their dictum against marital sexual intercourse is in fact absurd. Leyburn's *Frontier Folkways* upholds this erroneous supposition. The Cerescans most resembled George Ripley's communitarians at Brook Farm near Boston, with whom they held frequent correspondence. Morse's uneasy dislike may reflect his frontier independence and distrust of utopian communities, a common view of Brook Farm. The source of this research was an interview with the Archivist of the Wisconsin Historical Library in Madison, Gerald Ham, and his unpublished "The Fourierists of Ceresco." I am indebted to his courtesy.

21. Sanford Morse (1805-18?) was the third of Stephan D. Morse's children. He had purchased land from James I. Roosevelt of New York City, one of the largest speculators in Oswego County at that time (Oswego County Deeds, Book P, p. 282).

22. Morse's theme of innocence and experience has an interesting parallel in the prose writings of John Clare, the English "peasant

It was now 6 AM and we were told by the Captain that she would go out of Port at Eight—by Eight O'clock the gale had so increased that the Captain concluded that it would be prudent to wait till the wind abated—this was good news to me as I was in constant fear that we were sure to go to the Bottom—

The gale kept up its fury till the next morning, and the harbor was now full of vessels of all kinds as they had been coming in all day and none had ventured out—the water being in terrible agitation.

At 4 PM the Bell rung as a signal for all aboard and our trusty boat steamed out of Buffalo Harbor.

The water was still running high although the wind had ceased to blow for six hours.

I staid on deck and watched the City of Buffalo till it looked no bigger than a Soldiers Blanket and then turned in to wait Developments.

I actually slept well that night and when I awoke I felt of myself to determine for sure if it was really myself. I finally ventured out on Deck and looked about me to see naught but the Blue Waters which were as calm and tranquil as a sabbath morning in a New England town!

The day was pleasant and passed very agreeably. We stopped at Sandusky[23] and one or two other ports, the names I have forgotten and in due time arrived in Detroit, Michigan.

For some reason, and I never could tell why, I was Homesick from the first moment that we sighted the city and I never recovered from the first attack while I staid in the state.

We left Detroit at 8 AM on the train bound for Jackson [Michigan], the terminus of the Road at that time and if I remember right was called eighty miles from Detroit.

A great part of the way the road runs through swamps, marshes and low timber lands—which most effectually in-

---

poet," as well as in many American writings of the time. The reader should keep in mind that the innocent and untraveled backwoods mind first encountered unfamiliar country with a fear comparable to that of Columbus's sailors braving the edge of the world.

23. Sandusky, Ohio, about eighty miles west of Cleveland, remains a port city.

creased my dislike to the country and I saw nothing in the distance which had any charms for me or that looked the least inviting or homelike! We stopped at Ypsilanti, Annebar [Ann Arbor] and some other small towns of small dimensions and finally reached Jackson at 4 PM in the Spring of 44. This was a town of small proportions but in after years became quite a point—

I staid in Jackson that night and in the morning by inquiry found a Farmer by the name of King from Eaton Rapids[24] where I expected to find my brother whom I had not seen for 11 years. I was lucky to secure a passage with him and at 7 AM we set out for our destination—the actual destination from Jackson to the Rapids was only about twenty miles but the roads were fearful—mud, mire and more mud—which made nearly an all days drive!

[The ink changes here from brown to green.]

We arrived at Mr. Kings Home at Sundown and I immediately started to find my brother Sanford—it was a short distance and in a few moments I was standing at his shanty door a perfect stranger to him and family. I was a lad of 9 years when he left his home in Oswego Co, New York and the time had changed me so much that he had little idea that I was one of his own brothers. I found him in poor Health and poor circumstances. The Michigan Ague and Fever made sad Havoc with the inhabitants or early settlers and you could hardly find a family at that time but what a part and in many cases every one was on the sick list—I was not at all taken with the prospect of things and the whole surroundings served to give me a longing for my Home that I had left far away.

My attachment for Home and its surroundings was one of my failings as some term it but I consider a love of Home and friends and early associates One of the greatest blessings that mankind are possessed of! Michigan in them days was considered a long way off and almost the extreme West! When I presented myself before my brother and his family which

---

24. Eaton Rapids, is now a small community located in the south central part of Michigan on State Route 50, some forty miles from Jackson and seventy from Ann Arbor.

consisted of his wife and three small children—the oldest five the second three and the little lad of ten months without a penney in my pocket, far from Home in a wilderness—all strangers—I had that peculiar but very unpleasant feeling called Homesickness and I never wholly recovered and felt reconciled to my surrounding while I staid in the state.[25]

As it is my object in part to give my children a brief history of my Family as it seems to be the only possible means of their becoming acquainted with Each other I hear speak of this brother and his family as it seems to be the most appropriate time and place. The cause of his leaving his home in the state of New York was on account of his persecution by the Church—The Old Baptist of Colosse, Oswego Co—NY—He was always from Early Boyhood very touchy and of rather a pious nature and with all had a mind of his own somewhat more than usual for Boys of his age [and was] given to inquiring into the whys and wherefore's and having joined this church at quite an early age was naturally led to think and Examine into the requirements of church Organizations and the teachings of the Bible for himself. He soon found that the association or church was governed by creeds and manmade Dogmas that in great measure done away with investigation and free thought and the honest open expression of Opinions. He did not propose to take the say of priests for his guide nor be measured by man made creeds but use reason and the Bible as his only counsel. In a short time this led to difficulty between himself and the leading apostles of the church.

They called a counsel of wise men to examine into the case. The result was [that] after preferring certain charges and hearing his defense they considered him a dangerous man and in advance of the times. He must be squelched or as they termed it silenced—cut off—Excommunicated—thrust out.[26]

---

25. Morse's love of family and friends shows us the true settler. The restless frontier adventurer was a different breed from this home-loving pioneer whose goal in life was a family farm.

26. Sanford Morse's independent religious views were a kind of deistic frontier nonconformism. His emigration to Michigan to seek religious freedom places him in the tradition of his Puritan ancestors,

This led to his emigrating into the state of Michigan in the spring of —[18]33 where he found a more congenial soil for the reception of what his Baptist Brethern termed his Infidel Principles. In 1835 he married a young lady by the name of Mary E. Thomas. At the end of one year she died leaving him with a little son which after a few short months followed his mother—after a few years [he married a woman] of the same name of [as] the first with whom he was living at the time of my arrival at his Home near Eaton Rapids, Eaton County, Mich.

I made my home with them during the summer and found an acquaintance with his wife, a person of very quiet disposition, pleasant and agreeable in all her walks. In fact she done everything in her power to make my stay with them as pleasant as possible.

The two little girls, Alzina and Mary, were fine children, well behaved and kind to each other and their parents. The little lad, Allen by name, was I suppose very much like all chicks of that age, being the Baby and the only son, the pet of the family.

My Brother as I have already intimated was in very limited circumstances, having had a great deal of sickness and ill luck one way and [another] and during my stay with them was unable to do but little labor. He at the time I went there was trying to build a more commodious and comfortable dwelling, living at the time in a very rude rough sort of Shanty about 12 feet square— Between us or more properly with my assistance we were able [to complete] his building so far as to be able to occupy it some time in June merely enclosed and in this condition it remained at the time I left which was in October following—

At the same time he was trying to get up a Shop on a little

---

as well as the nonconformism of Roger Williams and quite possibly of his grandfather, the Rev. Gamaliel Barnes, who protested the rigid conservatism of his congregation. Barnes was able to reconcile his differences, it would seem, and continued to serve his backwoods parish for many years. See Simpson, *Mexico, Mother of Towns*, 434 for further details about Barnes' resistance to his congregation's narrow self-righteousness.

Spring brook. [With] water power a short distance from his dwelling, [he intended] to run a Lathe and some other small machinery necessary to carry on chair and cabinet making. I found plenty to busy myself about during the forepart of the season on his works till some time in August and at this time I found I was elected for a term of the Ague and Fever. Of all the most discouraging and harrassing diseases this is the Boss as the saying is.

In September my sister Alzina arrived and to her I always felt indebted for my providential escape from the country which I was through her care able to accomplish about the 20th of October.

I had been shaking two months nearly every day and my day's Journey was performed in a Lumber waggon [with] the soft side of a board for a seat. [We had traveled] a distance of nearly 25 miles when we arrived at sundown.

The next morning it was raining—just the most uncomfortable time for a person in my condition to be out but yet I braced up and mixed with the crowd, securing tickets and seats on the train for Detroit.

That evening after a fatiguing Journey of 80 or 100 miles [from Jackson] we arrived safely at the Seaport [Detroit] and immediately secured passage on the Old Reliable United States Steamer destined for Buffalo, N. York— We had a very rough passage. [It was] the worst gale said to be for years and many a smaller craft was foundered or driven ashore yet luckily we were safely landed in the city of Buffalo on the third day and immediately took passage on the Erie Canal for Brockport [New York].

I stopped at Clarendon, Monroe Co., New York with C.D. Thomas and late in the winter I set out for Hastings, my old Home and residence of my Parents. I was still very feeble and in poor health from the effects of Michigan fever.[27] and

27. Morse follows the custom of naming the crippling fever of the frontier for the state in which it attacked: hence "Michigan" fever. Omar's experience was typical of the backwoods "ghetto." Poor and crowded living conditions bred disease and an inevitable depression and resulting inanition.

remained at home till about the middle of July having rested up so as to be able to go to work.

I then went to Monroe County and worked through the Harvest and fall and by this time began to feel something like a man again.[28]

The winter of [18]45 and 6 I spent cutting cordwood on the farm of old Sanford, an old Bach [bachelor] on the ridge road between a little town called Clarendon and Redmond Corners.[29] The spring following I hired out to an old Scotch farmer, F. MacBane by name, [who lived] one and ½ miles from Brockport—I commenced work for him April 15th 1846—for the two or three weeks previous I was employed by Captain Barker to assist in preparing a section of canal for spring Boating—

Of all filthy disagreeable work this takes the lead—the pay was the round sum of seventy-five cents per day without Board.

I found the old Scotchman a thoroughbred farmer and everything on the premises had to be done in its proper time and in a workmanlike manner. He was a close, shrewd, businesslike man—honest, straightforward in dealings and take him every day a good sort of fellow.

Here is where we put in long days and heavy licks. His two sons at Home were the real tough Hardy Scotch and I found later in the season that they had made a practice of working their men to the last extremity, thinking no Yankee was ever raised to match a full blooded Scotch man. They found their match this time and got enough of it, especially in harvest.[30]

They never had occasion to call me in the morning as I never

---

28. His "initiation" into frontier life appears to have been regarded as a test of manhood.

29. Clarendon is three miles south of Holley and five miles west of Brockport. Redmond Corners is possibly the present Parma Corners.

30. Unlike some other employers, MacBane, with his tough fairness, had Omar's respect. He likely engaged in a work competition, such as shucking corn or cradling wheat, as a test of strength. This was not uncommon on the nineteenth-century farm in the days before machines replaced labor. See Hamlin Garland's *Son of the Middle Border* and John Muir's *Story of My Boyhood and Youth*.

failed to be on time. Sunday mornings I made a practice of doing all the chores which excused me for the rest of the day and with a few Exceptions they never saw me from Breakfast time Sundays till Monday morning—

The women folks were a jolly set, sociable and full of fun, there were six of them and every one had her certain portion of the work. Peace and harmony prevailed and everything went on like clockwork. At the expiration of my term I was paid off and bid the family farewell and in a few days started for my home in Hastings from which I had been absent about 16 months—I went as far as Syracuse on the old Erie Canal and from there by stage—

I staid with my father and mother this time from Nov till March and spent the winter principally visiting and sleighriding, having a good time generally. In March [1847] I started for Monroe Co. again, taking passage with an acquaintance by the name of O. Rider and his wife.

We left Hastings on two feet of snow. Before night the first day the snow had then melted down to a little more than one half and the second day many places were nearly bare— The second day in the afternoon we crossed Irondequoit Bay[31] on the ice, a distance of 1½ miles and with about 3 inches of water on it. It was raining and we were told that It was not safe to go on to the ice but we decided to run the risk as going round we [would] make us from 9 to 12 miles extra travel. We barely got over without any mishaps but concluded after reaching the opposite side that we did not want any more of the same.

The ice was rotten and several times one foot would break through, but we were going with the wind and had no time to take notes of our surroundings as we made the distance in about Six Minutes—

Stayed in the city of Rochester the second night. The third and last day of our journey we travelled some 25 miles and arrived at our Destination, the town of Clarkson—[32]

---

31. The Irondequoit is the small bay on the southern shore of Lake Ontario on which Rochester is situated.

32. Clarkson is a village north of Brockport on N.Y. 19.

In a few days I went up to Brockport and hired to old Harry Backus for one year— He was a very wealthy man and one of the proprietors of the large Foundry, and engaged in Mercantile Business quite heavily and owned a large farm a few miles from Lockport on the canal where I was to put in my time while in his employ—

I was not at all acquainted with this man. Had I been I should have known better than to put myself under his tuition [tutelage? Morse's irony is obvious]. I commenced the first day of April 1847 and the first month I was kept hacking round doing a little of everything while making preparations to go on to his Ranch at Lockport.

I made one discovery during the first month and that was I was supposed to be the nigger and he the master, that was all right. In one sense I always supposed that a man Should be Boss of his own affairs but I never could see the propriety and don't to this day think it policy for any man Employing laborers to treat them like brutes and no man that is endowed with a proper sense of his manhood will submit to any such regulation—consequently I told him he made too great a distinction between Employer and laborer. It might do in countrys farther south but up in the free state of New York all men whether rich or poor had certain rights and if they were possessed of the right Spirit would maintain their rights whether congenial to the moneyed aristocracy or otherwise.

I told him I had my papers to show that I was a free man—had never been sold into bondage and no white man less than sixteen feet between the eyes could ever make a slave of me![33]

---

33. It is Morse's purpose not to demean blacks but rather to strike an analogy of his treatment with that of the slave. His use of the word "nigger" is colloquial, as in Mark Twain's use in "Nigger Jim," Huck's friend. Morse's antislavery sentiments are obvious. He probably reflects a farm hand's attitude toward "bosses" (often farm owners) whose oppressive, or unfair treatment of their employees was supported by the existing social structure. If the independent farmer, such as Morse aspired to become at this time, was the symbol of a free Jeffersonian-Jacksonian democracy, the myth concealed the everyday reality of class distinction. Cooper's landlords (Satanstoe, for example), whether or not authentic, were lords indeed and may suggest a reality.

This happened about the first of May and I made up my mind in about five minutes to pack for Wisconsin—and accordingly started the fifth—and after a pleasant journey of three days Landed at Sheboygan.

Took stage at Sheboygan and after an all days fatiguing journey arrived at Fond Du Lac—the road from Sheboygan to Fond Du Lac in them days was a terror even to the natives, passengers being under the necessity many times in the course of a day to foot it across swampy wet places—which made it very interesting.

Fond Du Lac at that time was in its infancy. It was situated at the foot of Winnebago Lake on a small low prairie which was but little less than a mud hole yet the proprietors of the town were very Sanguine in their expectations and I think they really believed that this would be a second *Chicago*.[34]

There were about half a Dozen small dwellings and the foundations laid for as many more and in addition one Hotel called the Badger House and another in course of Erection to be called the Lewis House.

Main street through the town running North and South was little better than a cowpath and the only thoroughfare leading west was an Indian trail, their being no settlement for miles.

The next morning I crossed the Fond Du Lac River on the top side of a log and when across the stream found myself without a sign of a road or habitation. I had learned that out in the direction I was to travel was a one horse Hotel and by good engineering or by good luck I struck the point. Here I made enquiries concerning the county on beyond but could learn but little, our Host being almost a stranger to the country as well as myself. Ceresco was my destination, run by what was called the Fourierites.[35] Soon after leaving this 7 mile station, I

---

34. The successful growth of Fond du Lac city from unpretentious beginnings is recorded in Butterfield's *History of Fond du Lac County, Wisconsin*. Morse's satire is probably not in error, however, as "land fever" was a disease that plagued rich and poor alike. Mark Twain satirizes such speculation in *The Gilded Age* (1873). Morse's memories here were of 1846.

35. Ceresco has been previously identified as the location of the Fourierist Phalanx. The fertility of the land in this area, then as now,

emerged from the timber and grubs and found myself on—as I thought—the most beautiful spot of country on Gods green Earth. The prairie grass was then about 4 inches high and the whole face of the country had the appearance of an everlasting grainfield.

I traveled till nearly sundown and finally weary and footsore turned in with a man by the name of Almond Osborn and staid with him till morning—

I found this Osborn and wife two wide awakes—they had been on their claim but a short time but were workers and making a good showing. I found by this man Osborn that I was yet about 4 miles from Ceresco and nearly seven miles from my brother Myron who had come on the spring previous. After partaking of a Hearty Breakfast I struck a B Line for M.E. Morses ranch where I arrived nearly at noon, unlooked for, unexpected, weary, footsore and hungry.

I was greatly taken with the country and thought it a perfect paradise. The next day in company with Colon [Colonel ?] Tom I went to the Fox River some fifteen miles to a little town called Algona 3 miles up the river from Winnebago Lake. This berg consisted of one building used as a dwelling and store run by Old Tommy Baker and a large boarding house about half completed.[36] This establishment was owned by a man by the name of Coon—stopping at this house was old Dr. Firman and his son-in-law by the name of Wolsey. They were superintending the Building of a stream saw mill which was put in running order sometime in July.

After a few days I hired out to this man Coon for the summer for $26 pr month. The work was a little of everything but principally gardening. This garden was on the opposite side of Fox River[37] which at this place was said to be 60 rods wide.

---

indicates that it was appropriately named for Ceres, goddess of grains.

36. Morse's reference is possibly to a village that no longer exists or changed its name. The area, however, remains Algoma Township and lies on the Fox River northwest of Oshkosh.

37. According to Chart No. 720, U.S. Army Engineers, 1967, the Fox River runs northwesterly through the city of Oshkosh to Lake Butte des Mortes and connects this lake with Lake Winneconne;

Here was another difficulty. The only means of crossing was in regular indian canoes or a hollow log sharpened at each end. I never took much delight in boating and somehow had a sort of dread of water. It may be that the narrow escapes that I had when a mere lad of being drowned was the principle cause of this dislike. When about ten years old at the old town line School there was quite a large stream called the south Branch. This frequently rose up in time of heavy rains and spread out making quite a sea and several times swept away all the Bridges—at one of these times the crossing near the school house was taken away and while preparation for replacing or putting in a new crossing was going on we Boys big and little set to work and made what we called a raft and undertook to cross over to the opposite side but after getting into the main stream in about twelve feet of water the current was too much for our craft or else we lacked skill to manage it. At all events we swamped and went down. As our treacherous craft gradually settled, and seeing there was no help for us, I bid farewell to all earthly scenes, gave the last look upon the face of the earth and sank, as I supposed, to rise no more, but through some unknown agency I found myself safely on the shore with just the breath of life left in my poor frail body. I have wished a thousand times that I could express in words what I realized while under the water as long as consciousness lasted. That scene is fresh in my memory today although it is nearly fifty years ago. But necessity compelled me to undertake any and everything in the "line of duty" and run all risks.

I soon became quite an Expert with my craft and had the satisfaction of hearing others say that I would soon be a pretty good Indian. I occasionally got a good ducking but luckily went through the season without any serious mishaps.

I continued in the service of Coon till the time arrived for harvest and finding him rather unsafe pay I left and went up the River a few miles to what was called the Whitmore Farm.

Here was a farm opened by a couple of New York men and

Oshkosh is in the township of Algoma; hence, Morse refers to this area and not the Lower Fox River which is at the head of Lake Winnebago.

women and a wheat Harvest and stacking for One Dollar and twenty-five cents per day—

All this grain had to be cut in the old fashioned way with cradles—

We started in—about 12 or 15 hands—Pell Mell without any system. Our Boss probably had never seen a stack of grain put up but he had sense enough to soon find that it needed an experienced hand to run the business successfully and soon retired leaving a man named Tuttle as overseer. Matters now went on farmerlike and after the first weeks cutting, two or three teams were put to stacking and before cutting was finished a machine was put to threshing. As soon as threshing commenced a few teams were put to plowing.

During the wheat harvest a force were put to haymaking. Some 200 tons were put in the stack—

The first of Sept [1847] I bought a yoke of cattle [oxen] for which I was to plough fifty acres. One month completed the job and I started for the prairie where I had a claim. This was in the town of Ceresco and Co. of Fon Dulac [Fond du Lac], 62 [miles] south East of Oshkosh.[38]

I put in 10 tons of hay to keep my team through the coming winter and when I got my hay secured I sold the hay and cattle and went out to Fairwater[39] to work on the Dam where a Flouring mill was to be Erected. The wages were only $15. pr month but there was no other business that paid any better as the country was not yet opened to any Extent.

After a few days I was detailed to work on the foundation which was being built of stone under the Supervision of a scotchman by the name of Robert Miller. My pay was raised to $1.25 per day late in the fall. When this job was out of the way, I left and went to work for D. Egliston making rails—

---

38. Rosendale was officially named and separated from Ceresco in 1846. Although Morse mentions the year as 1847, his use of both names suggests his residence in the area immediately after the change. See McKenna, *Fond du Lac County, Wisconsin*, 266.

39. Fairwater is located on the county line between Fond du Lac and Green Lake Counties on Wisconsin 44. At this time Green Lake County was part of Dodge County, which is now immediately south of Fond du Lac County. The entire area is due west of Sheboygan.

One thing I should of spoken of as reference will be made to the same subject hereafter. During my work on the mill I became acquainted with a young lady by the name of Delia Mason, her parents having just moved into the place from the Southern part of the state. She was employed at our boarding house as one of the cooks and remained there until sometime in winter— During the winter I occasionally visited at her house and found the whole family very sociable and good company.

The old gentleman and Lady were formerly of Pennsylvania—but the western fever had led them from one place to another till the fall of '47 found them settled in Dodge County, Wisconsin, six or eight miles south of what is now called Ripon.[40]

In the spring—of late 1848—I went to work on my claim Located on the line between Dodge and Winnebago Co's and in the N. West Corner of the town of Rosendale.[41]

About this time the discovery of gold in California was made and every body was nearly mad to go to the Mines. Several young men of my acquaintance talked California and I found I was getting the fever and we finally called a counsel to talk the matter over and the result was we decided to form a company for an overland Expedition. [However, after serious reflection] I could not conscientiously after hearing their entreaties do otherwise than give up my proposed undertaking. For one

---

40. The Mason family lived in the present Green Lake County, Wisconsin. Since Morse does not give his father-in-law's first name, the Mason family was impossible to research.

41. Fond du Lac County Deeds, Book K, p. 622. Omar purchased this land from his brother Myron in 1849. (He had entered a claim by right of the 1842 preemption law in 1846 or 1847 but did not file and purchase it until 1849.) His deed was recorded as "the North East quarter of the North East quarter, Section six, Range 16, containing forty acres" and "thirty acres of land off of the North West quarter of the North East quarter." He purchased the land for "Eighty-seven dollars and fifty cents" from his brother Myron E. Morse. Myron owned much of the land in this area for speculation purposes, as his brother Ansel had in Hastings Township, Oswego County, New York. They were land speculators, a common occupation in the frontier settlement that seemed to promise much wealth. It was often a sideline.

Delia Mason Morse
1830-1876

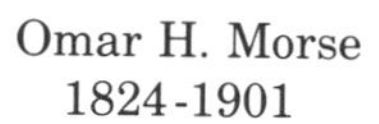

Omar H. Morse
1824-1901

cause and another others of the company gave up the job and others took their place— Some time in the early part of May [1848], the company moved, consisting of nine yoke of oxen, three waggons and nine men!

Out of this number only five ever reached the mines, the others turning back after a few weeks.[42]

After the departure of this company I went to work on my claim and in the course of the season made considerable improvement, so much so that I began to feel contented and more at home and finally considered myself lucky in giving up my California trip.

The winter following [1849] I was busy preparing to fence and further improve my Homestead and in the meantime renewed by acquaintance with the Mason family, visiting at their house during the winter.

1849

About this time my Father and Mother came from York State, also my youngest sister [Alzina Morse], during the summer. I worked on my land, Breaking [sod] and fencing, and commenced making preparation to build me a home— I hired a Dane by the name of Hanson and in the fall—about the middle of Sept.—he had got it ready for Lathing. I here give a plan of the cabin I was to occupy and in which I was to commence Housekeeping as arrangements had already been made and the first of Nov. I was set for our wedding day— This is a ground plan of the Building. Size 22—24, 12 ft. posts.[43]

---

42. Such ventures were common throughout the country, of course, and typified the expansionism and confidence of a still new and upstart nation. However, as Twain and Warner suggestively point out in *The Gilded Age*, land, not gold, was the real basis of that American disease, "speculation fever." Paul Gates's *Landlords and Tenants* supplies historical verification of Twain's "gilded age" observations. Gates's speculators were more successful in forming land companies than Twain's Colonel Sellers.

43. The ground plan shows a main room measuring 16′ × 14′, two bedrooms off the main room measuring 8′ × 9′ and 8′ × 7′, an 8′ × 11′ summer kitchen, and an 8′ × 7′ pantry. Between the summer

[A ground plan appears here.]

In October we had a party at the new house. As a large company assembled supposing the wedding was coming off, I hired a set of musicians from Oshkosh and a jolly time we had. Made a supper which was pronounced superb.

The first day of Nov I commenced plastering and finished on the 4th— The fifth I went in the afternoon up to the Masons and the sixth, according to arrangements, quite a goodly number of our friends gathered at the house of J. Mason where we were married by the Rev Barnum and after partaking of a dinner we went over to Green Lake[44] to a little town called Kingston in company with F.R. Sterrand and my sister Alzina.

The week was spent visiting and riding about and at the end of the week I returned to my future home to finish up my cabin preparatory to Housekeeping— The latter part of November we took possession of our new Home and commenced every day Life, Setting out with a very limited supply of this worlds goods but full of Hope and Ambition! hoping and believing better days were in store for us! In building my house I had laid plans larger than my means would warrant, consequently [I] became somewhat involved and the failure of my wheat crop made this embarrassment doubly severe—and all the difficulties combined to harass and torment me sorely— I saw no way out of it but to hire Money at a large pr-ct as money was uncommon tight.[45]

This of course necessitated giving a Mortgage on my home

---

kitchen and the pantry are stairs leading up, probably to a loft, and down to a cellar. A well is shown near the north side of the house. Although the dimensions of this cabin are small by modern standards, it was a large home for the area at the time.

44. Green Lake is a town immediately west of Ripon in the present Green Lake County.

45. Part Two, Chapter 1, demonstrates the historical and cultural background of the Morses' economic struggle. Their experience was not uncommon.

which in 9 cases in every ten results in misfortune and disaster as it eventually proved in my case.[46]

1849-1850

In December I threshed my wheat which was almost a total failure and the proceeds came far short of meeting my expenses—

In the spring of 1850 I put in another crop of wheat and labored hard to regain what I had already fell behind but somehow everything went wrong. My entire crop was the next thing to a failure and money was so tight—I could bearly raise the interest due on the Mortgage— My wheat was not worth Harvesting and instead of raising from 500 to 1000 bushels as I hoped to—I went to work in harvest by day for the Old Man Dustan.

The middle of August I was taken sick and was unable to do anything for two months. August 22 of this year our first daughter was born. During the time I was sick we saw pretty tough times for help and even for the necessaries of Life, being wholly without means which means in this country without friends!

Late in the fall of this year my father and mother moved from Ceresco in with us and staid through the winter.[47]

1851

Sometime in April at a school meeting in our District, Father had the misfortune to get a hurt which proved to be the means

46. Recorded in Fond du Lac County Mortgages, Book GG, p. 28. The mortgage is to Philatus Sawyer of Winnebago County in 1851 for $267 with 12 percent interst, due in three years. Sawyer was a United States senator from this district; see McKenna, *Fond du Lac County, Wisconsin*.

47. Omar's parents purchased land contiguous with his. This is recorded in Fond du Lac County Deeds, Book K, p. 624. Stephan D. Morse purchased this land from his son Myron in 1849: "ten acres off the West side of the Northwest quarter of the Northeast quarter" of Section 6.

of his Death which occured May 20th.[48] During the summer I hauled Lumber and flour to and from Ripon and Oshkosh—and in the fall Mother and my sister bought a bill of Lumber at Fox River[49] which I hauled and helped them to build a house on a piece of Land which they bought of Darius Goodrich.[50]

1852

The house was completed late in the fall and they left us and took possession.

About this time Mother was taken sick and finally died and was buried about the 20th of January 1852. Some time in April I rented my place to a man named [word illegible] and we went on to W. Goodrich's farm two miles from Our Own Home.

This seemed to me a hard blow—to be under the necessity of leaving a good place for the want of a little means and working out by the month but I could see no other way and it seemed the only way.

In the fall we moved to Ceresco to winter and in Dec I sold my place, my home, what I had hoped to keep and spend our days on for about two thirds what it was really worth rather than be in debt and paying interest.[51]

Well now for another spot that we could call Home—

---

48. Fond du Lac County records do not show the location of the graves nor the deaths of Stephan D. Morse or Polly Morse, his wife. Cemeteries were not opened in this area until later, and vital statistics records were not kept in frontier areas as a general rule.

49. He refers here to the village of Fox River, near Oshkosh.

50. A deed for this property was not located. However, the sale of this house to Polly Morse by the Morse children after Stephan's death is recorded in Fond du Lac County Deeds, Book 4, p. 15. A year and a half, approximately, following her death, the property was sold to Alzina Pierce, her daughter (in January 1853): Fond du Lac County Deeds, Book 4, p. 165.

51. Fond du Lac County Deeds, Book W, p. 290. Morse's sale to William D. Carpenter was recorded September 3, 1853, although sold in 1852. The sale price was $650. Although this was far more than he paid for it, his mortgage, loans, and other debts necessitated the sale of the entire property at less than its evaluation of $800. See *United States Census: State of Wisconsin, 1850*, Fond du Lac County, p. 227.

I bought one acre of Land of Woodruff between Ripon and Ceresco just south of the old saw mill and made preparations to build the second Cabin.[52] I dug a cellar and got my foundation ready in Dec and the weather got so severe I laid over till some time in March 1853 when I again commenced work on my house.

1853 [Date in margin of MS.]

I bought some tools and done the work myself and in thirty days got my cabin ready for business—the size of the building was 16 by 22—14 ft posts.

We had spent the winter in a garret and was indeed glad to get into our habitation which was ready for the mason— In the course of the Summer I enlarged our habitation by building on a wing 14 by 18 and in the fall plastered and painted the whole concern.

During the summer I worked with W. Crandel in Ripon and vicinity at Mason work.

1854

Through the winter of 53/54 I cut cordwood principally for a past time[53] and when spring opened sold out and moved on to T. Sheldons farm in Rosendale. This was a farm that Father Mason had moved onto the fall previous intending to carry on

52. Fond du Lac County Deeds, March 4, 1854: Block 8, Lot 3, on Liberty Street in the village of Ceresco, which was later incorporated into Ripon. The name remains Liberty Street. Omar purchased the southeast corner; Delia, the southwest corner. The sale of this property later enabled them to get a start in Dodge County, Minnesota in 1855, but the Morses were forced to borrow against their claim in Dodge County in order to purchase it. Pioneering thus became an economic trap for them as for many others in the West.

53. Here as elsewhere, Morse's bitter frontier ironies are concealed by surface humor, at times at his own expense. He implies that no other work was available and his family was in more serious need of cash than usual.

the year following. During the winter of 53 and 54 Every body became nearly crazy to go West.

Minnesota was all the talk.[54] The state or territory as it then was was but very sparsely settled and was inhabited principally by the Sioux and Winnebagoes—[55] St. Paul was the only point of much account although Winona, Red Wing and a few other towns were named and destined in later years to become points of interest.

I took possession of this place [the Sheldon farm mentioned above], moving in with Father Mason and family. Some time in May. The same spring Mason and his son George in company with a few others left for Minnessota to seek a Home where Land could be had at government rates—$1.25 an acre.

I soon found I had made a great mistake in going onto this place to fulfill another man's contract and only a verbal one at that. Misunderstandings was the result and this Sheldon being a strict Sabbatarian[56] and occupying the same House left in time wide differences and made the Summer pass very unpleasantly, I have no doubt, for him as well as myself.

However I made the best of a bad move and got through the Summer—saving next to nothing for all my hard labor. Determined to profit by sad Experience, looking forward to that time when I with my wife and two little girls would be by Our Own Fireside on a Home[stead] of our own in the far famed Minnesota.

About the middle of Oct after settling up with this man

---

54. "Land fever" was a contagious disease and contributed to frontier restlessness. However, Morse wanted a fresh start on his goal of a permanent homestead, not simply to be the proverbial rolling stone. More settlers than frontier historians are willing to recognize experienced loss of homes and the earnest labor of years; their migration was caused by economics, not shiftlessness and search for an easy life, as Morse here makes plain.

55. Wisconsin was also a Territory when Morse first set foot there. It became a state in 1848, although Fond du Lac County was formed in 1838. Minnesota became a state in 1858, five years after the Morses first settled there.

56. A Protestant fundamentalist who observes a strict sabbath and similar religious laws.

Sheldon—we packed our few worldly effects and started for the West. My wife and children took passage with Win Magee in a covered wagon and a good team of Horses as I was to travel with Oxen and heavily loaded.

Magee was eight days on the road while it required 15 days to make the distance with ox teams and was a tough hard trip at that—we had already had snows and a great amount of rain through Sept making the roads much of the way nearly impossible.

Our route lay through some fine country from the starting till we passed Kingston County from the west Over Land—marshes and any amount of good for nothing soil.

We crossed Fox River which was about 60 rods in width at high tide using an old Mud Scow for a ferry, the Bridge having been carried away a few weeks previous. We were obliged to operate this craft ourselves and make four trips to get everything over which occupied nearly all day which was on Sunday the fourth day out.

We were generally lucky in getting places to stop at night having to lay out in some strawstack only four nights in the whole distance—but we were going west so it did not matter. We must always Expect Some drawbacks to great undertakings and a man is no man unless he can adapt himself to circumstances and take Life as it comes, the bitter and good things as they appear—[57]

We arrived at Sparta[58] Saturday noon the 8th day of our pilgrimage and stopped, taking dinner with our Friend Alban Harrison and Lady— The next day we passed through Lacross Valley. This is a tract of country between bluffs and young Mountains varying from 3/4 to 1/2 miles in width and very productive and here we saw as nice corn, pumpkins and

57. Morse's code of manliness is highly stoic; Fortunately, he does not maintain the stoic silence of other pioneer families who suffered but did not record worse hardship than his. In oral tales and songs, however, hardship and bitter failure are evident, though concealed by humor or masked by statements of the virtues of harsh necessity.

58. Sparta lies east and slightly north of La Crosse, which is on the Mississippi River south of Winona. Morse may have followed present Routes 23 and 82 westward to the La Crosse Valley.

Squashes as can be grown this side of the Rockies. Sunday we arrived at Lacross at 4 PM.

Soon after our arrival we were in luck in chartering the Steam ferry to take us over the Mississippi.

We were landed on the opposite side after dark at a place where there was no road but much mud— Before we found where we were and how to get out, it being dark, the ferry had left for the City not even giving us time to chastise the ferryman for landing us in this out of the way place without a guide, road or landmark— Perseverence and good trusty teams took us over 2 miles of mud and mire and landed us on terra firma weary and hungry and it would be safe to add disgusted with our first introduction into Minnesota [October, 1855].

We staid all night with a Mr. Gillet who made us as comfortable as possible and after partaking of a good Substantial breakfast we again turned our faces westward.

For the next two days the country was anything but inviting to me. At least—however—when within about 10 miles of our destination we came onto nice prairie which began to look more like home— I was much dissapointed on my arrival at where I had expected to make my home.

The party that had gone ahead a few months to prepare for our arrival had done but little towards the desired end and we found ourselves 250 miles from Home and not even a stopping place for the Night.

I found Father Mason had struck his stakes and laid claim to a quarter section for himself and another for my benefit. It was a very nice prairie claim but not a stick of timber within six miles![59] Had put up about 20 tons of Hay which as luck would have it we arrived just in time to save from a prairie fire which burned over a thousand acres and as many tons of hay on the day of our arrival.

---

59. The Mason farm was likely a few miles west of La Crosse in Winona County; it is unusual that Morse does specify the location. Interestingly, both the needful timber and the familiarity of the land—both practical and aesthetic factors—are important to him in locating a new homestead, the familiar in the landscape now becoming a buffer in the family's dispossessed state.

This was not my abiding place by any means. I had come too far to be content [with] such a barren timberless region as this. I must go further or my object in going West was a total failure!

Mason was much displeased at my idea of going further and I consented to stay till he got his cabin so that he could get his family into winter quarters. This was a foolish move again as winter was so near at hand and where I might be Obliged to go to find a home I knew not and every day I was detained cut short my chances for getting a comfortable place for myself and family.

Two weeks was spent in completing his cabin and on the morning of Nov 12th, 1855 I started west again.

1855

I had heard a great deal about Rochester and supposing it to be Something of importance I made my way thither. I found the far-famed Zumbro River and a Log cabin on each side constituted the much talked of berg called Rochester. Here was territory sufficient for two cities but whether this was destined for a large inland Seaport was more than I was able to divine—

Here I took dinner and then bent my Steps toward the next Eldorado—Mantorville. That night found us at equal distances from Rochester and Mantorville—where we put [up] with a man by the name of Gilbert.

The next day we fell in with the Hurlbutts 4 miles from Mantorville—[60] These three brothers were from Wis. near where we started from and had been on their claims one year. They made good selections, locating near timber with water and as good soil as Minnesota affords.

These three Hurlbutts and their families and our party of three made the round number of 17 there. We staid 8 days in a twelve by 16 shanty and in the meantime turned all our forces toward constructing another cabin of better proportions for the Accomodation of One of the Hurlbutts and after seeing

60. Mantorville, the county seat of Dodge County, is just north of U.S. 14, about fifteen miles west of Rochester.

them into new quarters we Started once more for Mantorville and the home we were in pursuit of—Mantorville gave another surprise.

Everything was there but the town. The noble and far famed Zumbro, the rocks piled high on the East with a fine belt of timber Extending East for several miles and land worse than wild in abundance—this we were told was in time to be the great Center!

One mile north of this cite I found my friend Bardwell from Wis. He was living in a little Shanty and on his claim was a nice Spring and Brook, a Stone Quarry and a mile or so east he had 40 acres of very fair timber.

Staid overnight with him and the next morning went out about 2 miles north east of town and made claim to 160 acres of mighty rough land but an Excellent soil and about 5 acres of nice grove timber![61] Before night I had logs out for a cabin 12/16 and the next day with the help of One man laid them up ready for the roof—

It was now nearly the first of Dec and I set out for Chatfield [Minnesota][62] where I had left my family, knowing I had no time to spare as winter was liable to set in any day.

I found them all right and anxious to get Home. We were 2 days on the way and a rough time we had—bad roads, no bridges and many other impediments.

The day we arrived at our cabin I went to Mantorville, bought a few slabs for Roof and one green Basswood board which I hurriedly converted into a door and One light window on two sides, no floor and this we pronounced Home— A sorry looking place it was I thought and I think my wife and 2 little girls thought so too but not a word was said to that Effect!

If any poor mortals were ever lucky we were, for that same day it commenced storming and the next morning the Snow

---

61. Morse did not actually purchase a patent on this land until 1860. See Abstract of U.S. Land Office, Dodge County, Book 496, p. 164; also, Patent Book, Dodge County, Book 3, p. 45. His claim, however, was made in 1854, not as he states here in 1855.

62. Chatfield, southeast of Rochester, remains a village.

was 18 inches deep and the wind blowing a perfect Hurricane.

The storm commenced with a rain and grew colder and every bush, limb and twig was bent nearly to the ground and never got up for 90 days— There were 100 days commencing Dec 7th that it never thawed in the Sun.

After getting up a shelter for my Oxen and getting home hay which took several days it was so blustering and cold I began to look about for something which was to bring us in our Bread and Butter.

By mere chance I came onto a man by the name of P H Moses from the state of New York who gave me a winters job making rails.

This was an Exceeding tough Winter—provisions were enormous high as everything had to be shiped from the Bordering states south and much of it by ox team.[63]

1856

Flour was $6 [per barrel], fresh Pork 8 cts and groceries away up—but we lived it through and came out in the Spring all right— Some time in March my friend that came out with us Ansel Morse[64] found a timber claim and we built a house and moved on to his claim and at the same time were getting rails out of the woods onto the prairie.

We staid here till May and in the meantime I moved my shanty that we had occupied during the Summer [spring] while I spent the time Breaking—fencing and improving generally. In the course of the Summer I made preparations to build a more commodius habitation, getting Out Logs and [sawing them into] Lumber for a building 16′/24′ which I put up in the fall and moved into in November— The following winter was spent in making Rails, cutting woods, et cetera.

---

63. Morse is describing typical frontier conditions.

64. This Samaritan should not be confused with Omar's brother of the same name, who, according to Oswego County land records, stayed in Oswego County, farming and speculating in land.

1857

In the spring I put in about 30 acres to corn, wheat, oats and other crops which yielded very fairly and gave us provisions for the year and some to spare.

This season as building commenced I began job[b]ing occasionally at my trade, Plastering and Stone Laying.[65]

The winter following was Spent at the Old Business of chop[p]ing and getting timber, Lumber for the erection of a barn.

1858

I commenced in April to plan for another crop. Seed of all kinds were scarce and to be had only at very high prices but I finally suceeded in seeding and planting on May 18th.

At this stage of the proceedings Our third child was born and named Lydia A—from this time up to the spring of [18]61 nothing unusual transpired with us—it was Labor every day and the next the Same.

1861

March 4th was the inaugaration of President A. Lincoln—Exciting times in the Political World such as never had been experienced Since the days of Washington.

In April some time war was declared by the South and was followed by four years struggle for independence by the Southern states seceeding or withdrawing from the Union— It was thought at the beginning that a few would quell the disturbance and that the 7500 men called upon by the President would be sufficient to bring the belligerent partys to terms but it soon became evident that a serious Job was on hand and it

65. Like many pioneers, Morse was a resourceful man whose trades of plasterer and mason tided him over during lean years and supplied cash to pay that "everlasting mortgage." However, he was primarily a farmer, this time successful in using his soil productively.

was no childs play but an actual reality— War was the cry from Maine to California.

The Indians on our Western frontier it seems had been watching for an Opportunity or a pretext to commence Hostilities in the thinly inhabited portions of the state and remote settlers were hunted, killed and scalped by the savages without respect to age or sex till nearly 1000 had been annihilated.[66]

Repeated calls by the President were made for men till every available man was mustered into service.

A prolonged struggle of over four years with thousands of lives sacrificed and money without stint squandered and finally the South had to yield.

During the summer of 61 I had my hands full at Home. My wife was sick and almost helpless a greater part of the time and 2 of the children had a really severe attack of Lung fever right in Harvest time and no help to be got at any price—[67]

In October I made arrangements with Dr Potter for a Land Warrant to enter my claim and in Company with several from our neighborhood journeyed to St Peters where the Land Office for our district was opened. I located 160 acres N E from Mantorville, Dodge Co—[68]

---

66. Morse, like other settlers, was the victim of rumor and inaccurate newspaper reports. According to Carley, *The Sioux Uprising of 1862*, there were several causes not known by most whites at the time: (a) the Sioux Indians had been pushed to small reservations, and traders' claims had already encroached on these; (b) the winter of 1861-62 had caused starvation for this tribe of Sioux hunters, who had been given a prairie farming reservation alien to their culture; (c) because Inkpaduta, an outlaw chief of the Wahpekuti tribe of Sioux, had murdered settlers in Iowa and in Jackson County, Minnesota, the government had refused to pay its annuity on the Traverse de Sioux Treaty, an embracing tribal agreement (the government was also short of gold). A retributive series of Indian raids brought swift Army reprisal: well over a hundred Indians were taken as hostages and kept in foul prisons. Lincoln's clemency saved all but thirty from death, but their hanging was the largest mass execution ever held to this time. Supposition that Lincoln's clemency order was disregarded remains prevalent.

67. Morse's reasons for not volunteering are stated here explicitly. In addition, he faced heavy mortgage debt.

68. Dodge County Abstract of United States Land Offices, p. 28,

This Potter proved to be a dishonest cuss—and in order to settle up with him at any rate I was obliged to sacrifice 80 acres of Land which in a little time was worth $1000/oo and continued to rise in value and is now worth $4000—[69] In the fall I saved what I could of what I had raised though much of it went to waste for the amount of time to care of [for] it on account of sickness and other hindrances and the winter found us in pretty poor circumstances but still we lived and done what we could! October 9th [18]61 our first baby boy was born.[70] We had hard work to get any kind of help in the house and the Idea of getting outdoor help was out of the question as every available man had gone South—

The winter of 61 was spent at Home taking care of the sick and doing anything that come along but it was a hard tussle all alone as much of my time night and day was taken up with House Work and caring for the sick.

Through the summer of 62 I farmed what I could, work[ed]

---

recorded that in 1860 he purchased the northwest quarter of Section 10 of Mantorville Township (this abstract is considered legal evidence in this county).

69. Dodge County Deeds, Book 3, p. 45. Morse's homestead claim was entered in 1861, although he had probably entered this land in 1856 and had established his five-year residency. This was recorded as Land Warrant 89,225, originally owned by Qua Rick, widow of Shay O'Tuck, soldier in Captain George Johnson's Company, Michigan Volunteers, during the Black Hawk War. A land warrant helped the government aid a soldier's survivors. Morse was forced to sell half his claim before actually purchasing it, probably in order to pay for it. The record of Morse's sale to Dr. Horace C. Potter of New York (City?) for $400 appears in Dodge County Deeds, Book E, pp. 598-99. Morse calls Potter a "dishonest cuss" but gives no details. Conjecture opens two major possibilities: either Potter loaned Morse money at interest to purchase the government land warrant and took excessive payment ($400 for land sold by the government for $100) or Potter had an option on or owned the Qua Rick warrant for land in which Morse had invested five years of labor and improvements such as a barn and fences. He had not expected Potter's demand. See also Part Two, Ch. 1, for amplification of this barrier to viable settlement of the frontier. It was common.

70. His first son was Manly Morse, often a family provider, who became a blacksmith for the C.B.&Q. Railroad in Burlington, Iowa.

out job[b]ing here and there and managed to get along at some rate.

Groceries and store goods had taken a war boom and everything that we bought had got up as high as the crow flies yet farmers products was extremely low.

[A double zigzag line separates the insertion below from the text of the continuous narrative.]

Jan. 1888 This narrative as will be seen by the preface or introduction was commenced over 6 years ago, the writer being then fifty seven years of age and the events recorded are all from memory without any notes but on looking the pages over carefully I can see no mistakes as regards the dates yet many circumstances and things interesting to me have been purposely Omitted having in mind at the commencement that only the most prominent transactions which more or less served to connect the years and show a connected chain of events simple and easy to trace through all the following pages—[71]

It can be readily seen that a record of events extending back three score years written entirely from memory is no small undertaking and requires patience and perserverance, a good memory and a tolerable clear head.

[MS. shows the end of this insertion with three ruled lines in pencil equally spaced apart.]

From [18]42. Contributions and taxes to aid in the prosecution of the war were called for at every turn and every available man and every surplus dollar was called into requisition for the One great end.

From 62 till 65 or while the war was continued there were

71. Morse's conscious purpose is here stated. His "chain of events" which connects the "prominent transactions" (or central events in his personal history of dispossessions) implies his naive artist's sense of focus on the painful events of his struggle as a pioneer homesteader. As a result of his concern with his losses, the modern reader finds such frontier themes as innocence and experience, cultural loss, dispossession, illusion and reality, as well as his candid awareness of a lost cultural myth. Such themes have emerged consistently in later American fiction and poetry.

but little variation in my duties and Labors inasmuch as [it was] all I could turn my hand to to take care of the sick in the family and supply them with the necessaries of Life—

In Dec 65 my wife took a notion to go to Waseca[72] to her Father's, a distance of about 50 miles. This trip was made with an Ox team and sled with a bed of Blankets making it passably comfortable. Still it was a long tedious tiresome journey for a sick person and took two full days to accomplish it. George W. Mason[73] escorted her through and took pains to make the journey as agreeable as was possible under the circumstances. I had forgotten to mention that Lydia [the Morses' third daughter] then 7 or 8 years old accompanied them and remained at Mason's till nearly spring— The winter was long tedious and extremely cold and the snow very deep— I had my wood to haul two miles with an Ox team and break my road nearly every day as the snow was continually blowing with but very few fine days all winter—at this time I was continually behind in my financial affairs insomuch that it was a continual source of annoyance. Matters were getting worse and I could see no way out without a great sacrifice which is invariably the result of a forced sale. It was hard to bring my mind to the point that it was the only course now left—to sell out as best I could—save what I could and leave our Home again and begin anew, resolving henceforth if possible to profit by lessons learned in the past and makeone more effort to secure a Home, however humble it might be.[74]

1866

To this end I made some inquiries and soon found a customer ready and willing to take advantage of my Straightened

72. Waseca was a small community approximately thirty miles west of Mantorville in Waseca County.

73. This George Mason may have been Delia Morse's brother.

74. The pain of another dispossession from a homestead built for the care of a family who intended to be permanent settlers remained vivid in Morse's memory. The anguish it caused is masked by his stoic resolve to make one last effort.

circumstances, offering to buy the place providing he could get it for about two thirds what I considered it worth. We finally struck a bargain with a proviso—I was to go at once to Waseca where my wife was staying to her fathers and if the proposition was all satisfactory with him it should be called a trade.

Accordingly I set out one fine morning on foot leaving Alfredine, Minnie [Mary M.? See Appendix C] and Manly in the hands of my friend Page and his good wife—I made the entire distance by six o'clock the same day, a distance of 50 miles on a snow path—in the afternoon the road was full [and] the snow drifting which made it a tedious Job.

The trip proved a failure as far as the Sale was concerned—after Dinner the same day George Mason carried me [conveyed, perhaps by sled and team] to Wilton 8 miles from there.[75] I walked to Owatonna 18 miles and staid the second night from Home.[76]

The next day I arrived Home at 4 PM and found my little family all right and glad to see me back again. This trip was made—100 miles in three days, laying over one half day at Masons in the month of February on a snow path—

In March following I made the trip to Waseca again, this time with an ox team, to bring my wife and Lydia home, leaving the children this time with an old Lady—Grandmother Gilbert—

The fourth day at night we arrived at our cabin and were all once more in our own Home for which we tried to feel thankful—

Spring came at last and brought its usual routine of farm work, planting and seeding— My Wife was still under the care of the would be medical fraternity, a set of regular money suckers and with all I could muster my Expenses far exceeded

75. Wilton is unknown. Possibly it was an abandoned speculator's village whose name was forgotten after the plan failed.

76. Owatonna is a community located twenty miles west of Mantorville. When Morse was writing, such trips were less common; he was consciously describing events that he associated with pioneer life. His purpose in such a strenuous trip, as he states, was to recover loss by selling his improved land before foreclosure proceedings dispossessed him and his family.

my income and I could easily see that the time was not far distant when financial ruin would inevitably be the result. Under all these depressions and disadvantages no wonder that I was completely discouraged and at times ready to give up in despair.[77]

A faint ray of Hope of better days still kept the breath of life in my already worn out System and I continued to grope my way onward but not very perceptibly upward—[78]

The summer of [18]66 was spent in laboring to raise what I could on the place and jobbing around occasionally at mason work—when Winter came on we were just about where we were years before—hard run and still deeper in debt. Sometime in the winter we found we had got to sell out or do worse. In Feb [18]67 I bargained the place away to a man by the name of Paddock[79] and in March O.N. Page and I took a trip over to Goodline [Goodhue] County to look at ¼ section of land north of Pine Island which we bargained for for the sum of $1000 [160 acres, sold at government auction for $200].

At the same time I rented the farm known as the Sam Denton farm—but belonging to C. Townsend 2½ miles west from Pine Island [and] joining R Freeman.

We came onto this place in April about the 13th—the spring was wet and cold and at the time we moved there was ice and mud and all the little runs full of water besides raining all day and we had a terrible job in getting through.

Manly had been sick with Lung fever and was not suffi-

---

77. The heroic stereotype of the country doctor, like that of the one-room school, is corrected by Morse's observations: not all frontier physicians were "models of frontier nobility."

78. Morse's conspicuous lack of stoic silence indicates that pioneer or not, he felt the pain of dispossession deeply when mortgage and medical bills forced his family into another move.

79. Morse's financial problem is on record. His first mortgage on this property was to Augustus Barlow for $200 in 1864, during severe family illness: Dodge County Mortgages, Book F, p. 427. A second mortgage of $800 was incurred in 1866 to Elbridge and Martha Paddock for two promissory notes: Dodge County Mortgages, Book H, p. 212. To satisfy his debts, Morse sold to Martha Paddock for $1000: Dodge County Deeds, Book J, p. 352. Homesteading then as now was a high-risk "cottage industry."

ciently recovered to be moved. He and his Mother and Alfredine was left at the Old House.

We did not arrive at our new quarters till sometime after dark—wet—covered with mud and Hungry.

George Mason—D.F. Ingram was with me—we found a sorry looking old rickity—rotten—dirty Log House—a poor excuse for a Home if only for the summer—.

We had no matches, no stove up and no provisions that we could get at and we camped on the floor wet and Hungry. The next morning I was sore, lame and more than half sick.

I went to work and cleaned up the old Hovel making quite an improvement in the appearance of the premises and the next Sunday went back for the rest of the family. I found them anxious to depart from their present quarters. We arrived at our new quarters just [at] night So we were altogether once more.

I had about 30 acres to plant with an ox team and was a little late in getting my seeding done. I planted my corn—7 acres May 14th. We had a frost some time in June which killed corn down to the ground—and another in August which damaged it badly and then in Sept—so the corn crop was a failure—I raised 200 bushels of wheat and cockle [burrs], pigeon grass & other foul stuff and with all in all the crop was worth but little!

Well the section of Land that Page and I bargained for was a rough bushy grubby tract of Land with a spring of water near the South line—we failed to agree on the division as we both claimed the water So we gave it up.

I got my farm work out of the way about the 10th of September and went to work at my trade and followed it all the latter part of Nov. I earned considerable that way [but] some of the pay I never got. The biggest part was good.[80]

Some time in Dec. I bought a piece of timber of Burlingame and through the winter got out quite a quantity of wood posts and rails.[81]

---

80. The short supply of cash among homesteaders is evident in most writings. Prairie state farmers were similar in this respect to homesteaders on other frontiers.

81. The deed for this woodlot is not recorded.

1868

In March 68 I moved into another old log hut belonging to Geo Mason near where I had bargained for sixty acres of land of Geo Hayward.[82]

Through the season I got a little breaking [of sod cover] done by Peter Townsend. In the meantime [I] sold to Norm Dickinson a pair of oxen for 20 acres of Breaking and $50/ worth of Lumber for another Shanty. During the summer of 68 I worked at stone laying and anything that came along. I put up a foundation for a bridge East of Mantorville which took 25 cords of stone. I boarded with E.V. Canfield, one of the commissioners, while doing the work.

They had a splendid garden and were cultivating Strawberries, Raspberries and occasionally as I went Home I carried from 10 to 20 quarts of the fruit to the family which came very acceptable.

The winter season was spent getting wood and fencing for the lot bought of Heyward.

[18]69

In the spring of -69 sometime in March I commenced putting up a Dwelling house on my new Homestead size 14/by/28. I bought a set of Logs intending to build an old time Log cabin but finally changed the plan standing the logs on end as they were faced down to a thickness of five inches—Morticed and pinned into Sills setting them close together at a /height/ of 12 ft— For a foundation I [MS illegible] blocks as the ground was frozen which made it impracticable for digging a cellar. This imposing structure I put up without assistance one log at a time— It was a pretty tough job and occupied a month or more

---

82. The last Morse homestead was located in Roscoe Township, Goodhue County. Goodhue is immediately northeast of Dodge, the site of their previous farm. Although an error in the Goodhue index makes his deed impossible to locate, an early mortgage gives this information: "the Northwest corner of the Northeast of Section twenty-six, Town No. one hundred and nine": Goodhue County Mortgages, Book 21, p. 269.

to get it inhabitable and we took possession the first of May 69—

The inside work was left over till fall. Some time during the Summer I got out stone near by and completed a cellar under said building—14 by 18—and in the fall completed the inside work. I once more had 60 acres of Land with a very comfortable shelter for myself and family—but my team had to go for Breaking and Lumber to complete the house.

1870

The winter of 69 and 70 was spent cutting cord wood to supply the necessaries for the family. When seeding come I had no seed and no team but managed to get help enough together to complete the seeding in about 2 days—seed wheat I borrowed of James Parker—till fall, he obliging me to return at the rate of about 50 per cent for about 4 months—[83]

My crop of wheat was not all I could ask for being sowed after every body else was through and pastured till into June having the fence all to build new and alone! I had reserved 2 acres for potatoes—this my neighbor Twitchell furnished seed for—and planted— This was the memorable Potato Bug Season and it took all our available spare forces and time to gather the Bugs— I raised a little over 500 bushels of wheat which I cut the old fashioned way with a hand cradle and bound alone with the Exception of about 2 days help.

This wheat was marketed at the Forest Mills for 60 and 65 cts per bushel—

It rained from the commencement of stacking a good portion of the time till the ground froze up which was about the 20th of October, freezing in my potatoes.

In September I bought a pair of oxen of Dickinson for $125/ which took nearly half of my wheat crop. I was still to a heavy expense on acct of Sickness with little or nothing to turn off [up?] to meet Expenses. I was foolish enough to hire money and

83. Here as elsewhere, Morse's 50 percent seed loans increased his debts. Such explicit references are uncommon in homesteading narratives.

at a big interest and by Mortgage—this in time proved to be another great folly—as it had before— Experience is said to be a dear School and some are too big fools to learn even then.

[18]71

The winter of 1870 and 1871 was spent much the same as winters previous—doing a variety of work done at this Season of the year—and the summers were devoted to various duties principally on the farm with an occasional job of mason work.

Feb 29th 1872 another addition was made to the family by the advent of another son which we named O H Morse, Jr. Christmas Dec 25th [18]71 Alfredine [the Morses' first child] was married to V.W. Sterling from Indiana and settled on a small farm South East of Pine Island.[84] In the spring of 72 I helped to complete a neat log cabin for their use on this little farm of 40 acres and in March they took possession and moved their Effects into the same—

Through the summer of 72 farming and an occasional job of mason work was the business of the day.

Some time in April I contracted to build a School House in our district for the sum of $650/ and furnish all the material but about this time there was so much difficulty about the cite for said building that it was delayed till nearly June before I could get it under way— I finally turned the job over to a man by the name of Porter, reserving the mason work to do myself— The job was completed sometime in August or September.

This season I got considerably in debt again as usual and thought it necessary to hire money paying a big pr ct which as usual terminated in the loss of 40 acres out of 60. This foolish move reduced me down to a pretty small Homestead—only 21 acres left and pretty well discouraged.[85]

---

84. Victor W. Sterling later became a secretary of the People's party (or Populists) in Caddo Mills, Texas. A business card containing this information was found among Morse's letters. With Ignatius Donnelly (but living several counties north), Sterling was persuaded to join this party before he left Minnesota.

85. Morse's financial difficulties resulted in a mortgage sale: sixty

[A space of four lines in Morse's MS.]

1874 and 75

During these two years nothing unusual transpired. It was work here and there at anything that seemed to pay and much of it did not pay very much but being at considerable expense on account of sickness Something had to be done—every day—

In the spring of 75 I took a job of one Barnes in the town of New Haven, Olmstead County of stone work which occupied my time a month or more— The rest of the season was spent in jobbing and anything that come up—

The winter of 75 and 6 I cut cordwood most of the time! I was still employing Dr's and buying drugs which took every nickle that I could get hold of over and above a bare subsistence—pretty bare at that. In March Sim Dresback came over from New Haven and I engaged to do him a job of mason work—Stone laying and Lathing and Plastering, chimney, Buildings, etc.

When the time came to go my wife was getting worse, failing gradually but surely and it was evident to my mind that she was not long for this world— Through all of her sickness, much of the time suffering almost beyond endurance and not a murmur of discontent ever escaped her lips—always cheerful—always Hopeful and to all appearances reconciled to her fate whatever that may be— In April she wanted to be moved down to Pine Island and stay with Minnie [Mary M.?] a while thinking a change might rest her up and perhaps benefit her for the time being—undoubtedly she was well satisfied that the time was nearing (and that very perceptibly) which would terminate her Earthly career— About this time by the influence of Dr. Hill I employed R. McHinstry as a last resort. After a few visits we were satisfied that his skill and treatment was of no avail as she continued to get weaker and weaker every day—

---

acres of the northwest quarter of the northeast quarter of Section 26 in Roscoe Township in 1871 to James Hall for $316.38: Goodhue Deeds, Book T2, p. 292. Mortgage rates in this area at this time were 12 to 15 percent.

1876

I commenced my job at New Haven in May some ten or twelve miles away having to walk Home Saturday Evening and back to my work Monday mornings. After being absent a week I could plainly see a perceptible change in her condition for worse and I began to realize more than ever that her days were numbered although many times during her illness we had nearly given up all hope and believed the end to be near.

I removed from Home in june and went back to work satisfied that a few days or weeks at the most would finish her stay with us— I continued my work expecting every day and more particularly as each day passed and night came on to be summon'd home to witness her Departure—

On Friday evening July 27—1876 just as I had finished my work for the day I saw my son Manly come up the road driving at a pretty brisk pace— I readily divined his Errand and knew full well that the Crisis had come.

[Morse left a space blank and completed the following addition to his narrative in 1900, a year before he died.]

The Sunday before when I left Home to go to my job at New Haven I felt as though it would be my last trip before the final end—and I was very reluctant about going but she seemed willing and rather urged me to go as I was promised to be notified immediately of any change for worse but I could not shake off the belief but [that] I was doing wrong and it worried me constantly all the week and several times during them 5 days I threw down my tools determined to get home as fast as my legs would carry me but still I stayed, relying on the promise of being notified if my presence was needed.

But alas it was too late when I got the summons and when I arrived she was too far gone to recognize me, being unconscious and near the end— I then knew I made a great Mistake leaving her as I had at the last and justly blamed myself and no one else for the act. But O what would I have given for just one word or look of recognition—too late—too late. At 10 PM she passed away peacefully over the river and we were left without a mother— Only a few beside the family witnessed the departure, after nearly 17 years of suffering without a murmur or complaint the poor tired Soul was taken to her final rest.

Saturday the 28th all necessary arrangements were perfected and on Sunday the 29th at 10 AM a goodly number of friends and neighbors came to pay the last tribute of respect to the Mother and Companion of a bereaved Household—

A Baptist clergyman from Zumbrota spoke words of Consolation to the friends present at the House and she was then laid to rest in the Pine Island Cemetary—

The above record is entered in this memorandum this 14th Day of February in the year 1900 at 7 o'clock PM by O.H. Morse now in the 76th year of his age.[86]

[Morse's narrative resumes. He purposely left blank a space to record a memory then too painful.]

August 1st I went back to my job full of sorrow and loneliness. My interest and in fact ambition for Business seemed at a Standstill. I had toiled late and early through all kinds of Hardships and Disappointments still hoping that all would come right in time and this I said is the result

I completed my job at New Haven in August or the first days of Sept

About this time Manley went down to Cedar River after his oxen where they had been herded but by some mishap failed to find the herd. Soon after they were sent up being driven 35 miles in One day through the heat and unshod—which nearly ruined them. Lydia was with us through the winter and we got along finely.[87]

In Sept We had a call from Harry Thomas—staid till sometime in October. Through the fall Manly took jobs of

86. As this passage suggests, Morse's deep feeling for his wife and the mother of his children continued for twenty-four years. Neither his letters nor other family historians suggest that he considered remarriage, although it was common among pioneer families; see Angle, *Narratives of Noah Harris Letts and Thomas Allen Banning*.

87. Lydia A. Morse was his daughter, who became Mrs. Harry Thomas (see Appendix C). She is to be distinguished from Lydia A., Morse's sister.

ploughing with his young team of oxen, the first work of the kind he had ever undertaken.

The winter following we cut cordwood but made but little on account of low prices and culled timber.

1877

Through the summer of 77 we raised what we could on our limited little homestead and I jobbed around away from home much of the time, leaving the homework principally for Manly to do the best he could.

[One space in MS.]

March 8th, 1897

Today I resume my narrative once more it being several years since I have attempted to make any record and the above date shows 20 years in the rear [in arrears?] all of which I am obliged to make up from Memory and an occasional note made which must serve as a landmark or partial guide in making up the remainder of my narrative.[88]

The winter of 77 and 78 was spent as usual in caring for things at home, the family consisted of myself, Lydia [daughter; see Appendix C]—Manley and Omar [who was] now 6 years of age.

1878

The summer of 78—done an occasional job of Mason work interspersed with home gardening up to Harvest time—Manly went down and worked for Dickinson. Was away 6 weeks as till sometime in Sept. and during this time Lydia was married.

---

88. As he mentions, Morse wrote his narrative during infrequent moments of leisure in 1882-88 and 1897-1900, the latter period ending a year before his death. He is accurate in most details and is probably accurate here.

When Manley returned I was doing a job of Plastering for Jim Kane at Cherry Grove—[89]

This Dickinson cheated him out of nearly half he earned and what he got was forced and not till sometime in the winter following.[90]

It may not be advisable to make a record of personal transactions but in the above case I think it perfectly justifiable that such slippery dishonesty should be exposed and the perpetrators shunned as unreliable unprofitable people to associate with.

I have learned some things in the course of my short life by having transactions in a business point of view that had I realized earlier in life would no doubt have been to my advantage—But the lesson that I have learned all must learn for themselves—as individual Experience is what counts. [Morse drew an asterisk here, possibly for emphasis; there is no footnote.]

Lydia left us late in the fall and we got through the winter as best we could and during the Summer we Manly—Omar and Myself lived by ourselves. We cooked—Slept and Eat in peace and quiet and enjoyed life as well as might be expected under our demanding circumstances—being reminded only of the great change in our domestic affairs occasioned by the absence of our Mother and best advisor—

With the three oldest Children gone from the Home for all time I began fully to realize my lonely situation but still was thankful for the Companionship which the two left afforded me

---

89. Cherry Grove is a township in Goodhue County, near Morse's home.

90. Such references to "unsafe pay"—the results of the shortage of cash in the early settlements—are common in the journals, diaries, and other homestead writings that I have read. In one instance, an individual, a hard-pressed homesteader who wrote articles for a farm magazine was paid in land located several hundred miles away. He could neither farm it nor sell it since the cost of a journey to arrange a sale prohibited such recourse. The incredible paradox is that Ignatius Donnelly was the editor in question. See Ch. 2 for amplified analysis of his mind and works.

and I endeavored to make our Home as pleasant and cheerful as possible.

All this time and previous I was in pretty tight circumstances financially and had to Economize and forego all the luxuries and many of the actual necessaries of life, hoping some day to be more independent and better able to make what was left of my family more comfortably provided for—

This brings us down to Sept 1879—

The winter following was a long tedious cold blustering disagreable winter and about all we could do was to keep ourselves comfortable and care for stock, keeping up the same routine of daily work day after day—sometime in the latter part of winter Lydia came home and stayed a couple of months where she found much more comfortable quarters than where they had wintered.

In the Spring of 80—after getting things in as good shape as possible I commenced Stone laying and Plastering and Manly staid on the place entirely alone a good part of the Summer and a pretty lonely time he had but he done the best he could under the circumstances without a murmur and I must again acknowledge my thankfulness that I was blessed with so steady quiet good disposed and obedient willing faithful boy.

Sometime in the fall Mrs. Thomas[91]—my Sister—came and staid with us till the latter part of winter but finally went back to Wisconsin and in Dec Manly went from Fairpoint to Stillwater and hired to a Lumber Co and went up on the Moose Lake Country to work at a Lumber Camp. He was then 17 years old, totally inexperienced in such work and the winter was a severe one [with] deep snows and terrible cold.[92]

It was a tough winter for him and the Company that he was in was as rough and wild as the country and the weather but he happened to be fortunate in the way of health and soon had the good will of all the camp and got along all right. He staid

91. Lydia Morse Thomas.

92. Stillwater is located on the Wisconsin state line about twenty miles northeast of St. Paul, Minnesota.

till the first of May [and then] came down to Stillwater and hired out to a farmer near the city for 6 months and when the time was up came down home for a few days rest and visit before commencing a winters job at Brainerd in the employ of the N.P.R.R. Co.[93] This was the winter of 80 and 81—things went on much the same as in the preceeding winters. In the spring of 81, Thomas Robinson moved into the house and was to work the place and board Omar, the lad then 9 or 10 years of age.

This arrangement was for the purpose of giving me a chance to be away to work at my trade and at the same time make a home for boy Omar but bad luck to the day I ever took Robinson on to the place— He was decidedly the worst Specimen of humanity that I ever had anything to do with—

I found that by leaving Omar in his care and in his company I had done a thing that was much to be regretted—

We see and realize where we make a lot of mistakes after it is too late to help ourselves and it would seem as though much experience would open the Eyes of any person of ordinary intelligence.

I realized but little from the place this season except that every available thing that could be converted to his [Robinson's] use and benefit was nearly destroyed but by good luck I succeeded in getting rid of him late in the fall. About this time Manly came from Stillwater where he had put in a hard Summer—and had Engaged to go to Brainerd and work in the car shops for the N.P.R.R. Co

After staying with me a few days only, he went to Brainerd[94] taking Omar with him and I was to follow a few weeks later on as soon as I could arrange to leave—

In Dec I shut up the house and left the premises in care of old Father Townsend.

---

93. This was the Northern Pacific Railroad, which took over the Nebraska and Lake Superior Railroad on May 23, 1857. It served to connect Lake Superior with the Mississippi and St. Croix rivers. See Prosser, *Rails to the North Star*, 155.

94. Brainerd is in north central Minnesota, approximately 150 miles from Roscoe.

1881 and 82

This winter I made my home with old Sterling and kept Omar with me where he had the privelege of attending school a couple of months—the School was kept by a wild Irishman, a regular brute and intemperate, Disolute ignoramus in the bargain.

My time was taken up the forepart of the winter doing odd jobs and about the first of January I got word from Lydia—then in Swift Co—that she was left alone with her 2 children without Home or Shelter in midwinter and unless her friends came to her assistance she did not know what the consequences would be.

Manly was the boy to respond to the appeal to the tune of $100/oo of his hard earnings—and I was detailed to go and hunt her up and bring her and her two little Children with what few possessions she had to Brainerd where she could be cared for for the remainder of the winter.[95]

[Morse describes yet another cabin built to house his family in their dispossession.]

All went well for a time—but through the meddlesome interference of a certain old Hag that had professed to be a staid [staunch?] friend—the peace and quiet of our little family circle was changed into disorder, confusion, and finally into a shameful riot!!!

It is best perhaps to pass over what then and there transpired. It is a thing of the past and I would that it might be forgotten and I will only add this in connection with the matter. If there is a God and he sees and knows all things—directs and controls all our actions—wills all things for our good, why is it? and how is it? that things are unpleasant and so demoralizing and unprofitable to all concerned should be allowed to creep in and destroy the peace and happiness of the *family circle.*

In the latter [part] of the winter I worked for one Stinson

95. Harry Thomas, Lydia's husband, apparently deserted her. He later served a prison sentence.

and helped him on several cheap buildings put up to rent by employees in the R.R. shops and as the weather warmed up I commenced taking jobs of Lathing and Plastering.

Done considerable work for Mrs. Forsythe and later laid the foundation for the large School building in East Brainerd—finishing it up inside as soon as the joiner work was completed and from this time on there was plenty of work in that line which commanded fair prices and ready pay.

I made quite a little money this season but then at home was that Everlasting Mortgage and interest money that had to come besides some other debts and taking everything up and down I could always manage to get rid of every Dollar I could earn and more to go. When winter came I was as usual just about strapt—

In the forepart of this present Summer [1882] I had sent Omar down to Pine Island in Company of Hank Catlin—having made arrangements with my friend O.N. Page to board and care for him Supposing it to be just the place for a good home.—But again how easy to be deceived or mistaken in People and things—But this too with many other unpleasant things that come under my observation in those days might be passed over as a thing of the past and if possible forgotten—

Summer of 82

In August I found it necessary to make a new arrangement for a boarding place as mine Host Mr. Stirling Decamped.

I was at this time finishing up a house for a Mr. Hamiston—a mechanic in the car shops— I rented his house at $10/oo pr month and he and Manly came and boarded with us for a couple of months and at the end of this time Manly bought some lots of the old man Payne and we decided to build a house together in South Brainerd about this time— Manly left Brainerd and took a trip to Chicago, Bloomington and up to Pine Island while I was engaged on the building— He was away only a short time and by the time he returned I had it well under way and completed soon after and we took up our abode in our own Shanty— It was a neat little Cabin 14 x 22 [with] 9 ft. posts—painted and plastered and all complete—

It was getting near winter and after doing a few more jobs I decided to go down home to look after things and return with the other lad [Omar, Jr.] to winter with us.

I found Omar at Pages and glad to see his Pap once more and as glad to get away from his stopping place— I made a short stay at Pine Island and returned to Brainerd and found Manly all right and more than glad to see us both.

—We commenced housekeeping at once—and we were once more independent and as happy as you please— The old gent was installed as cook and maid of all work. Manly in the shop and the Lad at leisure to enjoy himself to the best of his ability.

Spring of 83

I started in this Spring Early to jobbing intending to put in a good Summers work—but Brainerd had seen its best days. Three seasons of Prosperity had overdone the Business and the building rush had done its Work. I staid till July and then [with] Omar left Brainerd for all time— We came down to Pine Island intending to occupy the Old Homestead but everything was upside down and the house and the whole outfit was in a demoralized condition and it took time and patience to get things in any kind of order!

Done some work for Batson, Hasbrook, Perkins and some small jobs but in the Country to finish up the Season—and during this time Boarded with Jim Howard and Omar staid at Frank Pennys.[96]

Winter of [18]83 and 84

We both made our stopping place with Howard—and in the Spring—or April 1st I rented a house of Old Man Perkins and we took possession and commenced housekeeping or more

96. Frank Penney was a son-in-law, the husband of the Morses' second daughter, Mary.

properly speaking Batching— This gave Omar a good chance—or Opportunity to attend School while I done some jobs at Mason Work.

[Morse describes moving from rented cabin to rented cabin through 1884 while struggling to maintain an inner peace within his family circle. He rented his "old homestead" in Roscoe Township, Goodhue County, during this interval in order to pay the mortgage.]

This brings us down to the fall of 1885—Sept 1st!

Omar was now about 18, a pretty good stout lad and much Company. It will now be seen that the past 6 or 7 years have been spent principally away from home and at various kinds of business and everything in a sort of unsettled, unsatisfactory, unpleasant manner— It seems that the home life has lost all its pleasures, all its endearments! and were it not for the Companionship of the few remaining Ones at home the pleasures of this life would poorly compensate for trials, hardships and disappointments.

After all I am well aware that such reflections are very unprofitable and not becoming an ordinarily intelligent being—

Winter of [18]85 and 6

This winter as usual seemed long and tedious but we still hoped for better days. The Bible says without Charity ye are nothing—But it is Hope in our case, Hope on Hope Ever shall be our Watchword—.

Thankful that we are still on Earth and Enjoying a good degree of Health—the greatest Blessing on earth—and reasonably provided with the comforts and necessaries of life and we realize that notwithstanding our situation and lot in life [it] sometimes seems a little tough. Still we have many things to be thankful for and in every case should strive to make the most of our surroundings—[97]

---

97. By finding an alternate occupation as mason and builder, Morse

[Two spaces left blank in MS.]

March 1899— 14 years more have come and gone since I laid this narrative aside to be taken up and completed at some more convenient Season—if ever such a time should present itself—[98]

I am now in my 75th year and I have for the past few months come to the very sensible conclusion that I have none too much time to complete my engagements with the outside world preparatory to my final taking off! Another thing I notice is that during this long lapse of time that this has lain idle I have been very perceptibly growing old and my memory of incidents and things that have transpired are not so forcibly impressed on my mind and it is far more Difficult to keep the dates of certain events in a continuous chain and in looking over the past it seems more like a dream than an actual reality.

[Morse's MS. leaves a three-space break.]

1887

I suppose it is to be quite natural that as the physical organism gets feebler and worn with care and anxiety that the mind too must suffer proportionately and become less active. This seems to be a law of nature and I find it holds good in my case.

—About this time (the fall of 1887) Omar and I took a notion that a few months spent in visiting our friends in Iowa and Illinois would be to our advantage in more ways than one—and we determined to make the trip— The last of October Omar started for Burlington, Ia.—Laid over at Rochester [Minnesota] 3 hours and again at Waseca for the South—

Our train was due at Burton [Burlington, Iowa] in the Early Morning—but through some unaccountable mistake I was left

---

was able to maintain his household; his son Manly, however, was the major source of family income. The loss of his wife and his last homestead in 1876 had obviously been blows that crushed Morse's spirit.

98. As he goes on to state, Morse's memory had begun to fail. He forgot that he had written more of his narrative in March, 1897.

at 4 A.M.—nearly 100 miles short of my destination and consequently had the pleasure of finishing my ride in the first freight Caboose and arrived at Burlington [when it was] nearly night. [However,] I had no trouble finding the boys although they were nearly a mile from the station.

Manly had married in Burlington about a year previous to this time and this was my first introduction to his Lady [Anna Schaeffer Morse]—which on further acquaintance I found to be a very fine woman indeed—

I staid with them a few weeks and then went on down to Knox County, Ill. to visit my Br Stephan who went from New York [Oswego County] to Ill. some 34 years previous to this time. During all this 34 years I had not seen one of the family which numbered from six to a dozen with an addition of a younger generation grown up to manhood. Here I found all well and enjoying themselves finely and they all seemed disposed to make my stay among them pleasant and agreeable. My arrival at their place was opportune being just in time to partake of a bountiful Thanksgiving Repast.

I spent the time visiting among the friends up to some time in March and then went to Burlington and staid with Manly another 10 days or there abouts—and then left them for home and Pine Island. I found it winter up here in Minnesota and colder weather than I had experienced any time during my stay in Ill. but I had become pretty well accustomed to our Minnesota winters after a stay of 35 years and so suffered no particular inconvenience.

Well here I am at Home again and found the folks on the place all right and had cared for things in my absence in good shape. There are a few persons it seems that can be trusted out of your sight and this old gentleman Coon and wife numbered among the few.

Spring of 89

Some time in the spring our people on the place took a notion that it would be a fine scheme to change their location and this left us alone again to get along the best we could which by the way was rather an uphill business as we had our grub to get and necessarily other matters of a domestic nature to look after which at best is not a very desirable or pleasant pastime.[99]

[A change of ink here indicates another interruption of his writing and resumption at a later date.]

This Season I occasionally done a job of Stone Laying as I had spare time from Home, leaving Omar to keep things in Shipshape as best he could—and when cold weather come on we were right where we found ourselves Every year, nothing ahead and not a verry pleasant prospect of the future!

I have asked myself a thousand times this simple question—what there is in a persons makeup to induce them to go on from year to year—combatting and striving against disappointments—and obstacles of all denominations [kinds] and still all this time remaining in the old beaten rut that has been traveled from boyhood.[100]

I think now that I have solved the Problem as far as my individual case is concerned—and of course I have no business to measure any one by my own shadow—So I shall be under the necessity of making an Explanation which seems particularly adapted to the case in point.

There seems to be something implanted in the organism of human beings—some call it Tact—some call it Luck—some say the will and determination to accomplish certain ends—is the main factor but I believe there is something back of the will—for we may will to do certain things and make as we think an Effort to accomplish this or that End and if every thing per-

---

99. Morse intends no disrespect for women; he merely reflects his pioneer's dislike of housekeeping chores. These were especially difficult for him as he was working at some distance from his home during this period.

100. Morse's philosophizing is not fully coherent but represents his narrative focus on incidents which reveal the several unifying themes of his autobiography: dispossession, innocence and experience, struggle, family values and so forth. We also find his ironic response to the change of the age from naive, mindless aspiration to the opportunism that plagued the era.

taining is favorable—all the conditions and influences harmonious—it is no great task to accomplish what we will to do.

If on the other hand we lay our plans to do certain things that we think is—within our compass or reach—providing every thing appears all harmonious and advantage[ous]ly [?] still at the proper time to make a move some unforseen obstacle confronts us—as also one after [another] in the line of mishaps or disappointments—and where now is that will that promised so much and yet when the pinch come was powerless to bring the desired Result.

The will is all right in its proper places; it lends force and energy to our undertakings but to place the whole responsibility on the freaks [?] of the will power leads us often into greater difficulties.

We know as little about this Law of nature that governs and controls Our actions as did a certain man called Joshua about the Planets Revolutions. It is said however that for some purpose He commanded the Sun to Stand still and it is recorded that it Obeyed him—

I think there is various opinions about the Truth of this little affair—certainly no sane man would put any faith in any thing so absurd—

I said I thought I had solved the problem of One Man getting rich or accumulating possessions without stint while another remained stationary—or apparently went back 2 steps to one gained and never got out of the rut of poverty. But I find I am at loss of words to make a satisfactory explanation to even myself—

I am satisfied on one point that a Boy and of course a man in time that has got business in his general makeup is agoing to show it when the time comes. I once heard of a certain Man that had been in business for a number of years and Every thing he took hold of in a business capacity moved like clockwork and he soon become famous as a money maker and in due process of time amassed a fortune.

This same man we are told had the misfortune to become Shipwrecked and alone, cast on a desert Island in the midst of the sea, an island peopled only by Savages—what did this man do, think you? Did he sit down and bewail his misfortune? Nay verily, not He. Before he had been on the Island half an hour he was selling sand to the natives—[101]

[Morse's MS. shows a one-space break.]

One more case in point—

Old man Sheldon tells a story on one of his neighbors; He said this neighbor of his was a farmer and contrary to general rule a money maker. While two thirds of his neighbors were in debt and some of them were mortgaged for all they were worth, He was actually coining money—could ride in his carriage and always had money in his pocket— Why this man would make money on his farm where the hardpan[102] come up to the third rail of the fence [is more than anyone can understand]

[Morse's MS. shows another one-space break to suggest a series of observations.]

There is an old saying that Poets and Statesmen are Born—such men as George Washington, Grant, Lincoln and others of equal prominence were destined from the beginning to occupy the very rich [important] positions in Lifes great drama that they did when the proper time come.

[A one-space break.]

Then there are thousands of others less fortunate that never seem to find their sphere and travel all the way through life and are blown about haphazard seemingly without any aim or purpose and finally go down to their last and final resting place and are remembered no more forever—Selah—

Some [who] would be wise old fogies content [contend] that the Moon has a powerful influence on certain vegetation and

---

101. Morse's point diminishes to commonplace complaint and a dull story of success that characterized the destructive power of the gilded age. Such false images deflect him from visualizing the effects on his homesteading of a grossly materialistic era of laissez-faire business concealed by a pleasant cultural myth.

102. Hardpan is a clay subsoil that prevents proper drainage and results in poor crops. Morse's exaggeration typifies the frontier humor of his style but implies a bitter wisdom.

Plants—for instance Potatoes planted in one particular stage of the Moon will grow all tops and blossom all the season while the same seed in the same soil planted a few days Earlier or later as the case may be so as to hit some other phase of the Luminary will produce fruit in abundance.[103]

I am not disposed to condemn this theory altogether for it is possible there may be some truth in it. Neither would I advise any one to plant in the moon. This being the fact, why may not people Born—as the phrase goes—under the ruling of certain planets have their whole Lives affected or influenced to walk in set paths in which they have no control. This seems just as plausible or reasonable as the vegetable Theory.

If this be true to any great extent it is better to be born Lucky than Rich or even Wise and the unlucky ones sadly need to be born again.[104]

I see I have wandered away from my original text—it being my purpose at the start to record only the actual transactions and happenings of Every day Life which I have pretty generally [adhered?] to and on looking over the pages of this narrative I am pretty well Satisfied with my undertaking. It has however the disadvantage of being written at long intervals and what I term odd spells in no mood for the work and to a disadvantage generally—

I am now writing up from the year 1890 to 95 from memory of passed [past] events—and I have to acknowledge that as the years come and go it is much more difficult to recall these daily transactions as my memory and mind both are not so clear as in earlier days—

[Morse repeats his earlier observation on the vividness of his youthful memory.]

Well now the fine years that have come and gone like all the years preceeding them have made no very great change in our

---

103. Morse is not one of the "old fogies," nor do we find other early writers advising the planting of crops by phases of the moon in this area at this time. Prairie farmers, as a rule, were pragmatists.

104. Morse's bitter disappointment here clouds his perceptions. His letters, excerpted in Appendix A, show less frustration.

wordly career and we have naturally jogged along in the old familiar beaten paths that we have travelled all the way up.

[Morse's MS. shows another one-space break.]

There is one thing we are sure of or at least has never failed us all the way through Life. Every day brings its Responsibilities, its never ceasing round of obligations and duties to be performed and we may look with reasonable certainty for the program to be continued to the end of our natural lives.

And when this old worn out physical frame shall have fulfilled its mission here it will necessarily be cast off like any other old worn out Garment. And if the promises contained in the Bible, the great Book of Books, and the belief of the Christian world counts for anything we are then to be clothed anew—take on new surroundings, a new or continued Life and Lives.

This of course is all in the future but if there be a God and he a God of justice, love and mercy we need have no fears but what we shall have justice done us in the end—So it be—

During all these intervening days we are doing just about what seems mapped out for us one day after another the year around, our aim and object being to live a quiet and contented Life and in peace and harmony with the whole world and—Let me in all conscience ask what more or better can we do—

In the Spring of [18]96 our old and reliable friend Mrs. Coon took up her abode with us once more and for the 4th time. In the meantime she, accompanied by old Father Coon and their two children had made a trip to Iowa intending to make [it] their abiding place in the future. The old gentleman sickened and died and things generally being in rather an unsatisfying condition she came back to Minnesota and engaged to stay with us for a time and do our work. We found it much more pleasant and to our liking than living alone and we got on finely again—

About July [18]97 we recd a visit from my Son Manly and his very much respected wife— They came from Fort Madison, he having a position there in the car shops of the Santafee RR Co. They made a rather short stay—only about one week—but we all put in the time to the best advantage and had a No. 1 visit but the time for their departure came all too soon and we very reluctantly bid them good by!

All things in this world have an End Especially the good and we need look for nothing permanent— Except trouble and disappointment of which we seem to have a goodly Share—

Soon after they left for their Home in Iowa, our old and trusty Housekeeper left, intending to make her permanent home in the state of Wis, having great inducements held out by a Br[other] in whom she placed much confidence—but like any unfortunate person she of course met with disappointment and [later] had settled in the state of Va.

The best we can do for her is to wish her Success in all her undertakings hopeing that in her last days she may Enjoy health and peace and have a sufficiency of the comforts of Life unto the end—Selah.

The years from 1897 to 1900 were years of Labor—Especially through the summer as we had started in on a small scale to cultivate Small fruit—

By the way this is a business that requires careful attention and a great amount of Labor—Every thing done in Season and well done—And to make a success of the business we must learn many things by Experience as we continue in the work—we must read up on the suggestion and practical experience of others that are working on the same lines so as to get the ideas and best results possible.

Every Family should grow small fruit if only on a very limited scale sufficient to supply their own needs—Dont get the idea in your head that a few rods of ground set apart in some obscure corner where nothing ever grew but weeds is going to make a Successful and paying garden with but little care and attention. If you do you are to meet with disappointment and perhaps entire failure—

Remember one thing; where there is a mul[ti]tude of farm work and every thing for one man to look after, see to it that you dont get any more plants, Roots or seeds in the ground than you can give proper attention. Prepare your ground with great care. Never let anything hinder through cultivation as often as may be necessary and never let a weed to to Seed—this is my advice if you wish to make a garden that you would be proud to show your neighbors—

While I am about it it may be well to state one fact which every body ought to know but I find many dont seem to—but a little experience sometimes is necessary if it is costly to open our Eyes

In starting in the fruit business get from the most reliable Seedsman your outfit if no more than $5.00 worth—Dont take plants from your neighbors garden that he could throw away entirely—because they can be had for a song—for they are dear in the end—go to work understandingly and whatever you do do thoroughly with an Eye to profit and success—

Study—work and Experiment and profit by experience and you may succeed.

[A space of some twenty-eight lines indicates the conclusion of Morse's narrative. He added a paragraph of observation toward the end of 1900, less than a year before he died.]

November 12th 1900

I find myself alive today at the good old age of 76 years—and [I don't understand] just why my Life has been Spared all these long years while so many of the human Family perhaps much more deserving—judging from outward appearances—have been summoned home and are now trying the realities of the Spirit Land to which we all Sooner or later will be gathered in—

PART TWO

1. The Dispossession of the Morse Family

Thomas Jefferson's agrarian dream would appear to have been sufficiently realized through the large number of farms established in 1880. Paul Gates points out that there were "969,679 farms in the public land states by 1860, and 2,185,492 by 1880, of which 76.2 percent were owner operated."[1] That is, by 1880 over 75 percent of western farms were ostensibly independent "family farms," while some 24 percent were large "factory farms" or "bonanza farms" corporately owned. A number of owner-operated farms, however, were one-family dynastics, small empires of thousands of acres like the King Ranch in Texas, whose fictional analog is Frank Norris's giant wheat empire, Los Muertos, in *The Octopus* (1901).

Gates qualifies this apparent success story: "These statistics do not reveal the hardships of pioneering: the failure of many who never acquired full ownership or even the status of tenants but who remained as farm laborers, the incessant worry over meeting mortgage payments and taxes, the fear of the loss of equities in land by foreclosure, by tax sale, or by controversy over titles."[2] The economics of homesteading, he concludes, led to needless dispossession and tenancy, caused principally by inadequately regulated land speculation. This, in turn, served to increase mortgage and loan debt.[3]

Although Alan Bogue[4] and Robert Swierenga[5] would contest Gates's conclusion, viewing debt as necessary to expansion, Horace Greeley anticipated the most recent scholars when, after a western experience that corrected his earlier optimism, he commented on the cruel struggle in 1860: "Tens of thousands have thus paid the Government price of their quarter section twice or thrice over [in mortgage interest and loans] before they could call them their own. Hundreds of thousands are paying enormous interest for them today, and hoping to pay the principle sometime—as perhaps they will.[6] Frontier restlessness, wastefulness, and shiftless irresponsibility—criticisms often leveled at pioneer generations—should be attributed to a needless economic burden imposed on people who, significantly, attempted to establish communities, but, disposessed or burdened by debts, sold out and moved farther west. They had little alternative.

Omar Morse and his family, clearly, are to be included among a once optimistic Greeley's "tens of thousands," helplessly unable to meet the demands of mortgage while farm-making under hazardous and unknown natural and economic conditions. Recent scholarship holds an enlightened perspective toward the Populists who, like Morse, suffered the cruel irony of the western homestead. *Populism*, Margaret Canovan's broad sociological analysis, finds a causal relationship between nineteenth-century economics and the history of distress that led to the organization of agrarian protest through the Farmers' Alliance and People's Party. This grass-roots liberalism, she suggests, generally placed the responsibility for merciless poverty on a cruel elite, an emerging "gilded age" aristocracy of corporate wealth such as the railroads—perhaps the largest landowner in this country and, through monopolistic practices, in control of the farmers' shipping costs. One of Morse's late letters of advice to his son Manly (see Appendix A) illustrates his advocacy of the People's Party; moreover, he finds the Burlington Railroad, Manly's employer, essentially undemocratic—"money-power," or authoritarian rule, is his term. Robert Klepper's objective study *The Economic Basis for Protest Movements in the United States, 1870-1900*, supports Canovan's theoretical perspective. Perhaps the most challenging of recent studies of frontier and agrarian culture is James Youngdale's theoretical vision of turbulence gathering direction and force (see his cultural history, *Populism: A Psycho-historical Perspective*), although Youngdale's persistent attacks on Richard Hofstadter's *Age of Reform* for his analysis of Populism as irrational occludes his significant contribution to western studies. Hofstadter finds that the Populists nostalgically invoke a Jeffersonian heritage, seeing themselves as the yeomen who carved a future nation through their hardscrabble lives on western homesteads. But lives of pitiless toil brought losses from which many homestead families had, literally, to walk away.

Youngdale and Hofstadter, taken together, suggest that the paradoxical western family farmer, in both the nineteenth and twentieth centuries, thinks and sometimes acts as an individual owner/operator yet also acts cooperatively, through various fraternal organizations and sales cooperatives. The paradox reflects a survival technique, inherited from an agrarian history of low incomes and high purposes, which characterizes regions where the continuity of the traditions of the early pioneers has made it possible.

The issue of the Morses' economic plight and its objective historical implications, central to our lives as contemporary sons and daughters of the frontier and its defining experience, asks us to suspend judgment of the western homestead mentality until the circumstances of their lives can be accurately presented. The Morse narrative seems the portrait of a luckless man and his family, a frontier loser, a voice who breaks the silence of the western code, but who is not representative. The aim of this chapter is to illuminate the reality of the economic causes underlying the Morses' and thousands of others' loss of homesteads and the resultant decay of the western myth. The tragic nemesis of an ineffectual land policy and insensitive usury and tax regulation, it appears, left the homesteaders to suffer needlessly on farm after farm that they had brought to fruition from the heartless land.

Morse's autobiography records three failures on land never before plowed and laments his resulting loss of equity and years of labor—understandably. The unanswered question is why the long silence? The Morse family's deeds and mortgages in Fond du Lac County, Wisconsin, and both Dodge and Goodhue counties in Minnesota indicate prevailing mortgage interest rates of 10 to 18 percent in a geographic area where county mortgage and deed books show foreclosures of three to twelve per page during their years of homesteading (1847-1870). Apparently, too, prices rose with demand for land and farm supplies when a homestead settlement experienced the pressure of an increase in population. Morse paid 11 to 12 percent mortgage interest and mentions 25 to 50 percent interest on other loans for seed, for medicine, and for hiring teams of oxen to break the sod for planting. I suggest that the basic law of supply and demand has a useful application to the Morses and, by extrapolation, to other homesteaders as well. That is, population increased sufficiently in each of these areas to create a demand for land with a resultant rise in prices and in mortgage and loan rates that stranded Morse economically. Although settlement naturally brought goods at a lower cost as a result of improved roads and transportation, flour mills, and so forth, Morse could not expand rapidly enough to increase crop yields sufficiently to pay his increasing mortgage and loan debts. A frontier mortgage was seldom made for a period longer than three or four years, and interest rates were variable. In addition, there were numerous techniques of manipulating sales and mortgage rates. Moreover, reform was frequently delayed or deflected and seriously compromised by congressmen themselves. A familiar historian's example is the legislator who speculated in land, mortgages, and loans and naturally felt justified in blocking all needed reform. Philetus Sawyer is a useful instance. He was a senator from Wisconsin who speculated in timberland and mortgages (one document shows a mortgage to Omar Morse at a then not uncommon 12 percent) as a member of a Wisconsin-based company; he used his power as a legislator to subvert reform, as others in political office had done.[7] The business and political strategies of such powerful men enabled them to dominate the lives of the average person—Omar Morse provides a lucid example. The liberal reforms generated by idealists from Thomas Hart Benton (Jefferson's self-appointed heir) through the famous

Greeley and the popular Henry George (the Socialist of the "single-tax plan") proved essentially ineffectual.

From even this brief analysis of the struggle to effect reform, the authoritative power of the land speculators in defining the shape of western society begins to emerge from the shadows of history. Many—like Dr. H.C. Potter of New York, Morse's "dishonest cuss"—were men of apparent probity and good reputation. Their power is evident in the failure of legislation introduced by such men as Benton and Andrew Jackson.

Early in the nineteenth century, Benton, a strong Jeffersonian, sought to redress the wrongs that complicated the lives of the homestead farmer. In his autobiography, Benton proudly records the achievement of state legislatures, principally those in the middle border states, during the panic of 1819: "No price for property or produce. No sales but those of the sheriff and the marshal. No purchases of execution sales but the creditor, or some hoarder of money. . . . Stop laws—replevin laws—the intervention of the legislator between the creditor and debtor; this was the business of the legislation of three-fourths of the states of the Union—of all south and west of New England. . . . Distress was the universal cry of the people; Relief, the universal demand of all legislatures."[8]

Benton's extravagant praise of state legislatures for restoring credit through stop and replevin laws (a legal stay of mortgage foreclosure) is an early application of the Jeffersonian principle that Henry George and the Farmers' Alliance leadership later sought to restore, but with little success. "Equal rights to all, special privileges to none" was the Alliance slogan. Negro and women's suffrage, anti-trust and monopoly laws, and protection of the individual's rights to land in the public domain were measures adopted for the Populists' platform in the 1880s. But in spite of Benton's legislation, in spite of Henry George's eloquence on the speaker's platform, the speculator continued his successful business in lands and farms.

The failure of two additional legislative measures illustrates the power of land speculators. Andrew Jacksons's specie circular of 1836 and the Homestead Act of 1862—both informed by principles of agrarianism advocated by Thomas Jefferson— aborted in spite of a popular mandate and strong leadership, suggesting the economic conditions that limited needed and farsighted reform early in the century (when it might have been effective).

Jackson's aim was to ensure the stable settlement of the West so that the people, in whom he sincerely believed (however contradictory his paternalistic administration), would not be hampered by banks and land speculators. Jackson revealed his Jeffersonian philosophical agrarianism in an 1833 message to Congress, among other documents proposing remedial measures: "No temptation will allure them [pioneer homesteaders] from that object of abiding interest, the settlement of their waste lands [unsettled public land] and the increase of a hardy race of free citizens, their [resultant] glory in peace and their defense in war."[9] Jackson echoes Jefferson's veneration of the small farmer: "Those who labor in the earth are the chosen people of God . . . whose breasts He has made His peculiar deposit for substantial and genuine virtue." Jackson's hope through the specie circular was to lower the existing $2.00 per acre minimum to $1.25 in order to ease the economic burden of the pioneer farmer. He also hoped to prevent manipulative and usurious mortgages and loans. But his attempt to legislate "a hardy race of free citizens" proved to be unsuccessful.

While the specie circular corrected some unsound banking practices, it did not remedy the economic conditions that hampered settlement, its major objective. The problem, Jackson believed, was caused by the several lending agencies used by the settlers: banks, mortgage houses, and individual land speculators like Senator Sawyer. The new specie circular stipulated that no one but the settlers were to use bank specie (bank notes issued as currency in a region); land speculators and agents were required to use more difficult-to-obtain eastern gold. But settlers at this time were generally legal squatters who customarily began to farm preempted claims they had not yet purchased at public land auctions and who had incurred debts in the process of settling and farming. After the crash of 1837, Jackson's plan became virtually ineffectual, as western banks had closed; gold and silver, which only eastern banks could supply, were legal tender. As a result, the frontier "loan shark," usually an eastern lender's agent, became a justifiably villified figure. In addition, he frequently bought claims at public auction on behalf of squatters without ready cash; he charged them about $30 per quarter-section above government price, then through clever manipulation collected on the one- or two-year loans at a usurious rate, well above the legal 12 percent.[10] It was never a question of old-fashioned "Yankee" horse-swapping in which the shrewdest trader won; rather, the homestead farmer was generally the sitting duck in the middle of the land agent's pond—lacking capital, he was the inevitable victim. (Homesteaders must have seen justice in the irony that moneylenders, land speculators, and town-lot gamblers were overloaded with unsalable land when the crash of 1837 came, an economic recession indicating the characteristic "boom-and-bust" periodicity of the century of western settlement.)

A second loophole that contributed to the failure of Jackson's specie circular has gone unnoticed by historians. Local Land Office authorities had the responsibility of setting the time of an auction and the kind of regional specie settlers were to use. The meetings held by the Rock River settlers in Galena, Illinois, in 1839 illustrate the fraudulent economic practices of the era. The settlers met in protest because they had been asked to buy their homesteads with either Bank of Missouri notes or those issued by the Galena bank. Their alternative to a trip to Missouri, expensive in both cash and time, was to exchange the Springfield and Alton, Illinois, bank notes they had in hand at rates set by the Galena bank. The *Chicago Daily American* of October 18, 1839, reported the first meeting of the Rock River settlers from a story in the Galena *Democrat*. Through these or other sources, news of the Rock River settlers' meeting reached the Galena Land Office Receivers, Colonel Derwent and Major Hackleton—or so it would seem, for on November 1 the *Daily American* ran the story of a second meeting in which the settlers reaffirmed their rights and with singular political finesse thanked these officials publically for accepting their Springfield and Alton banknotes. The officials prudently refrained from further serving their friends at the Galena bank by discovering that the Springfield and Alton notes were exactly the right legal tender. In this instance, organized protest succeeded.[11] Other homestead settlers were less fortunate. Jackson's hope of realizing Jeffersonian principles of homestead settlement during his presidency was subverted by the persistent history of shrewd manipulation, which his specie circular stopped for only a few years.

The Homestead Act, when it was passed after long debate in 1862, was a seeming triumph of liberal Jeffersonian-Jacksonian principle over its established conservative opponents. The act was intended to give legal teeth to the existing claim system by requiring settlers to "prove up": that is, to furnish evidence of a house and an acreage suitable for farming. Perversely, land speculation and mortgages rose in the public land states by the 1870s. Fred Shannon indicates that a rising curve of speculators' purchases from that period through the 1890s climaxed the growth of mortgage companies.[12] Their corrupt practices became public knowledge. A nineteenth-century cartoonist suggests the inventiveness of the land swindlers in his drawing of a speculator with a log cabin approximately the size of a dollhouse, conveniently portable, under his arm; another cartoon shows a land speculator with a wagonload of precut logs to be assembled on claim after claim whenever proof of residency was required. Another common practice of land speculators, legal though questionable, was to buy a right-to-purchase from stranded claim owners who had few options left. Their poverty furnished opportunity to purchase improved land cheaply, leaving a family to push on helplessly to another mythic garden in the wilderness.[13]

The western homestead appears to have been less viable economically than urban labor, although employment in industry suffered from both pre- and post-Civil War periods of acute recession. Even though the Homestead Act promised to correct previous abuses, farm dispossession and poverty increased after its enactment, while urban labor rose in income, thanks to the effort of the Knights of Labor to "level upward" the status of their membership. Increased industrialization naturally accounts for an increase in the quality of life for the laborer's family; however, in spite of heroic effort by legislators in both rural and urban reform, the economic ceiling on all lower-class family incomes severely limited the progress of settlement and left a heritage of urban and rural slums and destitution. The "safety-valve" theory of relief for urban distress, advocated by reformers who had accepted the garden model of democratic independence without understanding its inadequacies, served only to increase homestead destitution. Hamlin Garland's *Jason Edwards: An Average Man* (1892), a narrative of a laborer's losses, further illuminates the failure of reform and protests the loss of guiding cultural values. Protest actually changed little, and the capital gained from settlement financed the factory system of industrialization that changed a dominantly agricultural nation into an urban industrial United States of confused purposes. Morse's response in his letters to the Spanish-American war suggests an emerging citizens' awareness of poor leadership.

Frederick Jackson Turner, the historian, has long been considered the spokesman of the frontier ideal; on the frontier, he believed, the urban family would find relief. There democracy itself was to be renewed by contact with the wilderness, where hardship and danger would unify and equalize communities. Crèvecœur and Parkman anticipate Turner with this pleasing, somewhat decadent theory of wilderness and the renewal of democratic equality but omit the gamey toughness of the meat, the vulgarity of greasy fingers at the cabin table, so to speak. The unpleasant realities—the isolation, the violence, the barbarous conditions—were attributed, indirectly, to a lower class on the advanced parameter of the frontier. But even Turner recognized the economic hazards that could cause disaster on the homestead. Scholars have overlooked his cautionary observations. They have clear application to Morse's lean years on the prairie, and illustrate the obdurate law of supply and demand for land that obviously governed nineteenth-century laissez-faire economy in the settlement. In an essay published in *The United States, 1830-1850*, Turner points out that the boom years of the 1840s (when the Morses began farming in Wisconsin) substantially increased the cost of homesteading. The promised western "fresh start" on raw land cost "somewhat over a thousand dollars," which, he points out, was "considerable cash" for the average family.[14]

This indeed was the fact. Morse was then struggling with mortgages on his homestead farm in Rosendale Township in western Fond du Lac County, Wisconsin. His 12 percent interest rate could have been complicated, according to Turner's suggestions, by other expenses: the original cost of land (which frequently passed into ownership by land speculators before settlers arrived, thus raising the government's customary $1.25 per acre), erecting a cabin (often smaller than Morse's fourteen by twenty feet of living space), buying such needed equipment as sod ploughs and oxen, erecting barns and outbuildings, digging a well, fencing, seed, clearing and breaking sod—all in addition to the usual necessities. But Turner did not apply his observations. The Morses' years of survival from the 1840s through the 1870s were, in addition, made difficult by crop failures, the common problem of frontier "fever and ague," high mortgage and other debt payments, and, as he admits, his youthful inexperience in managing the economy of his first homestead.

We must remember, too, that his homestead was charged with the emotions generated by appeals, which none could escape at this time, to his sense of personal independence. He had married and begun his family with such expectations in mind. Even experienced farmers, it seems, could not anticipate the expense of becoming established on the homestead farm. But, as Turner suggests, the travel necessary to prospect for a good homesite itself was indicative of later expenses. Turner cites Horace Greeley's figure: a trip from Boston to Sheboygan, Wisconsin, in 1846 would have cost the traveler around forty dollars.[15] Omar Morse's trip one year later from Rochester, New York, to Sheboygan, (and then on foot across the prairie to Fond du Lac) would have cost an estimated fifteen to twenty dollars, probably about two months' pay for the young farmhand. As he himself points out, his skills as a farmer as well as the newly acquired skill of stonemason were crucial to his survival in Fond du Lac County, since he had arrived on the frontier with little cash to spare. Although he was industrious, he had only the small capital he earned himself in the yet new frontier community with which to begin homesteading; this, clearly, did not see him through. Turner's caution, not to mention the later studies of Shannon and Gates, implies the potential for dispossession that young homestead families like the Morses should have recognized but didn't because it was disguised by the potential fertility of the land itself and the shifting sands of the illusory homestead myth. Regrettably, Turner did not further investigate the economics of homestead farming.

There were, of course, some cautionary voices in Morse's early years as a homestead farmer. Josiah T. Marshall's *The Farmers' and Emigrants' Handbook* (1851) is one such example. Marshall's major caution to the prospective western settler was to avoid the purchase of more land than the individual could profitably manage. He suggests that seventy acres of improved land would be a more prudent investment than the customary unimproved government quarter-section of 160 acres because without "ready money," mortgage interest on unproductive land was a speculator's expense that the homesteader could ill afford.[16] He also warns against the dangers of mortgage: "It is the custom for private land owners to require one-fifth of the money down and the balance in four or five equal payments; the interest on the amount to be paid each year."[17] All seemingly prudent advice, surely, but impractical; for homesteaders like the Morses, the cost of improved land in addition to the mortgage was beyond their means. Some attempted to buy additional land for resale to help with mortgage payments, but it became an economic burden when it could not be sold advantageously, as so often it could not. Marshall all but assumes that the beginning farmer is a nascent capitalist, patrimony in pocket and a mind furnished with the dreams of success that the age readily furnished. Marshall's limitations arise from the fact that he was a gentleman farmer in New York, like James Fenimore Cooper, and relied on information from a western correspondent. Worse, he reveals the limited version of a landowning class, then without awareness of lower-class poverty and the limitation of opportunity this usually imposes. Similar misleading guides led many settlers into hunger and destitution.

Another example further illustrates the common limitations of such seemingly well-intentioned warning voices. The editors of the *Chicago Daily American* appear to have assumed that an increasing number of abandoned farms throughout the state were the fault of "shiftless" farmers who lacked initiative, mismanaged their farms, or neglected them because they drank too much—homestead Rip Van Winkles, as it were. Again, like Marshall, they did not understand homestead poverty. The newspaper's "Hints to Young Farmers" on June 4, 1835, for example, advised homesteaders to buy no more land than they could manage, and then preferably improved land; the writer added, "Consider your calling the most elevated and most important; but never be above it, nor afraid of the Book [the Bible] and apron [possibly "woman's work": i.e., churning, gardening, tending fowl?]."[18] Such edifying moral floss was probably thought wisdom by the writer, who hoped to encourage settlement by dignifying virtuous labor; and certainly it suited landowners and mortgage companies, who would profit from increased homestead stability and paid-up mortgages and loans. After pointing out such obvious practicalities as the importance of keeping tools in order, papers on file, and money at home rather than in the pocket where it might be spent, he continues with a temperance lesson: "Instead of spending a rainy day in the dram shop, as many do to their ruin, repair whatever wants mending—post your books."[19] The writer does concede that hunting and fishing might be acceptable leisure activities: "Should you be fond of the chase, or the sport with the hook, indulge occasionally, but never to the injury of important concerns."[20]

This seemingly fond avuncular advice appears to express greater concern for the work ethic (and, significantly, for money-lenders, who could only profit—either when the homesteader met his mortgage obligations or conversely, when he was forced from a farm and left improved land on which a speculator could profit from resale) than for the homesteaders' welfare. (Speculators usually made loans to homesteaders.) Such advice was not only insulting to the intelligence but often economically impractical for struggling homesteaders, whose reserve cash or credit was generally negligible. It suggests the mind that conceived reality—or "progress"—only as an investment in land, without apparent understanding of the settlers' problems. The labor of a hopeful emigrant frequently went to fatten the wallets of prosperous speculators on the resale of their improved land. For the shrewd investor, it was a plushy situation; for the advisors of hopeful emigrants, an opportunity to mint their dreams. The mentality behind such advice to new emigrants and immigrants seems to illustrate the mercantilism of the century. The speculator/investor had set the national ethos; he tended to limit reform through his insensitivity, if not actively oppose it, since his business ethic justified his laissez-faire capitalism. He saw no serious wrong in foreclosing on homesteaders whose failures he believed to be the consequence of shiftlessness. Chapter 2 analyzes a cultural and literary response to such philistinism. Because reformers were unable to effect changes in public land policy that would assist an economically trapped and struggling group of homesteaders, settlers like the Morses were trapped in circumstances over which they had little or no control. Like Philetus Sawyer, the senator from Wisconsin, some who had the authority and responsibility to effect change were corrupt; others were simply obtuse.

To further illuminate the controversial problem of dispossession from homesteads, let us examine the population expansion of Oswego County, New York, where Morse was born and where his father, he records, was forced from his land in 1839. From 1800 to 1815, a local historian states, the population of Hastings Township, where Stephan and Polly Morse homesteaded, was sparse; it had remained a near-frontier in a more settled county.[21] The first area census, in 1830, gives a population of 1,494, probably a sharp rise from 1800-15.[22]

Population growth increased steadily but not markedly; the 1840 census was 1,983 persons.[23] Several extant maps of the area illustrate settlement during this ten-year period: the Oswego County map of 1829 indicates there were two villages in Hastings Township, Central Square in the south and Hastings in the north. There was also a scattering of flouring mills, roads, schools, and other evidences of settlement.[24] The map of 1839, the year in which Stephan Morse was dispossessed from the "town line farm" (Omar's birthplace), shows a marked increase in all these evidences of settlement, although the county had no railroad, thus isolating farmers from the large urban markets of the East.[25] If, like most early local historians, the nineteenth-century chronicler of Oswego County assures his readers that the blessings of civilization had come to Hastings (by 1839),[26] he avoided the issue of its economy which was, we can assume, precarious. Ironically, the homesteader, that national model of fair and democratic opportunity, was jeopardized by the rising cost of farming as the population increased. Taxes, interest, fencing, and similar costs of civilization created unstable frontier communities.

Before we can ascertain with any degree of certainty the causal relation between Stephan Morse's dispossession and the increased demand for land in Oswego County, with its resulting price increases and rising farm costs, as suggested by the preceding pages, we must first establish the date of his arrival and the exact location. The youngest in a family of twelve, Omar, Stephan's witness, was naturally vague about such matters; he was obviously unable to recall early childhood events in detail. Moreover, research in Oswego County deeds reveals that Stephan's deed is not recorded, possibly because of a fire in the Hastings Town House in Central Square where early deeds were kept. A twentieth-century local historian, Elizabeth Simpson, fortunately supplies the necessary information. She states that Stephan D. Morse and his father-in-law, the Rev. Gamaliel Barnes, pioneered this area of Oswego County in 1803. Stephan gained a reputation as an able workman; he was often employed as a "pioneer" in the homestead sense of one who cleared land for others.[27]

Since Omar records both his father's and his grandfather's names in his family genealogy and includes his father's middle initial, there can be no coincidence: Omar's father is the Stephan D. Morse whom Simpson mentions. He arrived in 1803, among the first to settle in the area. Omar's references to his birthplace on the "town line farm" and the village school near "the tall Elm tree" are too vague to be identified with certainty; however, research has located the deed of Sanford Morse, Stephan's third child. Because sons and daughters liked to settle near parents for convenience and mutual assistance, Sanford's deed may offer a clue to the exact location of Stephan's homestead farm, the "town[ship] line farm" where Omar tells us he was born. Oswego County deeds show Sanford's farm as situated in "the East part of the Northwest quarter section of Great Lot #2.[28] The plat map locates the north line of Great Lot #2 on the northern town line of Hastings Township and to the west of Hastings Village. By extrapolation, we might assume that Omar refers to the northern town line and the Hastings village school. Sanford's farm would have been about three miles west of the village on the old town road. (The schoolhouse has been altered several times and now serves to house a fire engine. A tall elm, according to older villagers, stood near the school until it was killed by elm disease.)

It was most probably here, then, that Omar Morse's father was dispossessed in 1839. Omar records his painful memory of change to a new physical and social environment as well as his family's reduced circumstances. Historians have not as yet considered dispossession a serious problem for homesteaders before the mid-1850s, but records available in county courthouses and the Library of Congress suggest that the homesteaders' economic dilemma followed the Conestoga wagon westward from New England and the mid-Atlantic states.

We might assume, on Simpson's suggestion, that Stephan D. Morse operated the usual homestead farm, planting largely for his own needs rather than for cash crop sales. With a rise in population, which was coincident with a rising urban population in the markets of the seaboard cities, there was an increased demand for food production. But like others of his generation, he probably did not recognize the need to change to the more efficient methods of cash-crop agriculture—to plant a large wheat crop, for example, or begin dairying. He was a burdened homesteader whose obvious concern was a subsistance farm where he and his remaining children would be fed and housed, and their independence nourished. When the signals came, in the familiar terms of increased economic pressures, he was unable to interpret their meaning. In 1838, they came as two simultaneous events: first, the economic panic of 1837-38 caused both local and national distress (a suggestion of growing economic interdependency); second, the operative impact of the Welland Canal gave the one-crop wheat farmers of western New York a competitive edge over the central New York farmers of Oswego County because their transportation costs to the urban markets of the eastern seaboard had been measurably reduced.[29]

Let us also assume that Stephan Morse, like most others, was faced with some such economic demand as a mortgage payment, or an increased tax bill. He simply could not expand his subsistence pioneer homestead, since he did not have the needed capital to invest in land or machines. Or, to put this another way, a rising demand for food within the county as well as eastern urban areas—and the land on which to plant it—meant the necessity of changing farming methods—which Morse could not afford and probably did not understand. The Jeffersonian model of the family farm is now a faded if still visible historical symbol of American independence, but it was actually on the way to being economically outmoded early in the nineteenth century by a demand for more efficient production. The demand was for crop specialization. The agrarian dream had already become archaic by the late 1830s in New York.

Stephan Morse's dispossession indicates that he was forced to leave his homestead at a time when population had increased sufficiently to create a higher demand for land. Thus, in spite of the panic years of 1837-38, which reduced the cost of land and farm supplies, he could not survive; he had no capital reserve and was unable to borrow on a mortgaged farm. Change was out of the question. He went north to some "mighty rough land" (Omar's phrase) in Mexico Township to occupy another homestead subsistence farm, now of an inadequate ten acres. With a family of nine children to feed, Stephan faced the homestead bitter row to hoe—a "hard-scrabble" life, to use the settlers' phrase.

Omar's struggle to find economic independence—still our cultural norm of success, the American Dream, large and small—met a similar fate. We can assume that like Stephan, Omar Morse was faced with the classic problem of producing more food more efficiently without sufficient capital to improve his land, without even such basic farm technology as well-made steel plowshares, or money for cradles (for cutting wheat), hoes, barns, and similar needs. Above all, he lacked skilled farm hands. His reiterated complaint that his crop sales fell short of his expenses shows that he struggled to compete with those fortunate enough to employ the more progressive means of crop specialization, although he had sufficient acreage, it seems, to be a larger producer. Again, let us examine population statistics. When the young Omar Morse arrived in 1846, Fond du Lac County, Wisconsin, was enjoying a boom in population. It grew from a frontier of an estimated 139 persons in 1840[30] to 14,510 in 1850.[31] Attracted by the cheaper land in this unsettled township, Morse bought eighty acres from his brother Myron in 1847 for eighty-seven dollars.[32] (Myron had first come to Wisconsin to join the communitarians at Ceresco; when they disbanded, he became a land speculator, selling his share of their extensive, fertile holdings, as county deeds show.) In 1850, Omar Morse placed an $800 value on his homestead for the Wisconsin census,[33] an optimistic price reflecting the "land fever" of this speculative new county. By 1854, if not before, he was forced into a quick sale to discharge his three-year mortgage of $267 to Philetus Sawyer, the senator from Wisconsin mentioned earlier.[34] His subsequent purchase of town lots in Ceresco (now Ripon) in 1854 indicates the approximate date of his forced sale (improperly indexed by the County Recorder and thus lost). The surprising $450 that he paid for these lots,[35] acquired most likely by borrowing at high interest, would suggest his very real desperation. A land boom had threatened him, and he responded in the only way he knew. The rising population of the county, and that of Rosendale Township (where the Morses had located) after 1850 is coincident with his dispossession. The increasing economic pressures from such costs as taxes and mortgages, which rose with increasing population—and of course from the second mortgage—are a concrete index of a more indirect and theoretical pressure to feed an increasing number of mouths. He could not, to put it simply, feed enough people to survive in the time his cash reserve and credit allowed him to bring unimproved acreage, however fertile, into full productivity. Nineteenth-century reformers were accurate in urging more effective laws to protect the nation's food supply, but in the course of the century they lacked either popular and legislative support or an accurate perception of land-and-loan realities. The vulnerable people who were struggling against serious economic losses to produce food were never significantly aided. The problem for Stephan Morse and for his son Omar was how to feed a family as their costs rose and crops failed to meet expectations while the competition for markets reduced prices. In spite of the homestead promise of the century, poverty and dispossession seem to have constituted an inheritable disease.

Morse's ten-year struggle in Mantorville Township in Dodge County, Minnesota, shows a pattern similar to that in Wisconsin. The Morses arrived and entered their first claim about 1855. Omar writes that he was determined to profit from his mistakes in Wisconsin—this time he would be the diligent manager of his share of "everlasting grainfield" which was to be free and clear of the "everlasting mortgage." Their homestead near Mantorville in Dodge County, a government quarter-section of 160 acres, was purchased in 1861 at the Land Office in St. Peter.[36] By 1868, however, he was forced into another quick sale. Let us look at the population statistics once again. The first county census, in 1860, gives 3,797; the state census, 172,622. By 1865, the year Morse considered selling this homestead, the state population had risen to 248,848, a 40 percent rise.[37] No county data are available for this dicennial year. The 1870 census gives the county population as 8,598, an increase of 4,801 persons, which is over 50 percent.[38] Although Morse may have been a preemption squatter on his claim before 1861, even his approximate seven years on this homestead was inadequate time in which to bring his farm into break-even production. If the Morse farm resembled others at this time, quite possibly less than twenty acres of it was in pasture or crops—common enough in the northern states, where there was need for cheap farm labor but seldom any to be found except, of course, the family itself. As in the past, Omar's narrative explains, his problem was the mortgage. However, this chapter's analysis of local supply and demand for land, if unorthodox, suggests that homestead dispossession was related to the growth of population and the concomitant pressure to produce more food to feed growing towns and villages. We may assume, then, that usury, unethical land speculation, and the uncurbed opportunism long associated with early settlement apparently created an economic barrier for a significant number of homesteaders, the Morse family among them. Competition was the problem.

After 1868, the Morses moved to three additional homes, rented and owned, in Roscoe Township, about fifteen miles northeast of Mantorville in Goodhue County. On moving from Dodge County, Omar sold his farm for $1,000 which was apparently enough to pay off mortgage and loans, and after several seasons on rented farms decided to buy land in Roscoe (near Pine Island), this time from James Halloway, who accepted his mortgage at 12 percent.[39] By 1878, after his wife's death, he was forced to sell sixty of eighty acres to satisfy foreclosure proceedings, saving the remaining twenty acres for rental income. He then became a builder and stonemason in Brainerd, Minnesota, to support his five children, but returned in old age to become a subsistence farmer as his father had been. To further analyze population growth seems needless; the problem of an increasing demand for land by farmers raised land prices and mortgages, which in turn increased tax values. Morse's narrative suggests that another effort seemed another waste of an already wasted life.

The regularity of the Morse family's dispossession when population growth stimulated the demand for farm land, especially improved land, suggests an added index of economic conditions that hampered stable settlement in farming communities. If this suggests a competitive weeding process, it also implies the savage economic restrictions that settlement ironically imposed on the pioneer family. Omar had to supply more food more efficiently to remain a farmer, but like small businesses today, he lacked either the capital to survive the lean early years or the capacity to borrow capital at reasonable rates. The predictability of Morse's dispossession over a thirty-year period in areas of transition from wilderness to settlement suggests the effect of simple supply and demand for farm land and thus indicates the failure of reform laws to protect politically inactive and isolated people. Mortgage and interest rates were not sufficiently regulated. The western "fresh start" clearly required more capital than many families could acquire unless they became land speculators themselves, thus contributing to the already hazardous economic climate. In addition, quick sales like Morse's to prevent the total loss of investment were probably common, but the general estimate by historians of dispossession rates, which vary from 10 to 33 percent, does not include quick (or forced) sales since they would be difficult to find in county deed and mortgage records. Dispossession, then, is obviously a difficult factor to determine with absolute certainty, although analysis of Morse's lost farms suggests a major cause of unstable homestead communities and disillusion with the myth of the land. Neither Gates nor Bogue, it would seem, is conclusive.

Let us analyze Morse's dispossession in Dodge County, Minnesota, more closely. Here the reader finds him struggling with the "dishonest cuss" who took half of his public land quarter-section and thus deprived him of a source of capital for the farm improvement required for his survival. In this section of his autobiography, Morse looks back to his three lost homesteads with the pain of bewilderment. One disaster followed another, often at times when foreclosures threatened his homestead—family illness, scarcity of help at harvest time, low crop yields following adverse weather; in the midst of such struggles a baby was born, and Morse deserted his fields to care for the mother and new child as well as the others. Such detail has the ring of the actual, the human dimension, which the novelist attempts to capture; but for Morse, dispossession after years of labor was not a fictional experience.

The following passage indicates the problem other homesteaders encountered and illuminates the character of the land speculator.

> In October [1861] I made arrangements with Dr. Potter for a Land Warrant to enter my claim [to make actual purchase] and in company with several from our neighborhood journeyed to St. Peters [Minnesota] where the Land Office for our district was opened. I located 160 acres [2 miles] N E from Mantorville in Dodge Co—
>
> This Potter proved to be a dishonest cuss—and in order to settle with him at any rate I was obliged to sacrifice 80 acres of Land which in a little time was worth $1000/oo and continued to rise in value and is now worth $4000— in the fall I saved what I could of what I had raised though much of it went to waste for the want of time to care of it on account of sickness and other hindrances and the winter found us in pretty poor circumstances but still we lived and done what we could! October 9th [18]61 our first baby boy was born. We had hard work to get any kind of help in the house and the Idea of getting outdoor help was out of the question as every available man had gone South.[40]

He continues, the reader will recall, with the realistic details of a forced sale that illustrate an economic fact of life all homesteaders faced. If the hunter and scout lived wherever game was plentiful and the land unclaimed by white settlers, the homesteader of the prairies behind his oxen and sodbuster plow—in the vanguard of civilization—lived with an invisible enemy as deadly as the hunter/trapper's wilderness and its dispossessed, hostile Indians: an economic barrier that he could not climb, that reduced him and his family to poverty and resulted in the American "restlessness" for brighter western horizons. (The "wasteful" pioneer who cared little for the environment, with its offer of game and good crops, was not the thrift-minded survivor of economic and climatic hazards. Historians who claim that pioneer carelessness originated our wasteful society should reconsider the perception. Thrifty homesteaders like the Morses were disciplined by experience not to waste: not food—many families also ate local game and fish when they could afford the time and ammunition—not clothing, fuel, or any of the necessities of life. Tools they often made themselves; their creative ingenuity fills such farm museums as the unusual Cooperstown, New York, collection.)

For many homesteaders in the Middle West like Omar Morse, the organized protest of the Alliance came too late and did not press the mortgage and loan issues raised by the unethical practices of land speculators. For Morse and other dispossessed homesteaders, the Populists gave voice to the tragic experience that had already mocked their hopes of promised freedom and happiness with poverty and governmental indifference.

Morse's recollection of his Mantorville homestead records that family illness and the pinch of rising farm costs and low income during the Civil War brought him to the conclusion that a forced sale would be preferable to foreclosure. In 1865, he remembers, he made his decision to sell his personal symbol of democracy, a cabin approximately twenty feet by fourteen, and a partially cleared acreage yet inadequate to his and his growing family's needs: "Matters were getting worse and I could see no way out without a great sacrifice which is invariably the result of a forced sale. It was hard to bring my mind to the point that it was the only course now left—to sell out as best I could—save what I could and leave our Home again and begin anew, resolving henceforth if possible to profit by lessons learned in the past and make one more effort to secure a Home, however humble it might be" (Morse, 1865).

Research discloses several factors in Morse's dispossession from his Mantorville farm. He had filed a claim to the land in 1856, shortly after his arrival. Dr. Horace C. Potter of New York City, the "dishonest cuss" whose name appears in his narrative and on Morse's deed of sale for eighty acres in 1860, represents the pioneer's personal nemesis. Potter was probably a land speculator who dealt through a local agent, a customary procedure. Morse, who had preemption rights (having filed his claim in 1856 when he first arrived), was apparently forced into selling half of his quarter-section to Potter in 1860, possibly in order to purchase his claim (more accurately, to purchase the half not sold to pay Potter's loan) at the Land Office in St. Peter's. But Morse's unusual condemnation of this man implies his anger at an injustice difficult to forgive. From this we may assume either that Potter bought Morse's land for less than it was worth or that he or his agent used a more skillful manipulation such as the frontier speculators could legally or illegally (and sometime both) devise. We can either assume, then, that the disparity between Morse's date of sale to Potter in 1860 before his actual purchase from the Land Office is an error (Dodge County early records are cloudy here), or that he was legally able to sell, or arrange to sell, half of his homesteader's quarter-section in order to pay in cash for the remaining half.[41] Regrettably, Morse does not supply the interesting specific details of his predicament on his second homestead. Perhaps his western code of silence—already broken by his frank admission of loss—reawakened suddenly, or perhaps he felt a remembered pain and injustice too deep to allow his further description of this speculator's explicit methods. Tellingly, the manuscript breaks off at this point, with a note at the juncture. But Morse persevered; the narrative resumes. The Dr. Potters of a democractic society can never be eliminated, of course, but if they enjoy the power needed to define the limits of the ordinary person's income so that he or she labors only to provide for an affluent owning class, whatever the cultural illusion the individual suffers, that society must change or lose its guiding democratic myths in a purposeless civilization.

Morse's sale to Potter later forced him into an 11 percent mortgage of $200 on land originally costing $220, half of which had been sold. The mortgage was given by Augustus Barlow of Dodge County in 1864.[42] By April of 1868, however, he knew that his wisest decision was to sell his remaining eighty-acre homestead to Martha and Elbridge Paddock, offering them a 10 percent mortgage on $300, which he sold in turn to Barlow to clear his title.[43] In times when ten- and twelve-hour days of labor earned much less than one dollar, we recognize that the original cost of land from the government itself was the first barrier and served to stimulate investment by large speculators with capital rather than by the average person whose goal was a permanent home. When Omar first emigrated to Wisconsin, he had little capital for homesteading, and even less when he reached Dodge County; thus his third homestead of eighty acres in Goodhue County, an uncleared timberland, had small chance of success. We should not be surprised at the economic law of dimishing returns that held him to a mere survival level of existence and cost him the loss of sixty of his eighty acres in 1878. He was able to feed his family and had a little produce for sale, but he lacked the necessary capital to clear and plant a homestead where to achieve every square yard of plowed ground, a tree or two had to be cut, then uprooted with a chain and a team of oxen, and burned or hauled away. Farming virgin land in the nineteenth century, viewed from the Morse family's perspective, must have seemed to require more capital and years of brutal labor than the average person could acquire in a lifetime.

As the reader might assume, Morse's struggle with mortgages was complicated by his wife's medical expenses. High medical bills, according to a local history, were common in this area; an irritated county council halved the bills submitted by physicians for care of the poor.[44] Morse several times registers complaint against doctors' fees; in addition, a letter of Morse's (see Appendix A) speaks of borrowing at 25 percent in order to pay a pharmacist's bill of $100 incurred one summer. By the time of his wife's death in 1876, Morse had all but abandoned farming. Medical costs, impossible to estimate without additional information, may have put payment of the mortgages and the loans necessary to farming beyond his economic reach. His history was repeated many times by other homestead families.

The persistent mainstream culture image of the nineteenth-century friendly village druggist and the kindly, untiring country doctor seems to need adjustment to historical reality. So too does the popular image of the happy homesteader who had survived hardship that disciplined his virtue, elevated his thought, and encouraged a democratic American rebirth—a New World jolly green giant, springing from the dry husk of the wicked European, the Romantic's intuitively noble savage who was a natural gentleman and the plowman of the mythic garden. In spite of such scholarly historical correctives as Paul Gates's enlightening *Landlords and Tenants on the Prairie Frontier,*[45] the popular image of the homesteader seems to have thrived like the myth of happy blacks on the plantation, noble Indians on the reservation, and the gun-slinging sheriff or ranch foreman (like Owen Wister's Virginian) as the homesteaders' protective friend. The most insidious myth—the terrifying myth of success, still echoing a frontier image of gun-smoking righteousness, cabin door domestic virtue and wilderness courage, companionable neighbors, and assured wealth and happiness—continues to haunt the American consciousness.

Another objective index of dispossession lies in the physical characteristics of the land itself—wood (for building and fuel), water, soil, climate and general appearance. The towns in which Morse lived—Rosendale (Fond du Lac County, Wisconsin), Mantorville (Dodge County, Minnesota), and Roscoe (Goodhue County, Minnesota)—were once woodland and level-to-rolling prairie, and were likely fertile; their friable soils of clay and loam remain productive. Mantorville today is the most productive of the three, enjoying an average income, for townships of this area, from corn-and-hog farms. Hastings in Oswego County, New York, where Omar was born, is the poorest in farm income; its dairy farms are now in the soil bank because most farmers in this area were unable to find investment capital for the expansion needed to remain competitive as interest rates soared beyond their means. The more history changes, it appears, the more it stays the same.—a river of time.

But if the land seemed fertile, an "everlasting grainfield," it too could prove deceptive. The unknowns of soil chemistry and the soil-climate factor were then and obviously remain serious barriers to permanence; modern technology has not yet been able to solve all the existing problems. The variables of soil structure, for example, can alter from one farm to the adjacent one; indeed, they can vary within the boundaries of a single farm or field, because the several elements of soil—clay, loam, sand, muck, gravel, and so forth—vary in their proportion. If the homesteader on unfamiliar land in a new climate used farming methods that had been productive in the East or South, he probably experienced difficulty in raising sufficient crops to pay for his seed in the prairie and plains states. Aware before he settled that he was on unfamiliar soils, he tried to locate on land that seemed at once familiar and promising, but as with most farmers of the era, it was simply intuitive guesswork.[46] Morse's abrupt departure from Rochester, Minnesota, in 1847, for example, where his father-in-law had staked out a claim for him, may have been motivated by his farmer's intuition. He risked the oncoming Minnesota winter in late November to settle in Mantorville Township, fifty miles north and west, because the land "looked more like home." His terse idiom probably included the "look and feel" of soil as well as the lay of the land (or the aesthetics of place). He sought a new place in which he could feel comfortable after moving from Wisconsin. Because he complains of short crops "when the pinch came" and low market prices, he may have experienced problems of soil chemistry and structure that, in combination with a geographic distance from cheap transportation, still continue to limit farm income in these townships.

Prairie homesteaders like Morse knew farming was a gamble against weather and soil conditions. Like most farmers, he accepted the risk as part of his way of earning a living, but he did not expect to risk virtual starvation caused by an economic climate that daily threatened to dispossess him and his family. He had accepted the promise of the West as a statement of his right to an opportunity unhampered by the privileges of wealth. His experience with H. C. Potter of New York taught him wise distrust of land speculators, and town speculators, as the reader will notice, were among Morse's favorite targets. When he first came to Mantorville in 1857 he found "everything there but the town." His ability to laugh at the pretensions of these speculators and their bland facades reveals the good sense of early westerners.

In Morse's time, local speculators' hopes ran high in Mantorville, and they had political strength in St. Paul, the state capital. The village became the county seat as its founders hoped, due to political influence, and expected to become a large commercial center as well with this spur to business activity. An imposing courthouse with white wooden Doric columns, although of the usual midwestern courthouse-yellow brick, became a monument to their expectations. They lacked only a railroad to fulfill their speculator's dreams—a garden of easy dollars which the beneficient prairie would bestow—and believed they could convince St. Paul that the railroad should establish a shipping center at Mantorville. But the nearby town of Kassoon also had influence with St. Paul (and its known political influence with railroads), and so the railroad went through Kassoon. However, both towns had glimpsed their speck of American Destiny, a common piety in nineteenth-century society, and found it but a speck in their own eye. Both towns became museums of frontier great expectations, each with but five hundred residents.

Yet the ghosts of speculators past will not sleep. Mantorville has recently added a western board sidewalk, three Dodge City western storefronts, and a colonial-style inn with an attached buggy shed. They cluster at the foot of the not unpretentious courthouse, which sits on a small rise. The architectural simplicity of the first schoolhouse on the opposite side of the street wryly comments on this twentieth-century clutter. Mantorville today is another midwestern village struggling to survive its own pretensions. Villagers are as amused by the imposing courthouse and the small population of Mantorville, if not its recent main street clutter, as are visitors.[47]

The story of the midwestern village with pretensions of becoming a second Chicago is a familiar tale, in fiction and historical anecdote. For one early realist, Edward Eggleston, it served as a jeremiad against speculation. His Preface to *The Mystery of Metropolisville* (1873), discussed at length in the following chapter, contains this editorial message: "Metropolisville is nothing but a memory now. . . . The village grew, as hundreds of other frontier villages had grown, in the flush times; it died, as so many others died, of the financial crash which was the inevitable sequel and retribution of speculative madness."[48] The instability of nineteenth-century American society and the economy that supported it has an origin in the socioeconomic conditions to which Eggleston responded with his story and warning. While his novel purports to be a history of the 1850s—like Mark Twain and Charles Dudley Warner's *The Gilded Age: A Tale of Today*, also published in 1873—Eggleston must have recognized that land speculation created quick fortunes, which were sustained later by speculation in minerals and industry. He warns against the expected retribution of yet another financial crash and return to the sodbuster plow of the first generation. The prairie homestead schooled survivors in the bitter lesson that novelists like Eggleston, who were taught by frontier experience and its cultural response, knew was common.

Joseph Kirkland's *Zury; The Meanest Man in Spring County* orders plot material from history and, of course, with the artistic license of fiction, from possible history. Kirkland's book begins on a note of irony and continues to become involved with the ironies of early settlement conditions. We immediately learn that his protagonist's baptismal name is Usury, a name chosen by uneducated Yankee pioneer parents because they thought it biblical and dignified. A virtual giant in size and energies, Zury suffers deep psychological trauma due to the poverty (caused by high mortgages) that contributed to the death of his younger sister. "That evening was a sad one at the log hut. Half the section mortgaged and nothing to show for it *but this* [a freshly dug grave]."[49] He himself becomes a successful land speculator and moneylender and the "meanest man in Spring County," as Kirkland subtitled the book. The prairie school of experience, then, educated its students through "games" as cruel and destructive as those in Stephen Crane's urban slum in *Maggie: A Girl of the Streets* or Theodore Dreiser's wholly amoral city in *The Financier* and *Sister Carrie.*

Paradoxically, the prairie homesteaders were silent about financial hardship in personal narratives, journals, and diaries. When they wrote about the lean years in which they struggled with threatened loss and near or actual poverty, they usually followed with a success story of the new breed of pigs they could sell at a good profit or the additional acreage of corn that yielded bountifully in fertile Mississippi Valley bottomland or prairie. "Some Recollections of Thomas Pederson," for example, is a Wisconsin settler's memoir of success on his homestead farm; he asserts the triumph of the earnest, virtuous will of the yeoman over all obstacles to permanence.[50] The unpublished autobiography of Isaac G. Haycroft, a pioneer homesteader in Blue Earth County, Minnesota, contains a treasury of lost farming skills, and thus is invaluable history, but like most other homesteaders Haycroft grounds his narrative in a myth of pioneer virtue and agrarian self-sufficiency. He records his family's struggle against a plague of grasshoppers and days of near starvation, for example, but as his narrative continues, he becomes a late lyrical convert to increasing his acreage by buying out less prosperous neighbors and achieving the agri-miracle of economically successful Poland China hogs. He seems to overlook financial aid in need, meticulously recorded, by a helpful father-in-law.[51] Surprisingly, even such western writers as Hamlin Garland in *A Son of the Middle Border* (1917) and John Muir in *The Story of My Boyhood and Youth* (1916) view homestead life through the blurred romantic focus of nostalgia—yet Garland's "Under the Lion's Paw" remains the classic homestead protest against economic injustice.

How Morse was able to write his brief narrative at all, given his circumstances, remains an unsolved puzzle. Perhaps like other pioneers he felt the need to preserve his experience for his family. For him, it was a family history based on accurate details and observed life; he assumed that the truth would speak from this context. But was it also in part a tacit apology? Or did he hope to contain in narrative form the conditions that raised his doubts about the values of western independence and personal freedom? An undated letter (1890s) to his son (see Appendix A) raises the issue: "My object was merely to show to my family when on Earth I had a personality—did really Exist and that I tried to lead a sober and industrious life such as becomes a *true American citizen* and that in all the transactions of *life* I had for my object the betterment of mankind *generally*" [Morse's emphasis]. The major concern of his narrative, if we accept this statement, is to establish his identity as an American whose life represented the virtues of sobriety and industry, and his identity as a pioneer attempting the "betterment of mankind" as part of an experiment in democratic independence. In short, he believed himself the good citizen.

However, the economic climate demonstrated in this chapter had its effect on Morse; this late letter to his son (he was perhaps sixty-five) reveals an apologist. He may have felt it important to explain his failed quest for permanence in the West in the cultural context of his neighbor's real or imagined success story. The actual plowman of the West, like Morse, came to know that poverty could dispossess the individual of his or her land, and of freedom and independence as well. The experience could and did destroy the human spirit, but the farmer-authors usually concealed this dark truth in frontier stoicism. They did not write of such failures. Morse attempts to articulate his uneasy awareness of the moral collapse he faced in a society threatened by a disparity between its dominant model and its frontier reality. To retain his identity, he falls back on the Puritan values of sobriety and industry that Americans seem to feel are the bedrock of human character. In the narrative, begun when he was fifty-seven, he does not resort to evasion: he reaffirms the homestead courage and independence that manifests itself in the action of the narrative persona until the last pages, written shortly before his death. But his need to apologize for his life to his son as a "true American citizen" who had somehow contributed to the common good also illustrates, as I have suggested, his consciousness of a personal identity shaken by economic failure. In the pioneer settlement reality of the prosperous few and hard-pressed many, his voice becomes representative of the dispossessed person whose life adventure denied the promise of an American identity, or identifying source of an American reality. Yet by affirming his spirit in telling us of his struggle, he reveals the potential magnitude of the human character. Mark Twain's Huck and Jim are metaphors of the neglected heritage of cultural promise and dispossession of an ideal that the Morse narrative suggests.

Morse's dispossession reveals an ironic history of "money-power," to use his Populist language, which began with an authoritarian government; offering opportunity to white settlers, it dispossessed Indians and uprooted their cultures only to tacitly encourage—through corrupt administration and seriously compromised legislation—the dispossession of economically disabled homesteaders and thus delay the growth of agricultural communities. Labor to clear land and produce good crops, crucial to any society, was delayed; communities lost impetus toward stability and culture. A new wave of farmers, many with sufficient capital, replaced the pioneer and his culture, stranded such survivors as Morse on the island of historical witnesses of loss and desperate hopes. Research in county courthouses in each of the areas where Morse homesteaded suggests such irony and confirms the conclusions of Paul Gates and Fred Shannon. To their findings I have added the obvious law of supply and demand for land as a crucial factor in the Morses' dispossession and, by extrapolation, in the plight of a community of homesteaders who sought permanence on the land but were carried—by necessity—"somewhere else" to make one last effort.

2. The Morse Narrative and a Countermyth of Dispossession

James Fenimore Cooper considered the dispossession of wilderness values in his fable of civilization: Both red and white noble savages, Chingachgook, the noble Indian chief, as well as Natty Bumppo, the Leatherstocking, a frontier guide—all dwellers in the wilderness garden—were doomed by the progress of settlement that seemed to be represented by a white madonna, a woman-wife-mother figure of civilization. (Cooper's women are allegorical abstractions, not characters.) Her unspotted purity so dominated the Victorian male's imagination of western settlement that he—and Cooper—found it necessary to defend her against the untamed forces of good and evil that the wilderness and its people came to represent.

If an inviting target for scholarly ironies, Cooper's Leatherstocking fable nonetheless states the tragedy inherent in the deracination of a wilderness culture and its people. Implicit in *The Pioneers* (1823), with the aging Chingachgook dying of spiritual dispossession and an unheroic, garrulous Natty made to suffer the public disgrace of the stocks for shooting a deer, completed in *The Last of the Mohicans* (1826) and *The Prairie* (1827), with an aged Leatherstocking's heroic death among Indian friends, Cooper's idea of progress continues to shape the American imagination of the nineteenth-century wilderness. The frontier—residency of both white and red races, picturesquely and paradoxically a model of natural virtue as well as a symbol of dangerously unschooled and pagan forces—had to be replaced by the educated and refined society represented by white womanhood. This, of course, is also the cultural paradigm underlying Stephen Crane's "The Bride Comes to Yellow Sky."

The image of the garden, Henry Nash Smith believes, began to lose its social purity after the midcentury mark as the disparities between the western ideal and the actual West became a cultural experience. He qualifies this thesis, however, by pointing out the continuity of the magnetic all-purpose symbol in the commercial advertising of land and mortgage companies (railroads were the country's largest land owners).[1] While Smith's primary grasp of the West as symbol and myth has an unquestionable validity, especially in his response to Frederick Turner's ideal of nature as the source of cultural renewal, he fails to recognize the significance of the grassroots resurgance of the myth in the coin of Jeffersonian agrarianism, which the Populists revived. I have suggested that the garden myth is an ironist's weapon; the temper of the ideal toughens the steel of the realistic cutting edge; or, to extend the earlier metaphor, the spinning coin has two opposing truths—one abstract, the other an agrarian concretion.

Smith does not deal with the homely beginnings of the grassroots liberalism (the neglected continuity of this appealing myth and its ironic counterpart) that emerged in opposition to the Cooper women and the popular white frame house felt by the respectable Victorian majority (as well as wealthier farmers) to be the appropriate replacement for the little log cabin on the prairie or in the clearing. This early American political symbol (Morse recalls its use during Harrison's campaign) became the mythological home of uncouth and barbaric citizens; the vilification of Lincoln once he took office illustrates the cultural shift. Behind such screens of illusion, the frontier reality of dispossession and poverty went unchanged. As the Morse narrative and the previous chapter indicate, there was just cause for protest against needless—because controllable—barriers to permanency on the land created by usurious loans and mortgages. Although some loans were legal business arrangements, as previous chapter suggests, these and other less legitimate practices became commonly accepted techniques of manipulation that victimized the farmer. The stable community of independent family farms and villages, the inviting norm suggested by Grant Wood's twentieth-century Iowa landscapes, did not materialize until many in the pioneer generation had spent their lives to create fortunes, not permanent farms and towns. Yet as Morse's narrative demonstrates, even the dispossessed struggled to maintain their frontier sense of independence and personal liberty.

The purpose of this chapter is to analyze the emergence of a countermyth, the unweeded garden of dispossession, which like a Chinese puzzle box concealed within it the splendid dream of garden democracy; the homestead ideal and its ironic inversion remained a vital aspect of western imaginative life and became a meaningful legacy for twentieth-century American writers. The surprising popularity of "The Man with the Hoe" (1893), Edwin Markham's protest against the economic brutality of the homestead farm ("humanity betrayed"), illustrates the eruption of long-suppressed anger which the Populist Party held in check until its election campaigns of the 1880s and 90s. Markham's poem refers to Jean Millet's well-known painting of the same name.[2] In *Specimen Days* (1882-83), Walt Whitman remarks that Millet's paintings of French farm life seemed a visual social protest against an uncaring society; through reading Whitman, Hamlin Garland came to see his pioneers in *Main-Travelled Roads* (1891) as farmers oppressed by neglect and poverty. His descriptive remark that the American was but a "peasant among peasants" suggests the tenor of an art of cultural resistance in the oppressive context of gilded-age materialism. Garland's early works stand at the end of an evolving line of frontier writings: he had found his heritage.

The homestead countermyth—the unweeded garden—with its origins in the inhuman conditions of frontier life, deserves careful study: it represents the voice of the ordinary people and thus illuminates a cultural shadowland. The first section of this chapter looks at early nineteenth-century traditional songs and humorous stories that illustrate the beginnings of the countermyth. An analysis of the Populists' resistance to the overpowering materialism of an entrepreneurial elite (thought to be land speculators) then suggests the transformation of this theme into the rhetoric of protest. There follows an extensive analysis of American writers with frontier backgrounds—Eggleston, Garland, Kirkland, Donelly, Twain, and Norris—who found an accessible resource in the homestead culture of their youth. The chapter concludes with an analysis of the homesteader as the unheard voice of a moral past, a democratic past, which illuminates the configuration of a shaded society. It has, we may suspect, bequeathed a serpentine legacy that twentieth-century writers and modern scholars have found to be a knot of tangled aspirations and ugly realities. Several challenging knots, Gordian in their inexplicable difficulty, remain for future students. Whitman's "divine average"—the average frontier settler—would seem to be among them.

Earlier pages indicate Morse's reception of the dominant myth of the nineteenth-century West: "I emerged from the timber and grubs and found myself on—as I thought—the most beautiful spot on God's green earth. The prairie grass was about 4 inches high and the whole face of the country had the appearance of an everlasting grainfield" (Morse, 1847). He is evoking the memory of the awesome open prairie, yet to be plowed by a first homesteader, east of Fond du Lac, Wisconsin—then but a "mudhole" village. The "everlasting grainfield" obviously reflects his concept of the homestead garden and its associated egalitarian freedom. A half-century later, it echoes the eighteenth-century ideal. The context of his spontaneous departure from the employment of Mr. Harry Backus near Bridgeport, New York, to find his independence in Wisconsin illustrates his philosophy. He felt himself reduced to virtual slavery by the farm owner: "This of course led to a difference of opinion," he remarks. This deadpan humor, similar to Twain's more sophisticated style, reflects the vernacular culture, and its ability to laugh away real pain with controlled irony, in which Morse lived and wrote. In short, the quasi-religious wonder of an "everlasting grainfield," which follows his assertion of personal independence and ironic understatement, suggests the touch of the true folk artist upon the culture that shaped Morse's autobiographical imagination of the past. Morse disclaims all literary merit, but he has the ability to convey his views in a memorable scene or incident, even though he lacks a novelist's gift for character or family and domestic detail.

A folk culture—here defined as the ethnically and racially varied "colonies" of nineteenth-century Americans who often held common attitudes—may absorb the dominant metaphors of an intellectual elite even in the historical instant of one generation. Imagine, for example, a song collector discovering scraps of Beethoven in a Kentucky guitarist's "traditional" melody; such moments are not uncommon. Let us then examine the garden image in its original form: Morse and the culture he represents appear to have absorbed an intellectual legacy from the eighteenth-century Jeffersonian elite. For St. John de Crèvecœur and Thomas Jefferson, the ideal could be found in the writings of Abbé Guillaume Raynal, a French social theorist who had visited the United States. For the Americans, Raynal's *Philosophical and Political History of the Settlements and Trade of the Europeans in the East and West Indies* (1770) had transformed Virgil's idyllic pastoral and the Roman farmer into the figure of the independent man on his own land. As Smith points out, Jefferson and Crèvecœur, who dedicated his *Letters from an American Farmer* (1782) to Raynal, were instrumental in adapting this symbol to American social thought.[3] The natural right to ownership of land by those who toiled upon it, the primacy of agriculture in a nation's economy, and the independence that confers dignity and status on the freehold farmer became associated with Raynal's pastoral figure of virtue and independence.[4] Through numerous editions, John Filson's *The Discovery, Settlement and Present State of Kentucke* (1784), his popular travel narrative, lent its western locale and land-of-promise metaphors to the transition of Jefferson's thought into the symbolic garden of the West.[5] Thomas Hart Benton, Jefferson's vigorous advocate in the nineteenth century, inspired confidence in Jefferson's plan through his active legislation, speeches, and writings.[6] The compelling myth took a patriotic form.

Smith concludes that the mythical garden of the West was "a symbol that defines the promise of American life." He notes: "The master symbol of the garden embraced a cluster of metaphors expressing fecundity, growth, increase, and blissful labor in the earth, all centering about the heroic figure of the idealized frontier farmer armed with that supreme agrarian weapon, the sacred plough." If it is in fact a static model, a visual allegory (or a sort of verbal "pictograph" of the future), Smith contends that it fulfills the requirements of myth both in expressing the aspirations of a society—employing as an ethical model that heroic frontier plowman—and in its narrative hint of the wilderness.[7] However, it's flimsy pretext of western wilderness realities led later American writers to recreate the fable through fiction with authentic Western settings. Such early writers as Timothy Dwight in *Greenfield Hill* (1794), James K. Paulding in *The Backwoodsman* (1818), and Thomas Campbell in *Gertrude of Wyoming* (1809) struggled with fashionable sentimentality to graft the European ideal to narratives and topical descriptions of frontier American life and geography.[8] Chateaubriand's *Atala and René* give illustration of the European origins of the American garden in fantasy and its necessary romance.

Perhaps Crèvecœur's description of his travels in Pennsylvania, where he was himself an early farmer, best illustrates the New World garden model of independence as well as his sentimentalized egalitarianism.

> If he [the European visitor] travels through our rural districts he views not the hostile castle, and the haughty mansion, contrasted with the clay built hut and miserable cabbin where cattle and men help to keep each other warm, and dwell in meanness, smoke and indigence. A pleasing uniformity of decent competence appears throughout our habitations. The meannest of our log-houses is a dry and comfortable habitation. Lawyer or merchant are the fairest titles our towns afford: that of a farmer is the only appelation of the rural inhabitants of

our country. . . . We are the most perfect society now existing in the world.[9]

But Crèvecœur's patriotic excess of enthusiasm did not extend to the parameters of the frontier, where he found such indigent, restless, and barbaric people as Cooper later suggested (through Ishmael Bush and his devious family in *The Prairie*) inhabited the outer fringes of society. This perception has had a surprising continuity among frontier students, yet common sense indicates that courage, thrift, and hard labor, among the other virtues, were the essential means of survival on the pioneer farm.

Though admired as an abstract model—the plowman—the frontier farmer in the outlying fringe was in fact regarded as a barbarian simply because he was remote from civilization. The Daniel Boones were held to be uneducated, shiftless, violent, even potentially criminal by educated people. The attraction/repulsion syndrome riddled the upper-class American consciousness throughout the nineteenth century. That there was waste and terrifying violence is undeniable, but Crèvecœur's distaste seems gratuitous literary urbanity. He may not have intended to provide his reader with the thrill of romantic wildness by assuming an upper-class bias toward a lower class that usually settled on the homestead frontier, but this was his effect. It was Filson's Boone narrative, not Crèvecœur's *Letters*, that added a popular, if gamey, taste of the wild, which remained strong in spite of its sauce of biblical metaphors. One alluring description reads "the land of promise, flowing with milk and honey, a land of brooks of water . . . a land of wheat and barley, and all kinds of fruit."[10] These fictions created an image of the West that fed the aspiring dreams of the pioneers: this glamorous vision became the place of infinite (and always potentially commercial) possibilities by the mid-nineteenth century. Morse's "everlasting grainfield," clearly, reflects his, and a little-understood culture's, received perception of an American land of promise nearly a century later. For Morse, and obviously many others like him, a homestead was an opportunity for independence manifest in the glamorous image of a wilderness garden.

He could not have avoided a respectful understanding of this myth. The garden theme was central to nineteenth-century popular culture: local histories, newspapers, pioneer narratives, homesteaders' diaries, and similar documents suggest its centrality in their repetition of this image.[11] One example is sufficient to reveal the major cause of its widespread popularity. An address by G.W. Holley of Peru, Illinois, delivered in 1837 when the western portions of the state were still unsettled, illustrates a popular variant of the nineteenth-century garden: "The West, the mighty Valley of the Mississippi, with a soil of surpassing fertility, traversed and enriched by the noblest rivers of the earth, with exhaustless mineral wealth contains within itself the best elements of national wealth and power. With such advantages every free citizen so far as equality of condition permits might become a Rasselas [Samuel Johnson's discontented seeker of true happiness in *Rasselas: The Prince of Abissinia* (1759)] in all save his discontent; and beholding the happy valley a thousand fold enlarged might also behold it bear the palm of superiority even from this storied home."[12] Holley reflects the archetype of earthly paradise that underlies the garden of the American West by 1837. His scarcely edifying speech would appear to open vistas of unlimited opportunity; his commercial motive is flimsily disguised.

Obviously, this Fourth of July oratory alters and dilutes the paradise archetype in Samuel Johnson's *Rasselas* (Johnson's bored Rasselas would have found Holley's paradise insufferably barbaric). Holley suggests a second Eden in the West: the Mississippi Valley, a mythic idyl furnished with beatific rivers, an infinitely fertile soil, and "exhaustless" minerals. The eighteenth-century literary garden (of Johnson's allegory and Raynal's social theory) had become a popular folk myth, here highly commercialized. This materialistic garden of the West, with its promise of all things to all people—Edenic fertility, untold richness, chauvenistic power—invariably invites the homesteader to share the wealth of an open space associated with a vast unknown economic potential. As the quotation suggests, the Jeffersonian garden of democracy soon became the vehicle of land speculators' expedient means to wealth. The government's inadequate control of both public and private land sales exposed settlers to expenses beyond their pockets. Notice, for example, the orator's ambiguous "every free citizen so far as equality of condition permits."[13] This statement euphemistically conceals the fact that homesteading in the middle border territories would exclude settlers with insufficient capital to survive the early years.

The mild deception may have been unintentional; the statement may be rhetoric appropriate to the patriotic occasion, yet hopeful emigrants like the Morses—as hungry in spirit as in stomach—continued to believe that land would be their source of cultural and economic freedom. An ample cash reserve, not virtue, was the unwritten frontier rule for survival; the homesteaders' labor was an exploitable commodity when mortgage interest remained at 11 and 12 percent (and would have been higher if most states had not regulated interest rates). Possibly the able orator already owned a large tract of the paradise he found a compelling image. Mr. Holley's pleasing illusion reveals a game played many times over.

Morse's narrative suggests that the dispossessed and experienced settler took the Jeffersonian coin, heads and tails, in his hand and pocketed it; he had earned it, it was his—the ideal of frontier independence on one side seemed as necessary and real (if but an ideal and a strategy of defense) as the ironic obverse of the unweeded garden, rank with what seemed the choking political and social materialism of a corrupt age, the bitter weed of homestead life. Morse became conscious that he and his homestead friends were in fact exploitable commodities. His satire of the developers of the "mud hole" village of early Fond du Lac suggests that their pretensions masked the greed that characterized "land fever" throughout the "tame" West of most homesteaders. Fond du Lac, he recalls, was built on a swamp at the south end of Lake Winnebago, "on a small low prairie which was but little less than a mud hole yet the proprietors of the town were very Sanguine in their expectations and I think they really believed that this would be a second *Chicago* [Morse's emphasis]. There were about Half a Dozen small dwellings and in addition one Hotel . . . called the

Lewis House" (Morse, 1847). The ironic contrast of a "mud hole" with the "everlasting grainfield" of his mythic hopes suggests the ironic form of the homestead experience for many settlers, a configuration that shaped the inversion of the garden myth central to the frontier culture.

Morse satirizes the pretentiousness of these developers much as Twain and Warner satirize speculators and "speculation fever" in their fictional West of *The Gilded Age*. In his recollections of Minnesota we find a similarly acid comment, this time about Rochester. Here he is more conscious and subtle in his attack on developers' greedy expectations; he is more aware of traps set for the unwary settler, having experienced his first dispossession. Adopting the mask of naiveté, he writes: "I heard a great deal about Rochester and supposing it to be Something of importance I made my way thither. I found the far-famed Zumbro River and a log cabin on each side constituted the much talked of berg called Rochester. Here was territory sufficient for two cities but whether this was destined for a large inland Seaport was more than I was able to devine" (Morse, 1855). (The Zumbro is narrow and shallow; dredging would never have been feasible.) Colonel Beriah Sellers's attempted swindle in *The Gilded Age* seems no less pretentious when he himself all but believes in the future of Napoleon, a platted but unbuilt town in a Missouri swamp, and the Columbia River Slack Water Navigation Company whose purpose is to dredge a twenty-foot-deep channel in a shallow stream and straighten a river that bends a hundred miles in fifty.[14]

Like Twain's and Warner's satires, these excerpts from the Morse narrative illuminate the homesteaders' view and a style appropriate to their theme of protest. Morse had held a concept which gave his struggle purpose and dignity, but his homestead experience eventually made the "everlasting grainfield" of his emigrant's aspirations to the simple decency of owning his farm an unreachable goal, yet he clung to his ideals with a courageous tenacity. The theme of the "unweeded garden" evolved gradually among homesteaders and early humorists. Morse's irony implies a restraint that contained his disappointment in humor. Such a perspective characterizes the world of the transient frontier community. Frontier humorists were able to create a supple native style from such irony.

Johnson Hooper, in *The Adventures of Captain Simon Suggs* (1845), may have been the first professional writer and the first frontier humorist to satirize land speculation. He suggests that it was a cause of dispossession and a threat to the cultural ideal of the West. In two tales that satirize land speculators, Hooper's method is clear: he intends to laugh dishonesty into moral proportion with an inversion of the garden myth; in satire the national myth might by implication regain its original *cultural* dimension. In both sketches, "Simon Speculates" and "Simon Speculates Again,"[15] the transparently dishonest Suggs is highly successful, but such roguery could easily be exposed by the satirist's corrective lash. It was the optimism of hopeful satire. Somehow, in 1845, land speculation might be controlled by an aroused electorate of readers.

In "Simon Speculates," Hooper suggests that Suggs' tricks are those of an obvious rogue; to readers who knew the homestead frontier, Suggs's manipulations reveal the culpability of the Land Office in not sufficiently advertising public land sales, thus allowing insiders to acquire choice land, *and* encouraging their dishonesty. When Suggs discovers that another speculator wrongly holds advance information of a public auction, he lames the other man's horse in the stable, then overtakes him on the road to the Land Office. Manipulating the land speculator's anxiety to complete the transaction, Suggs contrives to trade his own spavined bag of bones for the lame horse, learns the location of the land to be sold, and—leaving his rival to find the Land Office—sets out on foot by a back trail known only to him, certain that he will be first to lay claim. The land in question, incidentally, is important to the future development of the community, since it contains a mill site.

To Hooper's homestead readers, Suggs was amusingly transparent, providing a needed corrective exposure of both land office failure *and* rehearsing the horse-swappers' methods of actual land speculators. Suggs's success is also a deliberate ironic inversion of Jefferson's agrarian myth of the garden. The homestead egalitarianism and prosperity of Crèvecœur's description has been placed on the balance beam by Hooper's sly manipulator and found virtually weightless. As homesteaders later discovered, few settlers were immune to "land fever," however strapped for cash. Trapped by an economic climate to which they were unable to adjust and by a self-deluding society, they came to exploit each other through legal (and illegal) mortgages and farm sales. Frontier neighborly cooperation rapidly became a quarrelsome bargaining over land boundaries, hard-driven agreements on land sales, and creditors dunning each other for unpaid mortgages. Early narratives reflect this destructive element. Morse's narrative suggests such a world when at the end he protests the futility of his thirty years as a homesteader.

In "Simon Speculates Again," "land fever" seems to have spread throughout Hooper's settlement. An Indian chief's widow has promised to sell her land to Simon, for whom she has a moon-eyed love, in spite of offers from three other speculators. (Hooper, like John Robb, another frontier humorist, recognized the primacy of the Indian claim to land.) Impecunious as usual, Simon contrives a plan to out-swindle the other swindlers. Their intention, we learn, is to promise the plump widow everything, but to pay only a fraction of a fair price. Appearing with bulging saddlebags stuffed with old iron, Simon takes advantage of the other land speculators' assumptions and sells his "option" to the highest bidder among three greedy men. Having had the moony widow's promise of sale, Simon has only to complete the transaction with the other speculators' cash and surrender to her charms, at least for the evening. Everyone is happy in this little settler's "paradise," Hooper's parodic garden of the West. In this tale, Hooper's irony is more than slashing: greed threatens to undermine settlement ideals when Simon shines, not in virtue, but in false sentiment and cleverness, and seems in this way to outshine the rest. The chief's widow enjoys a night of happiness in spite of dull-minded, greedy speculators.

John Robb's "The Pre-Emption Right; Or, Dick Kelsey's Signature to his Land Claim" in *Streaks of Squatter Life* (1847) suggests that greed among a new "breed" of homesteaders, who take squatters' rights on existing pioneer squatters' homesteads and file legitimate claims, threatens to undermine the values of a frontier community that believed in a simple democratic first come, first served claim system.[16] Early homesteaders did not understand the Land Office regulations and thus evolved their own. Within a decade the threat implied by dishonest speculation in a largely unregulated frontier economy had obviously materialized when the famous scout, Jim Bowie, had gained a valid reputation as a land swindler.[17] Like the "Michigan" fever (or frontier fever and ague) that Morse suffered, "land fever" seems a crippling disease.

Folk songs of the Civil War period (and earlier) and through the turn of the century contain a more potent attack on landowners and speculators than Morse's gibes at town developers, which, like Hooper's satire, illustrate the belief that error so outrageous exposes itself. The most obvious example, "Starving to Death on a Government Claim," centers on a poor homesteader whose sod hut is his sole possession; he has neither a wife nor productive fields. He complains that life is barren on the "elegant plain": "You'll find me out west on an elegant plain," he laments, "A-starvin' to death on my government claim."[18] Like Hooper, this anonymous folk song writer (or series of writers, each contributing a verse or two) uses the comedy of burlesque exaggeration, a style characteristic of frontier humor.

Settlers had little difficulty in recognizing the satire and understood that at least some gardens were indeed barren. To be certain, the last verse resolves the settler's plight by suggesting the bliss of marriage as the solution to his real problem, loneliness (the couple will live in town, however—Topeka, in one variant—and solve the social and economic problem.) But although prairie isolation was probably more destructive than the grasshopper infestations, marriage would neither bring rain during drought nor pay off the short-term mortgage common at the time. Pain has been masked by humor. Many were trapped by the homestead, with few options. The theme of dispossession in this song was probably used to warn the innocent against the illusion of the garden myth conveyed by landowners; whether they were speculators or government Land Offices—they could be equally deceptive.

"The Old Settler's Song" is another satirical inversion of the garden intended to correct a myth that could easily be manipulated by speculators, officials, and at times the homesteaders themselves. This folk song begins with a typical pioneer who treks west to the California gold fields. When he finds that mining does not "pan out," he leaves for a less fabulous land near Puget Sound, intending to homestead and settle down. But the forest grows as thick as corn on his far western claim, a fact of which no one had warned him. After a year of chopping trees, he is unable "to see ground"—the chips and stumps are too thick. He decides to "starve elsewhere," and leaves his first claim for the shore and a new homestead "surrounded by acres of clams."[19] The futility of this settler's struggle burlesques the government sales of such impractical terrain as rain forest and dry plains at the same price as potentially productive land. The old settler does eventually find a garden of ease where life is simple on his "acres of clams" (clams, however, provide a monotonous diet), but the irony is obvious: he has become a drifter. His alienation and dispossession suggest an inversion of the garden symbol originally intended to guide citizens toward a democratic society of homestead independence, and thus serves to demythologize the ideal yeoman of the Jeffersonian garden while retaining an image of the potential of the land, still the directive model. The satire of this folk song applies to all homestead frontiers, since the "old settler" becomes free and independent only by becoming an outsider, alienated and wise. The bitter humor of alienation suggests the reason for its revival in the 1960s and '70s. The song expects no hopeful change; its suggested alternative is disillusion and a realist's stoic shrug. The intent is to demythologize a false symbol, yet, clearly, Huck Finn has a friend who also finds "sivilization" cruel and absurd.

"The Farmer Is the Man" is another instance of the dispossession theme and its protest against economic distress, the root of the homesteaders' disillusionment. Carl Sandburg collected this song in Illinois from a singer who believed it dated from the

1860s, but determining the origin of folk songs is usually difficult. The characteristic homesteaders' inversion of the garden appears in the use of a fallen hero, the model plowman, who must live on credit until the harvest and then is led from the land (the central metaphor of the fallen earthly paradise in dispossession songs) by his creditors. The bitter lament of the following verse reveals the farmer-persona's lost sense of social value as producer of his country's food as well as the composer's ironic view of the homestead model of independence.

> The farmer is the man
> The farmer is the man
> He lives on credit till the fall;
> Then they take him by the hand
> and lead him from the land
> and the middleman's the man who gets it all.[20]

For John Greenway the song is a hard-times ballad in which the persona surrenders his frontier idealism after painful experience of economic reality. Greenway also identifies it as a Populist protest song of the 1880s; the Populists' political target was indifferent state and national governments that neglected pioneer homesteaders and failed to assist farmers who became victims of the railroad's stranglehold on the shipment of crops to the more profitable urban markets. The self-sufficient family homestead had begun to give way to the one-crop farm, with a loss of independence common in more technologically sophisticated societies. This song was appropriately revived in the hard times of the 1930s.[21] Such direct irony provides a useful illustration of the elements characteristic of the homestead unweeded garden of dispossession.

This cultural theme is essentially a strategy of defense against the encroachment of poverty and official neglect. The art of the folk singer or storyteller generally takes form in a bold moral melodrama of good and evil wherein a type of the "middleman"—a satanic figure who lurks on the periphery of the garden ("and gets it all") until the innocent farmer is ripe for the picking, as it were—serves the ironic thrust of the narrative. These central features, the fallen or inverted garden and its satanic destroyer, appear and reappear in songs and tales of the settlements, as well as in such forgotten sources as the campaign literature of the Populists and in the works of the midwestern literary realists whose agrarian backgrounds fed their sophisticated literary expression of the homestead irony. The central focus is of course the farmer, an alienated and culturally dispossessed figure. Edwin Markham's brutalized farmer, like Hamlin Garland's Haskins in "Under the Lion's Paw," parallels the painfully dispossessed orphan of the river frontier, Huckleberry Finn; all are types of the frontier homesteader cast adrift by his lot as the cultural hero of a democracy. This is sadly ironic aloneness in the context of mythically perceived solidarity (perhaps it is also the tragic loneliness of mankind in the universe, or perhaps the existential separation of the individual from society). The loss of communal values had a serious impact on the pioneer family.

A little-known stanza of "The Wayfaring Stranger" contributes an additional insight into the countermyth of the garden. The anguish and futility in the lines quoted below are the emotions of an aesthetic that both nineteenth- and twentieth-century novelists—Joseph Kirkland as well as Faulkner and Steinbeck—transformed into themes of alienation and dispossession. Contemporary novelist Joyce Carol Oates's little-known *Garden of Earthly Delight* also captures the legacy of the homestead frontier in its migrant farm laborer family, three generations removed from homestead grandparents, even though her title came from that of a Hieronymus Bosch painting of a post-lapsarian Eden.

The concluding verse of the song illuminates a folk culture's consciousness of its loss of values and ensuing destructive ignorance.

> My father lived and died a farmer
> A-reapin' less than he did sow;
> And now I travel in his footsteps
> A-knowin' less than he did know.[22]

The persona (son) instinctively knows that there is no hope (except money) of saving the farm and the farming community. Civilization obviously falters in this song of dispossession. Oates leaves her reader with a comparable folk song futility when a homestead granddaughter's marriage to wealth ends in an ironic disaster through her son's accidental murder of her successful husband. The failure of the early settlements have left an unrecognized legacy of a dark fate in much of its significant literature. The countermyth of the garden, implied by Oates's ironic title, is in a nineteenth-century folk tradition that the novel and this little-known verse both reflect. The garden symbol dissolves in a cultural failure: a pioneer generation has only its economically barren land to hand as a legacy to its children; there is little money for schools, churches, town governments; a second generation founders in squalor and ignorance. The twentieth-century legacy is too clear: Sinclair Lewis in *Main Street*, for example, was chilled by the raw winds of Hamlin Garland's prairie villages, culturally eroded by land speculators' greed.

This verse dramatically reveals the decay of pioneer ideals, and implies that the wayfaring stranger who travels through this "land of woe" is an alienated prototype of the former gardener. Like the old settler with his acres of clams, he finds that the struggle to achieve permanence on the land is wasted effort. This is the bitter lesson that Americans could not fully accept yet were unable to deny. Such songs bring home truth beyond the power to refute. Economic conditions in which settlement eroded, then gullied into pockets of distress, are an unrecognized frontier cultural heritage, a national shame.

"Mary's Little Lot" also inverts the garden symbol to imply widespread social distress caused by an ineffectual government. Popular at the time of Henry George's *Poverty and Progress* (1879), with its suggested land and tax reform, the song uses a "quite contrary" Mary as a satanic figure who starves helpless tenants in the garden with rentals increased above each rise of farm prices. Once a poor owner of marginal land herself, she has by renting it become "wealthy, refined, and wise," a satirist's portrait and ironic commentary on the Horatio Alger success myth. Here, as in other satiric songs of dispossession, a frontier moral vision attacks human greed. The frontier irony is obvious when the listener is advised: "If you had only hogged some land, / And held it for the rise."[23] Expediency is wisdom in such a society. Gates's studies of landlords and tenants in the Middle West suggest that the origin of this song could easily have been among suffering tenants in the prairie states—but "land fever," of course, was a national disease.[24]

A similar theme appears in "The State of Arkansas," a variant of the "Arkansas Traveler" or hard-times motif. Sanford Barnes, the narrator, tells of his employment by Jesse Herling, the skinflint owner of a farm that is half canebrake and half swamp. Barnes tells us he takes "corn dodger pills" (a corn dodger is fried cornmeal bread, sometimes called "johnny cake") for the swamp fever he contracts while working the canebrake for Herling, whose "hair hung like rat tails / Down his lean and lantern jaw." Herling is meant to be a representative figure; he is "the photygraph of all / the gents in Arkansaw." After six months, Barnes "gets as drunk as a biled owl" and leaves forever, advising us, "If I ever see that land again / I'll hand to you my jaw, / It will be from a long long telyscope / From here ["hell" in some variants] to Arkansaw."[25]

Greenway believes that songs of this type extend from the post-Civil War era to the Great Depression years of the 1930s. They are songs of protest about farmers who suffered as Omar Morse did the loss of independence at the hands of landlords, farm owners, and mortgagers alike. Greenway comments: "The better songs in this category [the hard-times motif] turn the lash of his [the farmer's] anger against the inanimate land and the people foolish enough to farm it."[26] Like the old settler, Barnes learns that the loss of a job on the land has the unsuspected advantage of the only garden possible. He can best find independence by becoming a drifter. As Morse's difference with Harry Backus of New York suggests, freedom comes at the cost of employment—although for this young idealist at the time, the West still promised both. "Starving to Death on a Government Claim" and "The Old Settler's Song" imply that the expense of acquiring independence on the land is too dear. Research also indicates that such reductive aspects of homestead life as isolation, disease, ignorance, squalor, hunger, brutal labor, even cannibalism, as well as the outrageous manipulation of homesteaders' land, can change the purposeful settler into a shiftless transient. The unweeded garden gave expression to the homesteaders' sense of the cruel illusion and naive trust which sent them west.

Newspapers, too, afforded opportunity to publish satirical treatments of the homestead theme generally visualized in a symbolic land of lost western promise. *The Falls Evening News* (April 3, 1858) of Little Falls, Minnesota, printed "A Trip to the Frontier" by its "roving reporter," in which the now vanished town of Humboldt draws satirical fire. W.A. Croffut writes:

> "The name is on all the maps. Here they have studied centralization and consolidation with astonishing success. From this point of view, Humboldt is a perfect model. So compact is everything, indeed, every residence and building in the whole town of Humboldt—stores, factories, schools, taverns, blacksmith shop, and church—all are contained under one roof! Not a large roof either—about twelve by twenty or so, and just about high enough for a man to walk upright. . . . The door opens with a hempen latchstring, and the gentleman who ventures in and out of it with a short pipe in his mouth, comprises all the male citizens of the town. Blocks and 'parks' and 'squares' are staked out far and near on either hand, but there are no improvements, the nearest approximation to a saw mill being a three-legged saw horse reclining in a graceful posture at the gable end of the town.[27]

Croffut concludes with a well-aimed parting shot at the state legislature, which incidentally had made Humboldt the county seat. "Happy dreams and a pocket full of rocks to the members of last year's Legislature who own corner lots in Humboldt."[28] Clearly, it was politics and business enjoying connubial bliss in the happy security of Humboldt's settlement humbug. By contrast, the other settlements receive Croffut's blessing; they seem models of industry and progress. In short, he recapitulates the smiling side of the Jeffersonian coin, the popular garden of the West, as well as its pathetic failure. The seedy proprietor of Humboldt (and its humbug) illustrates the satiric method that characterizes most presentations of the homestead countermyth: the inverted garden of the West. But the garden myth associated with the progress of civilization has not simply dissolved; the same person, like Croffut, could happily contain the whole of the frontier coin in his mental wallet.

Without doubt, mortgage interest was a spur to the resistance of the Farmers' Alliance and the People's Party in the 1870s, 1880s, and 1890s. While the central issue remained the high cost of transportation to larger urban markets, their anger had ripened in other and earlier issues, most significantly the high rates of mortgage and loan interest that had begun in frontier Midwest settlement.[29] Morse's dispossession was no isolated case. Homestead humor and protest in tales and songs—a humor that may mask the folk artist's sense of the tragic—have a direct relation to conditions that worsened as settlement increased. Songs of dispossession and oppression were implemented by the literature originating in a culture with a Puritan-Calvinist sense of justice and a fresh, if at times pointed, humor. Sparse notes came from this underground—the literature of homestead dispossession is not as ample as that which expresses the farmers' dream of a bountiful land—but its mark of humor and open, if strenuous, crude democracy was a literary source of direction in an amoral nineteenth-century society seeking to find its conscience and identity. (Perhaps all frontiers are indeed a moral and legal no-man's-land: international conflicts over oil and fishing rights in the oceans, as well as the uses of space, remain unsettled.) Since needed reform laws often came too late to relieve privation and hunger, they proved small remedy. State and interstate mortgage regulations are an important example. Populist leaders recognized that dispossession and even literal starvation among their membership meant a bitter loss of national goals.

Although strident and at times verbally blind with anger, at times ethnically prejudiced (Ignatius Donnelly, for example, feared Jewish, European, and American bankers alike), the Farmers' Alliance and People's Party gave needed though futile protest against a gilded-age commercial class and its power of control over such poor legislative action as there was. Their expression of loss forms an important aspect of the unweeded garden.[30]

The rising anger erupted in the 1880s because drought and economic conditions had caused starvation and related tragedies, especially in the western wheat regions. In a letter to Congress in 1889, President Edwin H. Atwood of the Minnesota Farm Alliance begged for relief from an obviously corrupt Senate and House of Representatives. Sensing the helplessness of his membership, Atwood's frustration breaks out in what seems an excessive and strident rhetoric. Note the symbolic value of land in the following quotation, however. In his need to arouse an apathetic Senate, Atwood inverts the mythic West of peaceful agriculture into a bitter land of war between the haves and have-nots, an Alliance concept that echoes the theme of dispossession. The comparative restraint or stoic acceptance demonstrated by such early treatments of the homesteaders' disillusion as Simon Sugg's adventures or "Starving to Death" become the loud anger of moral outrage—more accurately, an orator's melodrama—as the satirical garden changes in the turbulent ocean of nineteenth-century oratorical protest. This political world had no place for shades and subtleties.

> While we demand revision and cutting down of the present high tariff, we do not want to be diverted from greater wrongs by a clamour as to the duties on imported goods. The master thief of the continent is monopoly. Where we lost one dollar by the tariff, we lose ten by watered railroad stock, high rates of transportation, land grabbers and coal and oil trusts. The poor workman of the country [may desire and] gain some benefit from protection [i.e., higher tariff regulations, or duty] on foreign

agricultural imports but [as matters now stand] only the rich profit from monopoly.[31]

Atwood reflects a similar pattern in his uses of the theme of dispossession: the land of the Jeffersonian garden has been spoiled; the "master thief of the continent," the satanic figure, lurks everywhere, specifically "on our land"—which, even to the stoic farmer of Minnesota, meant "our place in the scheme of things," the promised garden of the West. They could not have escaped knowing its promise, however glossy or sophisticated the form in which it was presented.

The first paragraph of Atwood's letter to Congress shows the reason for his emotional urgency in the paragraph quoted above, with its echo of Populist evangelistic fervor. He writes: "The other day a thousand farmers in western America perished by the cold and storm; and we ask the representatives of the people in the Senate and House to come to our relief."[32] But relief did not come, although Atwood and the Farm Alliance membership proposed two potentially effective legislative measures: first, the enlargement of the Sault St. Marie Canal to provide a direct water route from Minnesota to European markets; second, the enactment of interstate commerce laws that would limit railroad shipping costs and thus help to prevent future starvation in homestead settlements. These farsighted proposals suggest the logic behind Alliance platforms, to which reform government from Theodore to Franklin Roosevelt has been indebted.

The Alliance proposals would likely have brought economic relief to starving people in the future and mitigated erosion of democratic values in the West. Atwood's rhetoric, however excessive it now seems, was justifiable in light of the homesteaders' desperate plight; moreover, his outrage suggests the farmers' perception of their actual unimportance in a society that had claimed to model itself on the homestead farm. The Populists contributed governmental reforms at once practical and idealistic to a then indifferent society. Their unusual contribution, however, can never be perceived as an unmixed blessing. The cruel perversity in a democratic idealism that included equal rights for women and black people was an anti-Semitism which, although limited in extent, remains indicative of American xenophobia. This perversity can be seen in Ignatius Donnelly, who—whatever historians may decide—is an interesting type of Populist leader. At once brilliant in logic, experienced in legislative warfare, and painstaking in legal research, he was nevertheless capable of a demagogue's tyranny for which there is no defense. His fear, shared by others in the Farmers' Alliance, first took shape in a demimythical monster, the Corporation, which he believed had historically usurped the rights of the people: "There is neither soul nor conscience nor even gratitude in corporations. Popular liberty, I fear, in the grasp of this monstrous cuttlefish will be stung and poisoned unto death."[33] He had earlier described this monster to his audience at the 1871 Anti-Monopoly Convention in Rochester, Minnesota, as a Briareus, the giant of many grasping arms. Certainly, the farmers' complaint was justified; their economic situation had steadily worsened—a direct result, they believed, of such land and mineral monopolies as the larger western railroads. Moreover, popular democracy was in transition on the homestead frontier. It was as if the ordinary person had never thought to challenge "money-power" and, by doing so, free his or her mind from an undemocratic subservience to the authority of wealth. Their poverty had long driven away their personal autonomy.

One terrifying aspect of Donnelly's fear, as I have suggested, was his seemingly incomprehensible anti-Semitism. *Caesar's Column* (1890), one of his best-known novels, uses the Jewish stereotype (Prince Capano) to represent the corporate mentality he thought would seize control of government and destroy the fabric of American society. (Prince Capano, Donnelly's monster of corporate degeneracy, plots—thematically—to seduce George Washington's granddaughter, preposterous as that may seem.) Such once popular books as Coin Harvey's *Tale of Two Nations* (1894) and James Woodward's *Life of Thaddeus Stevens* (1913) are comparable instances of this undemocratic and irrational ignorance.[34] Erza Pound's foolish anti-Semitism, as well as his wiser dislike of usury, seems to have historical precedent. To label all Populists and their social thought anti-Semitic would subvert the importance of their contribution to American culture; nevertheless, such severe limitations cannot be overlooked.

Donnelly had emigrated to Minnesota with an idealist's conviction that the garden of the West would also be an intellectual's paradise. Nininger, his one-home utopian community and farm in the present suburbs of Minneapolis, had an exceptionally fine library invariably full of his and his wife's friends. Idealists, it seems, are inadequate as farmers. Like Brook Farm, it failed of high ambitions and unskilled workers, unlike such nineteenth-century communitarian ventures as the successful Zoar, Ohio, and Oneida, New York, where a Shaker sect practiced a form of eugenics. As the son of Irish immigrants in Philadelphia, his American belief in the garden had not prepared Donnelly for its existential sterility. Hard pressed by creditors, he later tried to protect himself from the shock he experienced when his dream failed to materialize by locating the cause of his trauma in the farmers' demons of land speculators and—in addition to Jewish bankers—the railroad (a landowning corporation), and gilded-age government (the scheming brain of this monster was, in several instances, the archetypal Jew). His prejudice stemmed from his response to the European House of Rothschild and other banking firms who he believed should be distrusted—a popular phobia of the age.[35]

Donnelly never fully forgave the world—more accurately, the economics of Minnesota farming—for the loss of Nininger. Although his career took him to Washington as a United States senator, to his family's home in Philadelphia for periods of rest, and to remote Minnesota settlements on campaigns for the Populist candidates (including himself), he invariably returned to his debt-shadowed home, a spiritual sanctuary in what seemed a cruel society of heartlessly indifferent people. Like Omar Morse and thousands of other farmers, he also had suffered dispossession. Out of this emotionally wrenching experience came his passion to cure the ills of his chosen pioneer society near St. Paul. "The world is a garden of beauty filled with the stench of injustice," he writes in his yet unpublished diaries.[36] His remedy for existing inequities of wealth is roughly analogous to Edward Bellamy's allegory of the stagecoach in *Looking Backward* (1888), popular when Donnelly wrote the following: "Society is a waiting room in a railroad station in which one-tenth of the seats are cushioned, the rest bare boards . . . the remedy is not to abolish the cushions but to cushion all the seats."[37] The socialism of his remark is undershot with a western democracy of egalitarian thought, anticipating a modern liberal vision.

In addition, the loss of his own garden and its model motivated his Populist concept of the land as the true source of the viable community. In Donnelly's *The American People's Money* (1895), a tract in the once popular form of the dialogue, the homestead theme of protest reappears to lend structure to his statement of the farmers' problem and a remedy. The problem is given image in the visible terms of everyday reality; that is, a realistic surface conceals a rasping satirical burlesque that barely falls short of travesty: "Nothing is profitable now-a-days but your business of money-lending," a farmer tells his traveling companion, a banker. The farmer, like Mary of "Mary's Little Lot," has found that renting on shares and moneylending are more profitable than working his farm: "If I had farmed it myself I should probably be in the same boat with the rest [of my industrious neighbors]. As it is I have a good lot of land and some money out at interest."[38] Others starve on productive land without an acceptable recourse. A fact of homestead life—perhaps the most brutal—comes to light: the economic system also created usurious neighbors, not simply remote land corporations.

The Golden Bottle: The Story of Ephraim Bednezet (1892) offers an additional instance of Donnelly's imaginative treatment of the homestead theme. This novel, however, suffers from the stridency of extreme haste. Rushed to completion during his unsuccessful campaign for governor, the work begins with the melodrama of the unpaid mortgage (at this time, usually 11 to 18 percent). Ephraim's parents wait helplessly; his future dims in the austere perspective; his hopes of marriage to Sophia, the neighbor's daughter, gradually dissolve. Frontier humor and pathos have been replaced by Donnelly's popular style of melodrama; folk irony and deadpan understatement disappear in a drama of grand utopian solutions to the farmer's struggle to remain on the farm. Although the novel opens with a realistic description of the social problem and its western setting—Butler County, Kansas, the town of Eldorado, in the 1890s—it remains primarily the allegorical vehicle of an obvious social message; it departs from all pretense of realism and becomes an Edward Bellamy dream vision, not only of technological progress but of a new world economy that Donnelly believes is possible.

The troubled Ephraim falls asleep and dreams of an angel who offers him a bottle of magic liquid that will transmute base metal to gold and enable him to hold the power of all government. At the end of the novel a different angel, The Pity of God, explains its symbology: "The Golden Bottle represents the power of government to create its own money. With that power it will do all you dreamed the Bottle did."[39] The dream takes Ephraim from Eldorado, Kansas, his inverted garden, to the U.S. presidency and ultimately the presidency of the world. He evolves a plan of making 2 percent loans to disadvantaged families; this cash flow, spent in home and farm improvements, so stimulates the American economy and democracy that he receives a popular mandate. By waging war, he is able to put his plan into world action. *The Golden Bottle* is a flawed work, certainly; however, it illustrates one of the several modes of transforming the pioneer farmers' experience and an emerging cultural theme of protest into the larger scope of a then popular form, the utopian novel. The inverted garden, Eldorado, here concretely becomes a pastoral garden-vision of remarkable virtue and independence.

If Donnelly's extravagant, even militant imagination would seem to lack any responsible sense of reality, any grasp of "Eldorado, Kansas" as an actuality, entries in his journal while campaigning in raw farm communities suggest his understanding and stubborn idealism; in Phillipsburg, Kansas, he sees "a great many harsh featured people—a race of battling pioneers, fighting nature and one another. Time and assured prosperity will soften these countenances."[40] But this journal entry merely hints at the extent of Donnelly's visionary political reform. Ephrain Bednezet's plan for an Irish Republic illuminates the author's hope of restoring the Jeffersonian idealism of the garden for the entire world. Once a prosperous United States has achieved true liberty under Ephraim's inspired leadership, he issues a proclamation for Ireland that will ensure all of the following: universal education, impartial suffrage, the separation of church and state, equality before the law, secrecy of the ballot, a graduated income tax (excessive wealth—notably that of bankers—will be confiscated), punishment of the bribery of public officials by death and of the intimidation of voters by life imprisonment—in sum, Donnelly's declaration of human rights.[41] When Ephraim wakes, however, nothing has changed. The Pity of God visits him to explain the symbolism of his dream: mankind does not exist effortlessly in a barren universe of material progress—all are workers whose strivings realize a "creative revolution" of spiritual values. A forthcoming revolution of farmers and laborers, he is told, suggests the dynamics of the world-spirit. No longer despondent, he decides to join these forces of civilization (the Alliance).[42]

Another journal entry crystalizes Donnelly's philosophy: "Civilization is the increased and steadily increasing power of spirit over matter. In the remote future man will control all the forces of the planets [psychic forces]."[43] Donnelly arrives at a characteristic nineteenth-century resolution in which a triumph of the spirit satisfies the conditions of the good while indicating the irreducible circumstances of reality. The ideal, however remote from Bednezet's unpaid mortgage and dependent parents, offers a redemptive hope for mankind. Morse's "everlasting grainfield" conveys a similar spiritual ideal. In sum, Donnelly's *Golden Bottle* is structured on a dual perception of the garden image: the irony of lost democratic aspiration suggested by his Eldorado, Kansas, contains an inverted garden; the dream-vision utopia is a Donnelly garden of political freedom, as yet unrealized. His incipient fascism, militant and expedient, spoils his beautiful plan, however.

In contrast to Donnelly's fabulous visions, which illustrate the later unweeded garden theme and its political melodrama, Edward Eggleston's humorous burlesque in *The Mystery of Metropolisville* (1873) reflects the earlier style of the garden used in folk song and frontier tale. This novel represents his most direct attack on "speculative madness" (his phrase, closely related to Twain's "speculation fever"); Eggleston's security in treating this theme suggests that he is using a cultural metaphor as familiar to him as his own face. Although *The Gilded Age* satirized "speculation fever" in the corrupt society of Twain and Warner's day, which their novel subsequently named, Eggleston remained the historian he had chosen to be in earlier novels. He could look back to the philistine outrages of the 1850s and, through the indirection of inescapable parallels, suggest corrective attitudes toward the present. He states his method and purpose in the Preface of this little-known work: "A novel should be truest of books. It partakes in a certain sense of the nature of history and art. . . . I have wished to make my stories of value as a contribution to the history of civilization in United States."[44] Superficially, he seems to accept the historian's myth of progress: a flawed past inevitably evolves toward the contemporary just society. But Eggleston's backward look was as contemporary as Twain's. The novel is a farcical tale about Mr. Plausaby, a land speculator, which is complicated by a melodramatic subplot. Plausaby speculates in a paper city, attempts to sell lots at absurdly high prices, builds one house (his own), and then—under Egglestonian retributive justice—suffers the loss of his hopes in prison. Like Morse in his satiric comment on speculators' towns in the middle border states, Eggleston felt he could laugh these past follies into proportion. The moral lesson is direct—indeed, simplistic. Eggleston states it in the Preface as a comment on Metropolisville, his fictional Minnesota village near the actual Morse homestead of the 1850s: "It died, as so many others died, of the financial crash which was the inevitable sequel and retribution of speculative madness."[45] But neither Eggleston nor his readers thought Plausaby would vanish with his village; he held too much power over the minds of his fellow citizens.

Metropolisville, lacking the control of style that Eggleston had shown in the *Hoosier Schoolmaster*, is an uneven mixture of history, local color, Dickensian comedy, romance, and satire; however, Eggleston succeeds when he borrows the homestead method of absurdity and burlesque in satirical protest of frontier conditions. Of his several novels of the frontier, this work most clearly illustrates his familiarity with an earlier satire on land speculators and moneylenders, that is, the unweeded garden, as I have described it. Mr. Plausaby is Simon Suggs in a Dickensian business suit, who, if out of context on the frontier prairie, makes a convincing statement of the fraudulence and vulgarity of land speculators and by implication of vapid deceptions by the American businessman. Eggleston all but succeeds in capturing the elusive substance of the American businessman whom Sinclair Lewis later defines in Babbitt. Mr. Plausaby, however, is the single gem among the many unpolished stones of the book. The pathetic subplot, a love story involving Plausaby's foster son (an insufferably righteous hero), distracts readers from the ironic realism of the speculator's vanished village. The humor is more subtle than that of the folk satirist; Eggleston dresses it in dark suit-and-tie ironies aimed at the feeble American conscience. The following passage displays Plausaby's approach to persuading Charleton Albert, his step-son, that he must buy town lots in the paper village.

> All the young men who were over nineteen had preempted [filed claims to buy land]. It was customary. Quite customary indeed. And custom was law. Of course there are some customs in regard to pre-emption that Plausaby thought no man could approve. Not at all. There was the building of a house on wheels and hauling it from claim to claim and swearing it on each claim as a house on that claim. Plausaby, Esq., did not approve of that. Not at all. He thought it a dangerous precedent. Quite dangerous. Quite so. But good men did it. Very good men, indeed. And then he had known men to swear that there was glass in the window of a house when there was only a whiskey bottle. It was amusing. Quite amusing these

> devices. Four men just over in Town 21 had built a house on the corner of four quarter sections. Swore that house in on each claim. But such expedients were not to be approved. Not at all. They were not commendable. However, nearly all the claims in the Territory were irregular. Nearly all of them. And the matter of age could be gotten over easily. Custom made law. And Albert was twenty-three in looks.[46]

Plausaby's flexible conscience, the source of his bland manner, finds Albert's age (he was not yet a legal twenty-one) a minor difficulty in view of the manipulations of other speculators. Here as elsewhere, the public Plausaby seldom offends, but merely generates rationalizations; the private Plausaby, however, sets up everyone for a swindle with unembarrassed aplomb, including his second wife and her son. In the tradition of Johnson Hooper, Eggleston transforms the homesteaders' demonic land speculator into a scoundrel, but one even more pernicious because more deceptive and hypocritical than the scoundrelly Suggs or Twain's maladroit swindler, Colonel Beriah Sellers. Plausaby operates from behind a screen of bland respectability like Sinclair Lewis's businessmen. He is as possible and convincing as the frontier setting itself, although his origin was probably in Eggleston's reading of Charles Dickens. To state Eggleston's pun explicitly, he is the too plausible citizen, whose mask of disingenuousness conceals his dishonest business practices.

Before Plausaby can reap the benefits of his one-house speculator's village, he is exposed and his "town" transported by wagon (as boards) to a nearby railroad station. Eggleston uses the device of the "seller sold," a frontier irony that Twain also had mastered. The book's Afterword contains an admonition: "Metropolisville is a memory now. The collapse of the land bubble and the opening of the railroad which a corrupt state congress decided should run elsewhere destroyed it. . . . Not only has Metropolisville gone, but the unsettled state of society in which it grew has likewise disappeared—the land sharks, the claim speculators, the town proprietors, the trappers, the stage coach drivers have emigrated or undergone metamorphosis. The wild excitement of '56 is a tradition hardly creditable to those who did not feel its fever."[47] Eggleston speaks in two voices here: the historian banishes the past to the long-settled dust of the raw frontier; the novelist, however, asks the readers of 1873—the year of Twain and Warner's *Gilded Age*—to consider the beginnings of "speculation madness." While Eggleston assures his reader that the *sturm und drang* of a comic historical adolescence is past, neither he nor his readers could escape knowledge of the historical past in the present. Clearly Eggleston reflects a frontier culture's ironic garden.

Although a flawed novel, Joseph Kirkland's *Zury: The Meanest Man in Spring County* remains a powerful story, and starkly reveals the pitiless economic conditions of the mid-nineteenth century homestead frontier.[48] Kirkland's Zury, a giant of prodigious physical strength and powers of endurance, masters these forces, but at a personal cost tragic in implication. Before Kirkland's characterization is discussed, however, an analysis of Zury's origins in a folk tradition offers suggestive insight. Zury, the "meanest man" in any county, clearly originates in folk humor with strong liberal implications. As illustrated earlier, songs on the Arkansas Traveler motif use an ignorant farmer who stays on his unproductive backwoods acreage to protest the myth of the land. Zury has an origin in such a crude landowner as Jesse Herling "whose hair hung down like rat tails / On his lean and lantern jaw."[49] Certainly the meanest man in Arkansas (the folk song Hell, so to speak, since it represents a place of those damned to perpetual ignorance and cruelty), Herling, like Zury, is a liberal folk artist's expression of cultural loss. His farm is half canebrake and half swamp; he pays starvation wages; but—most significantly—he stays with the land. His hired hand, Sanford Barnes, does not—wisely. Those who remain farmers, by implication, are doomed to poverty, ignorance, and cruelty.

Although Zury Prouder is not intended to be a Jesse Herling, he is nevertheless a mean survivor edged with a keen instinct for the upper hand. He gains his local reputation by using Yankee horse-swapping methods in land speculation and loans that are scrupulously fair but merciless. He lives by a code he developed in early youth to protect his humanity from other wounds. He too stays with the land, in appearance and manner a bucolic savage, and profits from his neighbors' mistakes in land deals. Moreover, to further suggest Kirkland's use of folk humor and his own, Zury's name originates in the limited culture of the frontier. The Prouders, his parents, name him Usury (which backwoods Illinois dialect shortens to 'Zury) because they believe it to be a biblical and dignified name. Kirkland thus adapts a homestead folk-song type to his liberal theme of dispossession. But this of course is merely the imaginative genesis of his uncivilized giant of prodigious energy who is, significantly, not dispossessed because he learns the methods of land speculation.

Kirkland's motivation for creating this complex protagonist (at least more complex than present criticism indicates) is the frontier theme of dispossession transformed by his realist's perception of society. Zury, prototype of the compulsive American overachiever, like Dreiser's Frank Cowperwood (*The Financier* and *The Titan*), experiences a frontier economy that causes him and his parents undue hardship. The Prouders suffer the effect of a usurious mortgage on the farm that is their living; they thus resemble the protagonists of early dispossession songs. In the first chapter we find Zury mourning the death of his young sister, Selena, who dies because the family cannot affort medical care. He broods with customary and eloquent granite silence, then flees into the night storm. Kirkland sees the death as the result of poverty caused by inadequate land laws. "That evening was a sad one in the log hut. Half the section mortgaged and nothing to show for it but *this*. Not one cent in money, nothing to eat, drink, or wear, a growing crop that might be worth ten cents a bushel three months hence, and a little unsodded grave without even a fence around it."[50] Zury never recovers from this youthful time of deepest loss, for he had loved the sickly girl profoundly. When he returns on that night of grief, he pledges revenge on society; within a year he pays his parents' mortgage and begins to speculate in lands and make loans. But his ambition comes at a deep personal cost: "He was without associates, ambitions or objects in life, except 'subduing' that farm; in the next place, clearing it of mortgages; in the third place, increasing its money-making capacities; and thenceforth and forever adding dollar to dollar, mortgage to mortgage, note to note, and gain to gain, with all the force of a strong intellect pent into a narrow channel."[51]

Kirkland, like Eggleston—to whom he acknowledged his debt as a writer of frontier realities—translates an earlier theme of homestead protest into Zury's cold passion for the upper hand in economic affairs. Circumstances that dispossessed the Morses and thousands of other pioneers change Kirkland's protagonist from a loving brother and son into a compulsively ambitious moneylender, a type of American success whose overachievement reflects a cultural slavish respect for the power of wealth. His source in "unweeded garden" humor undergoes sophistication into psychological realism. (Dr. Oliver Wendell Holmes's *Elsie Venner* [1861] may be a forerunner of this aspect of *Zury*, whose meanness has been conditioned by his social circumstances.) Zury's change from rural innocent to the "meanest man" inverts a prairie democratic garden of the West, Kirkland's recognition of western potential, into the ironic world where the individual may resist economic outrage through skillful and amoral expedients, or, as Zury does, with the stoic durable acceptance of his personal code and hard bargains. In either case, the maleficence of needless economic pressures appears inescapable. Kirkland may perhaps be described as a moral determinist, if I may be allowed that term.

In ambiguous contrast, the narrative of Zury's progress to wealth and a country squire's estate invokes the garden myth with its ideal of a democratic western civilization on the American frontier. This is the conservative aspect of Kirkland's art. The image of the Illinois prairie—fertile ground, a test of pioneer courage, a source of community—pervades the novel. Its symbolic values are made explicit: "In the prairie, Nature had stored, and preserved thus far through the ages, more life-materials than she ever before amassed in the same space. It is all for man, but only for such men as can take it by courage, and hold it by endurance. Many assailants are slain, many give up and fly, but he who is sufficiently brave, strong, and faithful, and fortunate, to maintain the fight to the end has ample reward."[52] Zury's rise, ostensibly, is the result of Nature's "life-materials," a kind of *élan vital* originiating in the soil itself, an original energy to be rewarded by a pioneer's share of the noble garden. (Morse left New York with similar expectations and the innocent energies of the hopeful emigrant.)

For Kirkland, the Conestoga wagon is the epitome of pioneering; it is the "Mayflower of the West" carrying a new generation of the decadent but civilized East into the romance of homestead promise. Kirkland is also a romantic and an idealist. The symbolic prairie schooner as a "carrier of virtue, honesty, intelligence, and freedom, and an incredible appetite and capacity for toil"[53] is the symbol of civilization, the now transported garden, which fuses the ideal with the future reality, preposterous as this may seem today. For Kirkland, burdened by a Victorian literary conscience, the pioneer's redemptive gift had assured the refined present of genteel society. This society was the renewed civilization of the East, somehow still to be emulated, feared, distrusted, admired, revered, and deified as the only true source of culture by its rebellious (but vital) child, the West. Kirkland endeavors to hold the two in harmonious balance. On the one hand, he generates the style of a historical romance through the primitive, Zury Prouder, a homestead "noble savage" whose human goodness has been subverted by the trauma of his sister's premature death. Within the setting of the potential garden of natural (intuitive) virtue, a Jeffersonian romantic garden, Kirkland is able to clarify the ugly blight of speculation that attacks his hardiest of plants. He has, then, inverted the popular image of the West by suggesting its effect in Zury's maimed character.

But when the garden thus falls, how is it to become the source of a new civilization? Kirkland, like others of his literary generation, does not attempt to resolve the ambiguity;

perhaps he could not, since in this respect he is much like Twain. Cooper's romances seem to have led the way; the white madonna of the East—civilization—dominated yet another generation's literary imagination of society. But as I have suggested, the vital Zury is a subversive character; he retains the intuitive virtues of the democratic plowman who is the hero of the garden (like the Leatherstocking). Even as he becomes the hardened, crude, amoral son of a harshly materialistic society, we see compassion and leadership in his character. Kirkland's boyhood on the Michigan frontier may have instructed him in the cruel authority of an economic plague, land fever. Intensely conscious that he had located the historical continuity between a less-than-perfect gilded age in the wild and the philistine speculation that distorts Zury's humanity, he nevertheless felt the need to maintain a genteel literary decorum. The barbarous age of vigor—Zury's crude world—had passed, and with it the democracy of merit and human worth that Kirkland himself knew was the cornerstone of American aspirations; an intensifying materialism had become characteristic of society. Yet Kirkland refused to impose that view on his readers. His letters and early journalism show his dislike for speculation in the Illinois coal fields in his own time.[54] This seems a clear suggestion that he understood the power of an economy to shape and motivate character in any age. With his readers, he may have wished for the triumph of another vigorous Zury, warts and all, because civilization—the East—had become insufferably rigid, but he did not really allow himself the luxury of that optimism. When the cruel frontier passed, the cruelty remained, but a rare wildness (Zury) passed with it.

In letters to his then young friend Hamlin Garland, Kirkland illuminates the puzzling contradiction of his stance as realist and romantic. Garland, at the time serving a literary apprenticeship in Boston, had sent Kirkland the first draft of a story titled "Boomtown: A Social Study"; the older writer criticized the piece, calling it a sociological essay rather than objective (or dramatic) narrative. "Our fiction is a social study, but we must conceal the study part. You might as well call it an essay, and so damn it at once. And if, as I fear, your study is perceptible in your *treatment* of it, you must write it all over again to eliminate self and make your characters seem to act and talk with perfect spontaneity. The 'art to conceal art' is the only indispensable thing in realism."[55] Kirkland's "art to conceal art" in his practice reveals character through personal interaction as well as a more general relationship with society, in this instance a morally turbulent society. Thus Kirkland's "concealed art" is, so to speak, an unbalanced tension between two gardens: one heroic if nobly primitive, the other harshly and coercively "unweeded." With Garland, Kirkland revered William Dean Howells and his new realism. It had enabled his creation of a society appropriate to his crude protagonist, a homestead society that he had evolved through listening to the memories of early settlers in central Illinois where he lived as an adult. That is, Howell's moral realism had penetrated Kirkland's social view. Such fiction needs the aesthetic complexity of structural metaphor; the ironic garden of the homestead supplied the motivation for Zury's conduct and emerges as the dominant symbol of the novel. The realism Kirkland wanted was inherent in the homesteaders' view of their own predicament.

Another comment in a letter to Garland suggests Kirkland's troublesome interplay of two gardens. He rejects his younger friend's suggestion that he transform his novel into a play, but in doing so he indicates a brief potential schematic. Again, we encounter the tension of an ideal implicit in frontier history but not realized until Kirkland's own time, a logical difficulty in view of the disabling cruelty of Zury's society. He holds, on the one hand, that progress is as inevitable as sunlight: "Let us see—four acts—the hardening suffering of youth—the rude and grotesque features of prosperity—the grievous awakening on being refused by his lady love—the country gentleman."[56] Zury's rise from suffering youth to reformed gentleman, stated here, is as surprising as Kirkland's apparent belief in the inevitability of his reform and the progress of his society, yet the two are closely linked in his mind. Taine, Tolstoi, and Spencer had suggested to Howells and the school of realists that a scientific law governed the progress of society. Their theory of four dynamic stages was easily adaptable to the historian of the Illinois frontier, whose four-act play, although merely conjectural, reveals his perception of "Howellsian" (Tolstoian is more accurate, perhaps) progress.[57] Fortunately, the artist in Kirkland controls the scientist. The "hardening" of the young Zury remains an aspect of the mature, suffering, "reformed" hero. In youth he has been psychologically maimed for life—dispossessed, as it were, of the intangible and abstract; certainly only of that which he can see and touch. Moreover, human affections—even for Anne Sparrow, who becomes his common-law wife—is never to be trusted or openly expressed. Kirkland had come to understand the interaction of the individual and society that led to the pragmatic American.

Zury's relationship with Anne, central to Kirkland's thematic focus on civilization, deserves fresh analysis. The ideal garden of democracy and primitive virtue becomes allegorically significant through this relationship, serving as a norm as Zury and Anne change along with the crude society emerging from the raw frontier. Her entrance into the central action of the novel—that is, into relationship with Zury, who represents power in Spring County—seems gratuitous, a mechanical device used to symbolize civilization in her role as a schoolteacher from the East. Personally independent and intelligent *and* well educated, she is also associated, as Zury is, with the perpetually juvenescent garden: she lends her moral authority. As her relationship with Zury becomes more intimate, we recognize the limitations the frontier has imposed in his character. Anne, as teacher, tames an ignorant community. Her success is realistic; she is industrious and perceptive, an individual who sees her responsibilities in an uncouth community and acts purposefully.

She is less successful in taming Zury. In spite of her effort, he remains a person of unusual energies whose hold on Spring County is through his power as landowner and moneylender. Allegorically, he represents the unweeded garden. The ideal is thus juxtaposed to the real. His rise to country gentleman is realistic; the hardscrabble existence of his early years leaves no room for significant change; his grim materialism has its rewards. Unfortunately, he becomes a diminished character, a bumpkin who speaks an unintelligible dialect, a character without force. His purpose in the novel seems ended. The hope of true progress, of de Tocqueville's democratic vigor expressing itself in the creation of a new civilization, seems to lie with the next generation. Although Zury becomes a respected county judge, he fails to win an election for state senator because his speech betrays his lack of education. As the idle country squire, Zury loses the unique vitality of the aggressive frontier gardener—however psychologically maimed by an economic system—whose survival ensures the democratic vitality of the future. Yet he is the father of Anne's twins and, by implication, progenitor of the new civilization, whatever it is to be.

Kirkland enjoys a sparkling modernity in his drama of sexual relationships; they become a pantomime of human misunderstanding—mute, confused, desperate. A climactic scene offers evidence of Zury's concealed emotional depth and thick outer shell: Anne, neurotically fearful of the dark (Kirkland suggests it is fear of her unconscious), leaves an evening meeting at the school determined this time to make her way home alone. She fails, camping for the night in a rude shelter by the river she also fears. Early the next morning Zury comes to her rescue, as indifferent to the scandal her disappearance for the night will cause as to the river he must ford. But the tender moment of his concern for Anne, bringer of light to his darkness, abruptly ends. Misunderstanding her confused behavior, he forces his attentions on her, then solemnly leaves her in the darkness by the river—but not before he has fathered her twins. When he learns of her pregnancy, he takes responsibility, offering his home and marriage. Independent and courageous, firm in the conviction of her own responsibility in the matter, Anne refuses marriage but accepts his offer of a home during her pregnancy. (The dull wife he had previously married—because she inherited an adjacent farm he had long coveted—has died of perceptible emotional attrition due to Zury's understandable neglect; Anne has replaced her.) Anne lives openly with Zury in the domestic happiness of a companionable arrangement. If this was acceptable in a tale of a barbaric past, Kirkland would have offended most readers had he dared to suggest that such a companionate marriage held a greater value than the frozen virtue of the conventional Victorian marriage. The couple live in mutual respect, a form of love and understanding. Allegorically, of course, the warmth and authority of true civilization has reached the unweeded garden of Spring County; Anne's twins imply a vital future—yet Zury's diminished stature as a personality, it seems, negates that hope.

Zury shows none of the lover's redemptive passion; stoically but unconventially, he never again offers marriage. Nor does the independent Anne desire his offer. In this as in other ways, Kirkland suggests that the barbarity of the past causes a cruel "hardening" of youth; he is the vigorous philistine of frontier society. In sum, the inverted garden dispossesses human personality, although Anne and Zury, to their credit, survive the cruelty and find together "life, liberty, and the pursuit of happiness" that would not otherwise have been possible for either. In addition, the allegorical union of the East (that is, of Anne, the schoolteacher and civilization) with the West (that is, Zury and the new democracy reborn with vigor and freedom) now occurs in a context of true human warmth, although the fruits of that union would seem to remain of questionable moral legitimacy. Intended or not, Kirkland's suggestion of happiness achieved in a society of morally uncertain lineage retains a lively contemporaneity.

The son of Caroline Kirkland, an early literary realist, Kirkland had absorbed her interest as well as the culture of the Michigan frontier in his youth. Later years in central Illinois awakened his desire to write a truthful fiction about the frontier world while its echoes were still bouncing from the walls of living memories. Like Eggleston, whom he respected, he lacked Twain's supple style of portraying western life, yet this work remains his payment of debt to his fellow midwestern novelist. In turn, Kirkland's well-known relationship with Garland served to transmit a native cultural theme as well as a usable style of perceiving that theme.

While the Morse narrative was not intended to be read as serious literature, a brief examination of its narrative rhythm indicates the cultural source of these writers' imagination of human loss and failure. Morse originates his "story" in a nostalgic comedy of boyhood life in New York that ends in the revolt of young manhood; then moves toward the freedom of the West, toward the responsibility of marriage and purposeful work; suggests his disappointment as he is forced off the land by debt and his sense of loss in Delia's final illness and death; and ends with an attempt to find the reason for loss among the scattered and fading memories left in the years during which he wrote. Yet the shape of the homesteaders' garden has a clear outline here; the homes and farmland he had lost clearly represented to him the potential freedom of the economically independent person as well as his measure of personal worth. In the story of his lifelong failure, Morse offers a focus for additional studies of frontier society, historical and cultural.

The tragic potential of the dispossession theme may not have been fully realized until Faulkner explored the failure of democracy in his Yoknapatawpha novels—especially *Light in August* and *Absalom! Absalom!*—but both Kirkland and his understanding student, Hamlin Garland, made significant attempts. Analysis of Garland's "Up the Coulee" in *Main-Travelled Roads* (1891) and his *Jason Edwards: An Average Man* (1892), both infrequently read, suggest a treatment of this theme that intends a tragic vision of man in society. Garland's is a world of human suffering and wasted lives like Omar Morse's. "Up the Coolly" (to use its original title) begins with the return of an affluent Howard to his prairie home after his New York success as a playwright and director. The land and its people at first seem a bountiful garden of the West to him. Grant, Howard's elder brother, who has stayed at home to support their parents, discloses the reality: his years of exhausting labor have failed to provide more than mere subsistence after mortgage payments; indeed, he had previously lost the family's homestead (and their years of collective labor) to the destroyer, the "everlasting mortgage" (Morse's term), and moved to another farm. The rhythm of the Morse narrative has an interesting parallel here.[58]

Grant thus reflects the homestead protagonist of the dispossessed garden theme in the futility of his labors. The folk demon of the land speculator is again offstage, but his works are manifest in a mortage. Garland's parable is obvious: he does not invert the garden theme; he rushes at it with the perspective of a doomed prairie Quixote and thus discloses the chaotic windmill whirligig of economic realities. Irony, not heavy satiric message, serves Garland best, however. Howard, still complacent, self-congratulatory with his recent success, had not realized how desperate Grant's need for relief truly was. Remorseful at his failure as son and brother, Howard bursts into a stark metaphor: "What was it worth anyhow—success? struggle, strife, trampling on someone else. His play crowding out some other fellow's hope. The hawk eats the partridge, the partridge eats the flies and bugs, the bugs eat each other, and the hawk, when he in turn is shot by man."[59] Such despair, here as elsewhere in the story, suggests that Garland's tragic vision includes an all but fatalistic (or Darwinian) view of economic competition, which, interestingly, seems to have inspired William Dean Howells's remark about "Up the Coolly." Howells felt that Garland's portraits of the complacent and the bitter brothers revealed the truth about America's "vaunted conditions" (Howells's phrase): "The upper dog and the under dog are everywhere, and the under dog nowhere likes it."[60] Howard, made aware and remorseful during a visit too long delayed, writes a New York friend that if the world were in his hands, he would "crush it like a puffball," so fleeting is the happiness of those on the main-travelled road (the ordinary person's road of life) on which his family had journeyed.[61] The austerity of a tragic vision crackles through Garland's prose.

A final scene deepens protest to honest pathos. Howard again offers to help, with tears of remorse at his failure, but it is too late. Grant knows that he has neither the time nor the money for the education he needs if he hopes to leave the profitless farm. His life has been sacrificed without apparent reason; there are no rewards for virtue. The brothers' mutual anguish reconciles them to an understanding of their situation and renews their love and respect, but nothing changes in Garland's random universe of murderous economic warfare. Like Dreiser, Garland implies the fated catastrophe of classical tragedy through a Darwinian "trampling on someone else." The resolution of the story, Grant's acceptance of his life for what it is, suggests Garland's bitter knowledge of dispossession in wasted lives and cultural erosion. Crane's dark story of suicide in *Maggie: A Girl of the Streets* has comparable social realism. Garland had earlier found that Whitman's praise of Jean François Millet's paintings suggested the kind of realism he and Kirkland wished to capture. Millet's famous *Man with the Hoe* had already supplied Edwin Markham with a source of inspiration. For Garland, such brutalized peasants had their American counterparts in Grant and other characters in *Main-Travelled Roads*. But the memorable tale is "Up the Coolly," in which the homestead countermyth gives structure to the narrative; here the merciless prairie sunlight on bountiful acres of wheat illuminates the stooped lives of a homestead family. The life of the successful New York playwright invites dramatic contrast. Howell's acute perception of the continuing economic battle of haves and have-nots powerfully and directly illuminates Garland's "man with the hoe." America's "vaunted conditions" had not relieved the ancient social burden of poverty. Garland holds the whole coin of the frontier ironist; he sees the smiling face of the weedless garden in the golden wheat of the prairies *and* the hunched figure of the American farmer dispossessed in spite of his bountiful crops. The grassroots Populism heard in youth became the "concealed art" of his mature narratives.[62]

In addition to "Up the Coolly," Garland's "Under the Lion's Paw," "The Return of Private Smith," and "The Branch Roads" in *Main-Travelled Roads*, as well as *Jason Edwards*, a novel, suggest his uses of the unweeded garden theme. Edwards is a Boston foundry worker whose low pay, tenement life, and rising rent assessed by avaricious slum landlords motivates his desire for the relief of a change for the better promised by the idea of the West. He has seized in dire need on the vague cultural promise of his Boston workingman's society that a family may be independent in the West. He finds this promise floating with an illusory but hopeful and boyant élan in the desperate society of his laborer's daily realities. Like his friends, he perceives the West as a tangible place with its happiness and freedom evident in acres of ripe wheat. The marketplace truths have no place in these dreams, of course, but in such naiveté lies the cause of human helplessness and social failure. Jason migrates westward with the aspirations of the earlier homesteader. As in "Up the Coolly," Garland indicates the sources of the destructive illusion that the garden myth has generated. (In Jason's world, the garden is simply "the West.") Garland's transvaluation of the lurking Satan of the unweeded garden, the land speculator Judge Balser, has but to wait; he knows disaster will overtake Edwards as it has overtaken others to whom he has sold land and given mortgages at increasing margins of profit. A summer storm as fierce as the unleashed furies of Dante's and Milton's underworld destroys Edwards's first wheat crop and with it his hopes; his cash reserve is gone. For Garland's Jason there is no golden fleece: no wheat and, within a summer, no homestead. His moment of understanding his loss, wandering alone through his wheatfield, has the dimensions of the tragic, although this novel is seriously flawed by its sentimentality and too obvious message.

Both *A Spoil of Office* (1892) and *A Member of the Third House* (1892) attack legislative apathy, for Garland a major cause of homestead failure, but *A Spoil of Office* continues his powerful focus on the land and its worn people, universal in its scope. These works imply his knowledge of America's failed quest: the promised rebirth of a new western society had aborted; its bones were scattered like the lost graves of his dead forebears, the pioneer mothers and fathers whose cultures were now extinct or threatened. Garland sees, intuitively, that such losses speak a tragic wisdom of suffering such as Kirkland's Zury experienced, and that the future will prove as barren as the frontier past. Garland's theme of dispossesision, much like Zury's, was first transmitted by his parents in Wisconsin coulee country (low rolling hills and valleys); it intensified in Iowa and South Dakota during his young manhood, and in his experience with the Farmers' Alliance and the Populists.[63] Perhaps Kirkland's realism, too, stimulated Garland's thought and style, although such songs as "Starving to Death" and "The Old Settler's Song," possibly heard in youth were later the seed crystals of the writer's experience. Garland refers directly to "The Arkansas Traveler," analyzed earlier, in "Up the Coolly." The melodramatic contrast between the good but helpless farmer with his deserving family and the lurking figure of villainous intent congenial to Populist rhetoric is central to the narrative of *Jason Edwards.*

A helpless, mute Jason, waist-deep in his drought-wilted wheat, waits for expected relief from the gathering clouds on the horizon, but they prove instead to bring devastation. A torrential rain washes out his crop, and his home is all but afloat; then, although he recovers from the shock, his farm must be sold to satisfy a mortgage held by the bland villain, Judge Balser, a smiling hypocrite. If Garland sees mankind existentially, he seeks order in civilization—specifically, in the democratic society of the new West—but this ostensibly manifest hope remains illusory.

Yet Garland and Reeves are undaunted: that is, Garland uses the novel to proselytize but thus spoils the drama of the conclusion. His successful Boston reporter, Walter Reeves (a wooden and inadvertent Horatio Alger hero), decides to use his influence and wealth to aid the helpless Jason and his family. Reeves has been converted to the Farmers' Alliance by hearing Henry George speak at a Boston union meeting. In love with Jason's gifted daughter, a singer, he travels west to ask her to marry him, after waiting out the Victorian year of obligatory probation she requested. This contrived plot sends Reeves to Garland's Boomtown just before disaster strikes. He finds food and shelter for the pathetic Edwards family, aided by other Alliance members, but cannot prevent their dispossession. Pathos, unfortunately, becomes bathos. An Alliance white knight, Reeves magnanimously adopts the whole family and takes them to Boston to live with him and his aged mother, happily anticipating his forthcoming marriage to Jason's talented daughter. If Reeves and the Alliance are the benevolent society of the future, the present hope seems the East and its symbolic model of civilization. Although seriously flawed by mawkish emotion, the conclusion, if unintentionally, illustrates such an intent. Jason feebly raises his head to peer through the train window at a Boston suburb. Although physically and psychologically paralyzed by his losses, and a victim of the homestead garden of the West as well, at the sight he begins to revive. Boston subsequently restores him to sanity and health, and Walter Reeves exults in his marriage.[64]

The "cure" for western ills, then—or so it would seem—is to become a backtrailer. Unions were providing better conditions for laborers than the Alliance was able to generate for farmers, the rural workforce, many of whom—like the Morses—had pioneered the west. The powerful figure of the smiling Balser remains triumphant. Some of Garland's refugees go to the state mental asylum; others survive to seek again the magic "somewhere else" that remains such a familiar aspect of the American landscape. We can forget the tacked-on ending, but remember that in spite of all nobility and good intention, in spite of Alliance cooperation in Garland's Boomtown, the Edwards farm was lost to the harsh effect of nature and Balser's kind of economic laissez-faire. Clearly, then, the unweeded garden has a vivid image in Jason's desolate, flattened wheat. In *A Spoil of Office* (1892), in addition, the final chapter achieves its powerful climax with an Alliance meeting and protest demonstration through the streets of the town. Although Garland's major concern here was not simply the poverty and despair caused by an illusory cultural myth, it again motivates his strongest dramatic scenes.

An earlier novel, Mark Twain and Charles Dudley Warner's *The Gilded Age* (1873), is closer to the satire of frontier songs and humorous tales. This transitional work illustrates the devolution of the unweeded garden from Morse's fading hope of a viable farm through folk materials into Eggleston's, Kirkland's, Garland's, and Donnelly's works. Twain's irony, gained in the western experience described in *Roughing It* and the early practice of frontier tales, encompasses a pre-Civil War theme of dispossession from land through wild speculation and extends it into postbellum speculation in railroads and villages in the hazy West of the age. As a satirist Twain aims his protest at the corrupt Grant administration. As humorist he collects now familiar characters into a novel as loose and baggy as a pair of homespun jeans—the greenhorn Easterner, Brierly; the bungling confidence man, Sellers; the country gallant, Washington Hawkins. As sentimental romancer he creates a sustaining love interest that includes the blonde heroine as well as the dark lady of ill-fated character. The unity of this novel, if unity is possible in such astounding variety, lies in Twain's concern with dispossession as the symbolic event that implies the loss of cultural health (or moral order) to "speculation fever," to use his term.

However, we find here no helpless farmers struggling against an indifferent government and an intractable nature. Nor do we find a prototype of Huck Finn on a symbolic raft with his black friend, both dispossessed of "sivilization," the unweeded garden of Twain's pre-Civil War shore society. We do find Twain's perception of the wilderness garden in an image of a yet unspoiled West, a symbolic garden of potential culture, as well as his satire on land speculators who destroy the western opportunity.[65]

Phil Sterling, Twain's romance hero, discovers an Arcadian wilderness on his first trip into the Mississippi Valley, then westward. It is Twain's happy valley of the homestead, an archetype, but it proves an Eden tottering on the brink of the Fall. Although the characters are but types, easily recognizable, they wear the authentic costumes of moral Bedlam. Beriah Sellers, perhaps the most obvious Bedlamite, has long delighted readers because he is recognizable yet. Costumed with Twainian originality, he seems as relevant as one of Saul Bellows's more desperate and inept confidence men. He first amuses because his deceptions are humorously transparent. No one seriously believes that Napoleon, Sellers's speculator village, is a true threat to responsible settlement. Like Suggs he exposes his own chicanery, though he is seldom as successful. Later he becomes a more shadowy character, less the amusing and harmless fool than a henchman of the frontier demon who has triumphed in earlier folk songs. Twain and Warner, I am convinced, only *seem* to remain mere satirists intent on laughing fools into moral perspective; Sellers's later machinations suggest that satire on occasion darkens into near tragedy.

He becomes a successful lobbyist for Senator Dilworthy's Tennessee Land Bill, legislation airmed at the reconstruction of the post-Civil War South. An obvious farce, the bill is sold to the public as a means of obtaining land for a black vocational school, but Dilworthy's bill is another land swindle. Since he arranges matters by covert dealing with the landowners themselves, his friends Laura and Washington Hawkins, we understand why the price of land alone precludes building the school.[66] Twain implies that the unweeded garden of speculation encourages a continued slavery by diverting funds needed to relieve the poverty of black people.

Twain's moral irony is obvious: Sellers, Dilworthy, and Laura Hawkins, Dilworthy's sexy and successful lobbyist, are exposed by accident. These swindlers, closely and thematically linked to Congress, rehearse the concrete details of the homestead countermyth in their cleverness as satanic "landgrabbers." The popular melodrama of the novel seems to have been borrowed from the folk theme. Although Twain did not apparently read Hooper's satire, and there is no record of his interest in dispossession songs, he understood the cultural attitudes that shaped the countermyth. Like other satirists, he could visualize the ideal while lampooning the actual. And his experience supplied images. While Twain's dark perception of land misused for fat and corrupt profit foreshadows the later pessimist of *Letters from the Earth* (published posthumously, in 1964), he cannot believe that civilization—or the symbolic madonna of white civilization that he could never quite forget or forgive—in the United States was doomed to undemocratic and authoritarian rule. Yet he could never resist the saving grace of his own humor. While the swindlers receive their punishment and are properly banished from Washington, at the close of the novel we learn that Dilworthy intends to continue to manipulate his constituency, although no longer from the Senate. Behind the illuminating brilliance of his wit, Twain delights in a charade in the shadowland where mad deception parades as public righteousness and sanity. The unweeded garden here finds a zenith of satiric irony. It is this aesthetic that is best described as moral Bedlam.

In Frank Norris's *The Octopus* (1901), as in *The Gilded Age*, the central features of the western homestead countermyth hold the epic sprawl of incident in focus. Like Garland, Norris was an artist, not an apologist for a cause. Yet he seems to have grasped the loose strands of a cultural countermyth and woven them into the matrix of his narrative. With his western childhood and memories of Populist rhetoric, Norris could not escape an understanding of the ironic garden. While I find no evidence of Norris's interest in or reading of their literature, his novel shows highly complicated changes of the earlier midwestern novelists' treatments of this theme. With the advantage of historical perspective in 1903, he was able to adjust the familiar melodrama of satanic "land grabbers," their hopeless victims, and alienated, thwarted heroes to his scheme of an ambiguous tension between social idealism and the naturalistic novel form. Garland had struggled to unify these contradictory modes.

Two symbolic gardens manifest the central metaphor of the homestead theme and give sophisticated literary structure to Norris's design. The Seed Farm, a central symbol, is a translated mythic garden of the West resembling Morse's hopeful "everlasting grainfield." In the walled garden of the Seed Farm, the Jeffersonian virtues of industry, human dignity, and moral life seem possible. Here the young and lovely Angele, the spirit of the Farm, meets her love, Vanamee. Vanamee and Father Sarria of the Spanish church nearby may hold conversations at their ease. It is a nostalgic old West, as yet unchanged. Nearby is Los Muertos ("the dead ones"), a wheat empire built by Magnus Derrick and managed as a mechanized "factory farm." Norris suggests that Los Muertos ought to become the old Seed Farm made new. Machines promise to fulfill the garden myth, having also acquired the appeal of the myth of technological progress so congenial to Americans. But Norris's thematic Seed Farm is symbolically lost in the rape of Angele by an unknown attacker. Her death completes the symbolism. Without "seed" (the fruit of the farm, Angele and Vanamee), cultural change is doomed. Los Muertos, the second garden, has no other source of "life," no "seed." The allegory of the second garden is stated when "the dead ones" literally multiply at Derrick's wheat ranch. To the extent that Norris's allegory utilizes materials from Garland and the Alliance, he implies social protest; his fallen gardens may be understood as unweeded gardens that protest cultural and actual dispossession. Thus, if the homestead farm became a disabling ideal, the mechanized ranch—the new vision wrought by progress—proves equally destructive to the human personality.

At the risk of elaborating the already obvious, let us further analyze the garden symbol parallels. S.N. Behrman, a railroad agent, manipulates Derrick's and other ranchers' shipping costs, ensuring that the railroad (the octopus of many-branched tentacles) can claim its legal right-of-way (government land grants were given to railroads during early settlement), which Derrick and his ranchers must buy at the present market price, not the original Land Office price that they believed had been promised. A man as devious as Faulkner's Flem Snopes, Behrman also resembles Garland's Balser as a satanic figure, the homesteaders' "land grabber." As the result of his devious manipulation, Los Muertos becomes government property. Derrick's faith in himself and his ranch—the agrarian/capitalistic source of a free nation in the future—proves illusory: the Seed Farm, like the homestead garden of the West that it represents, is an American dream that ends in tragedy; Los Muertos, although adjusted to the dynamic of technological change, is dispossessed by the railroad, armed by the government to claim land Derrick refused to buy when the railroad raised the original frontier price.

Norris releases the energies of suspense in a dramatic shootout at Los Muertos in true western style. Derrick suffers the loss of his wheat ranch to United States marshals led by Behrman, having previously endured public disgrace after attempting bribery in order to save his ranch. He witnesses the death of friends and of his son Harlan, experiences his fall from eminence, and loses his home to his enemies. Norris thus completes the symbolic rape of the second garden; here he echoes the "he was taken by the hand / And led from the land" pattern of the homesteaders' countermyth, evident when the railroad "middleman"—represented by Behrman and supported by the government—"gets it all." Society, symbolically the progressive West, will decay into slum ignorance. Norris's transportation issue and land manipulation too closely resemble early prairie homestead realists' and the Alliance's theme of dispossession to be dismissed. Critics who have pointed out the tension between Norris's protest against lost cultural ideals and his naturalistic sense of fate have overlooked his sources in a cultural theme of protest.[67]

Norris's ambiguously skewed idealism holds an additional dimension that unifies his sprawling, sometimes tendentious novel. When Los Muertos falls into the hands of the railroad through Behrman, Norris's allegory of gardens is yet incomplete. Through Presley, a survivor at Los Muertos and a close friend of Derrick's family, he implies that the wheat ranch can never be won or lost; it can only be left behind. Staying with the land, even in nostalgic memory, is fruitless, Presley comes to realize. He must reconcile himself to his loss of friends at the wheat ranch, to the shattered social ideals stated in his poem, "The Toilers" (Presley is an obvious Edwin Markham), and to a society that he believes is a race of "cannibals." He is a dispossessed person at the end of the novel, somewhat comparable to the persona of the Arkansas Traveler songs, having decided to become a traveler like Huck Finn—at home nowhere. For this alienated poet, leaving Los Muertos is preferable to staying where he and his friends have lost an agrarian way of life. His ideal of cooperative society now seems foolishly naive, utopian; for him, cultural values become—figuratively—Scott Fitzgerald's boats against the stream. The wheat from Los Muertos is sent to feed starving people in India with funds raised by fatuous socialites. By accepting such ironies and recognizing the mystery, Presley accepts the meaning of the garden of Los Muertos. Out of catastrophe and cruelty, paradoxically, starving people will be fed, though millions will continue to starve. And good friends, who dreamed the new agriculture, had ruined their lives in pursuit of justice.[68] For Norris, the West was a symbol, a good dream, but a dream humanity could not achieve. The tension between protest against its failure and a naturalistic view of human nature remains, but the futility and despair that nineteenth-century folk culture captures in its theme of dispossession echoes in the darkness of Norris's tragedy of lost cultural values. The tragic potential of *The Octopus* is never realized in this sprawling book, but Norris has located the frayed blossoms of the garden myth, which he considers for objective study. In Norris's failed work, we thus recognize the abortive promise of the land through its fated victims.

In his autobiography, Omar Morse does not register protest against his dispossession. He does, however, offer homestead themes of grassroots realism while struggling to keep his "everlasting grainfield" model alive, perhaps fooling only himself and aware of it—or, as Mody Boatwright suggests of western farmers, stoically risking another homestead in the spirit of individualism, believing that a new homestead would at least be no worse than his last.[69] Perhaps Victor W. Sterling, Morse's son-in-law who became a secretary in the People's Party, and perhaps the Rev. Gamaliel Barnes, his grandfather and former chaplain in the American Revolution, imbued him with their sense of individual and democratic rights.

Whatever influenced Morse, with other homesteaders he absorbed it into his way of life. In 1882, when he began to write his narrative, he had suffered the death of his beloved wife Delia, the breakup of his family, and the loss of three homestead farms. To maintain his ideal, he contrived to live on the last twenty acres of his third homestead. He called this his "Old Home in the Woods," a symbolic garden of the West. From this vantage point, he could begin to visualize his life in terms of a faith that he had kept but that had not kept him. Early on, he tells us he will select incidents that seem to him connected. Thus his deliberate contrast of a youthful "garden" innocence with his later struggle against hardship to realize his dream in tangible acres and dollars illustrates his literary awareness of the ironic trick life and his hopes (and his culture) had played on him. Like the hero of "Starving to Death," he had all but starved out while suffering Minnesota winters on his government claim, yet—foolishly perhaps—he persisted in cultivating his land, more land than he could properly manage. A permanent home was his cherished symbol, his last reality in a mirage of hopeless hopes, which kept him and his family inwardly alive in the desolate cultural space of failure in American society. (Dreiser's Hurstwood illustrates this kind of cruel exile.) Huck Finn, the archetype of dispossessed persons, seems to share Morse's hopeless hope when—is it from boredom, desperation, a need for freedom, or the longing for a magic "somewhere else"?—he decides to "light out for the Territory ahead of the rest." In motion there may be ease for the anguish of dwindling expectations in an eroding culture.

Thousands of homestead farmers—among them blacks, Indians, emigrants, and immigrants—speak through Morse's alienation in a narrative intended merely as a family record, as well as through the songs, tales, and novels that reflect the unweeded garden of dispossession. In such reflecting literary mirrors as Mark Twain's or, in this century, William Faulkner's, the common person is enabled to understand the dignity with which he must surrender to forces that wholly diminish the measure of mankind. The tragic history of wasted lives inherent in the frontier raises searching questions and protest against the loss of democratic ideals in corrosive, blind expansion. A resulting cultural theme has left a legacy of failure—or the psychic wolves of the fear of failure—which continues to haunt the American literary consciousness.

3. The Repossession: A Creative Recovery of Community

This book has offered three perspectives on homestead dispossession for the purpose of suggesting the values of a frontier community not fully understood. As a result of instability due to dispossession, it dissolved into legend before its norms and their adjustment to the realities of the homestead farm had become accessible to students of pioneering. The unweeded garden theme suggests the homestead culture. (As an unweeded garden is the centering metaphor in *Richard II*, Shakespeare's drama of willful misrule and resulting cultural dislocation, this descriptive term not only suggests the technique of ironic inversion but also the implication of the homesteaders' protest.)

To facilitate comprehension of this unusual transitory community, the book has been divided into two major parts. The first contains Morse's statement of his failed quest for a permanent home and his sense of lost goals and disillusionment. Part Two extends the Morse family's experience into the objective dimension of history so that Omar's dispossession, recorded only for his children as a witness of his life, becomes significantly representative. Chapter two offers an analysis of cultural dispossession, or of pioneer and later strategies of creative defense and recovery from lost homes and farms, with their implied symbolic value of independence, that is, the theme of the unweeded garden, which appears in folk and literary forms of social protest.

The homestead protest may first emerge in Simon Sugg's misadventures and/or in folk songs revealing the plight of the victims whose lives demythologize the illusory promise of the western homestead; Frank Norris's late statement in *The Octopus* (1903) of lost nineteenth-century promise reveals an American society whose pretentions to an epic manifest destiny are lost in a representative land swindle by the corrupt railroads, the *bête noir* of the then long-defeated Populists. Cultural memory is in general long lived. Unusual in his homesteader's reflection of Populist sentiment or, more precisely, of a frontier "unweeded garden," Morse declares his unofficial independence from an amoral society (the letters in Appendix A offer clarifying examples) as an individual who had been committed to the mythic ideal of the land as a source of his personal integrity and freedom; he then creates a narrative world at once his own and a mirror of a society that time has clouded over with the gray dust of nostalgic stereotypes. The reader discovers Morse's characteristic homesteader's courage and endurance in the test of his will to independence by an obdurate economy. In addition, the reader finds that Morse's later years became a groping but meaningful surrender of the pride that had once enabled him to survive his years of crisis but had also made him vulnerable to the depredations of land speculators with money to lend, who had used and would continue to use his labor to fatten their wallets. He sought to recover his losses, perhaps, by writing of them, thus invoking the historical context of values and the dynamic of inevitable loss in a causal economic climate. His is a communal and tragic statement.

Small farmers, homesteaders like the Morses, could not pay mortgages and taxes, hire added labor to increase planted acreage and pastures, *or* buy needed machines; they had neither capital nor borrowing capacity. Dispossession was as inevitable as weeds in the wheat. Without a fully articulated or implemented government control and in the resultant unethical society, a materialistic age confirmed in practice a Darwinian "red in tooth and claw" business climate that frequently benefitted the speculator but seldom the average homestead family. Such barriers of avarice were an impediment to growth; the potentially stable farming community faced an enemy more deadly than hostile Indians or marauding bears, because debt accumulated almost invisibly and certainly without scruple or recognition of the cultural effect. It was an "everlasting mortgage," as Morse called it. Even if historians are right in disputing the seriousness of homestead dispossession, we know that many homesteaders came to *feel* themselves the victims of usury and dishonest landowners. This study suggests there is ample evidence to support their feelings. The Populists, as well as western authors, reflect agrarian disillusion and a rising political activity that gave force to their anger and liberal concerns. If forced by neglect into strident rhetoric, a pioneer generation and its children were not an irrational people; they knew they had just cause.

Thus the historians' problem remains: a data base that includes a ten-year history of land sales and resales, of mortgages and foreclosures in representative counties throughout the country remains to be assembled. Such representative sampling is essential to even a preliminary estimate of homestead dispossession. None of the studies researched for this book were based on such extensive data; thus conclusions by various scholars remain educated opinion. The failure of the garden model to direct frontier settlement toward feasible economic controls had an unquestionable effect on an American perspective toward its ripening civilization in the "dangerous days" of the gilded age. The repossession of the true values underlying the garden ideal, values adjusted to homestead fact such as independence and dignity in loss, would seem the object of Morse's creative search for the truth of his and his family's experience. A similar concern underlies the folk art of the western humorist and song writer as well as the more complex vision of the novelist. The previous chapter has illustrated the imaginative shape of this long unrecognized artistic ordering of the western experience.

Let us consider once again the pattern of Morse's narrative. He organizes his thought about an archetype of the fall, a loss of ideality common to the human condition but for him obviously occurring within the homestead context. His vision of a promised land, somewhere in the mythic West, an "everlasting grainfield," led him to seek the farm on which he and his family might at last find the independence and happiness the West had promised him when a young man in New York. It did not seem a vague scheme, a pot of gold at the end of the rainbow, but the ordinary person's accessible American freedom. The price, however, was invariably the "everlasting mortgage" and a struggle to relocate, physically and psychologically. The disaster, of course, was not in an individual case, but in the thousands who had a similar experience. Yet history, at least this different kind of history, is made by individuals who live it out and fumble, as we all must, for some kind of meaning. This study suggests that a folk culture responded deeply to dispossession; in so doing it revealed those values of the heart and mind which the loss of homes threatened to destroy. We can locate Morse's struggle to recover losses in his later years and find a desire to repossess those truths on which he had built a life, however unrewarding in material terms that life had been.

Morse's preoccupation with the transactions of buying land, building a home, and then leaving years of effort behind implies the concern of an individual who will continue to search the rubble of his losses as if it afforded a key to some ultimate explanation. The probable cause of his dispossession was lack of capital and a willingness to discount the need for money. But the wisdom of acceptance and the ability to adjust, finding work elsewhere to support his motherless family of five, reveals a community with other dispossessed homesteaders who did not tell the painful story of their failures. In such resourcefulness, Morse, like many others, kept his valued independence. The candor of Morse's autobiography, I have maintained, makes it an invaluable document, authorizing research into historical records and an exploration of the heritage of dispossession from society in twentieth-century literature and culture. The full and definitive account of dispossession from pioneer farms and later established farms from the earliest days of the colonies through the ethical tumult of the gilded age has not been written. We have the results of varied regional investigations, but no coordinated and directed study of a historic problem central to our present society. However, the area of the widest concensus offers a reasonable focus of results. Let us put the matter to rest this way: the Morse narrative exemplifies a mode of perception, a state of consciousness born of harsh experience—the ordinary person's hope and growing disillusionment in an era of greatest westward expansion—which, in turn, tallies with such liberal scholars' views as Smith's in *Virgin Land* and Gates's in *Landlords and Tenants*, a cultural history and frontier history respectively. The Morse narrative thus serves to illuminate the homesteaders' and several nineteenth-century novelists' consciousness of cruel economic barriers caused by an ethically unstable society. I have contended that the cultural awakening of the homesteaders themselves, the result of extreme disillusionment, brought about a renewal of their homestead culture under the stress caused by the loss of guiding homestead models; that this renewal, at first evident in the humor and satire of frontier writers, became the individual farmer's strategy of defense against the loss of moral direction and purpose, as well as the central metaphor of a group of writers who may be appropriately described as prairie realists. Not all were enabled to survive loss; the frozen winds of prairie isolation left many a helpless person prey to inanition.

Let us rehearse in one event the exercise in human greed that government land auctions became and, in this way, offer persuasive evidence of the causes of homestead failure. A department store bargain day or the television giveaway show, perhaps, can excite the basest aspect of the human personality. Such was the land rush for the Cherokee Strip in the Dakota Territory, the unofficial closing of the western frontier. Robert Swierenga's chapters on the history of the Iowa land rush of the 1850s give useful information on the complexities of pertinent government regulations and their inadequacies.[1] The narrative of the Cherokee Strip in Seth Humphries's vivid *Following the Prairie Frontier*, a professional writer's memoir not published until 1930, gives dramatic illustration of the greed that followed in the wake of the guide-trapper and Indian. He recalls the land rush that opened settlement in the last unsettled land in the Dakotas. A race on foot, by bicycle, by wagon and train became a human stampede, a mad rush to secure choice farm and town sites that moved the Cherokees, once native to Georgia, to yet another reservation farther north. Without wild land, the Cherokee society—a hunting and trapping culture—was doomed to become weak and decadent.[2]

The Cherokee land rush, as Humphries describes it, illustrates the compounded irony of economic conditions that led to dispossession. Those settlers who could, bought land to sell at 300 or more percent profit while offering mortgages at equally absurd percentages. Neighbor preyed on neighbor while loan sharks hovered beyond the shoal of homestead debt, waiting their opportunity. The drama of American instant success was being played out before the eyes of such spectators as Omar Morse, who realized that he was also on stage, as it were, since he had little alternative. He had believed in a different drama. Humphries's experience as an agent for a Boston mortgage company in the Dakotas offers an empathic but objective view of prairie homesteading. He could remember that his father in Minnesota in 1857 survived the first years of homesteading by raising sheep, having the advantage of neighbors who lacked the capital for this survival alternative. There had been much hunger in the community, he recalls, because many families had come to the area with the expectation of low-cost transportation of their products to the large urban markets. But this did not happen; the railroad went elsewhere, leaving a community to survive as best it could. Only those with capital enough became successful farmers.

And out on the Dakota prairies, their immense distances intensified by an awesome Gothic isolation, people clung to each other in desperate need of companionship. Humphries recalled the homesteaders' wives and their pleasure in his company. The price of civilization in the West has never been estimated; the psychological as well as physical hardships were often dealt with by concealing humor and desperate, stoic optimism. Those who like the Morses were several times dispossessed were recognized by Humphries as victims of a common circumstance—of course, economic in origin. But the intangibles of prairie silences and long winters, which must have deeply affected Delia Morse and the children as well as Omar himself, were significant forces in the settlers' struggle to remain on the land; thus, they remain a factor in prairie dispossession. Pioneers and their wives accepted these hardships, however; less comprehensible to a farmer without an informed knowledge of economic forces were the overpowering debts that led to the loss of homes. When values fragment and powder in one's hand because of cultural failure, the individual must fall back on his inner strength. Unlike others, however, Morse voiced his sorrows and his losses; few homesteaders told of their failures, because their culture, like our own, did not openly recognize failure. But the dark, rude truth that underlies one of the homeliest, most democratic and cheerful of American myths—the garden of the West—emerges from the honesty of a Morse, who could see and tell of his painful experiences of death, defeat, and failure. The emerging novelists of the prairie told a comparable story, having a comparable response to their society.

Morse's letters to his son (Appendix A) also hold significant interest for their revelation of the homestead community. He wrote them in the last decade of his life while another society, like and much unlike the one he had known, surrounded him. Omar and Omar, Jr. seem an echo of a harsher age, yet one that had kept its sense of independence—its freedom—through discipline in a society dominated by a gilded-age aristocracy of land barons and cattle kings, captains of industry and princes of mineral rights; in sum, by a vision of success. Fearful of his other son's dependency in the railroad repair shop, the father advises that he buy some land so he can farm should he lose his job or when he must retire. His language reflects the unionism inherent in the Populist philosophy, although it was more theoretical than actual, if he was similar in his views to other farmers. Yet the voice of the homestead community he had known is unmistakable: "You are nearly 40—about one half of your life has been spent in the hardest kind of servitude for an aristocratic corporation that cares less for your well being than we do for our stock—while your labor and sweat holds out to build them up and enrich them *you are all right*—if you vote right." He felt that his son, a railroad blacksmith, had become a mere employee, a person at the whim of his employer. There seems to him a loss of moral stature in this remunerative but suspect labor, though he himself, of course, had labored for the profit of a land speculator, if unknowingly. "A little Spot of Gods green earth" is all Manly needs to protect himself against the impact of urban industrialization and its interdependence.

"I say we are independent," he writes of himself and his second son, "in this sense, if we want a holiday—Or if we feel inclined we can sleep in the morning regardless of the toots of the Masters' whistles and the grass grows just the same—the corn beans and other products thrive and the chickens tend to their business just the same—we are our own masters as well as servants. This I call *independent what would you call it*." The values of another culture and an earlier generation (*and* a universal human desire) are voiced in his spontaneous outcry against an age of oncoming technological progress. While Morse's letters show his respect for progress, with that nineteenth-century spirit we identify as modern, he had also learned a wise distrust from an age of moot concern for individuals.

The era that produced *The Theory of the Leisure Class* (Veblen, 1899) as well as *The Man That Corrupted Hadleyburg* (Twain, 1900), an age of pessimism and revolt, also encouraged Omar Morse to collect his memories in an autobiography. He had no quarrel with society and seemed content to leave most moral quandaries to others; he was an ordinary man with but an ordinary man's literary abilities. He emphasizes this himself. Yet he was an insightful common man, an uncommon common man. He had perceived, as Thoreau and Whitman had, that he must repossess the factual details of his personal landscape and transform them into an order logical and honest. It must also have meaning. At first his facts must have seemed unwieldy and unyielding, or pleasing small exercises in nostalgia. But when his narrative line led from revolt from a cruel boss in New York to encounters with the open spaces of the prairies (a metaphor of freedom), he could recover the exhilarating releases of youth, and when he found this mythic space falling in as he recalled the plodding years of failure and death, with homestead after homestead left behind, he groped toward the figure of the inverted garden model. If he did not fashion it with the clarity of a folk artist, he suggests his understanding of the ironic "everlasting futility" that his society stoically accepted and concealed behind the several masks of its culture. He had of course understood that he lived in a materialistic society where "Things are in the saddle." The only acceptable reality was success, a cruel truth for a farmer who had at best managed to survive. Pathetically, at the close of his autobiography, he philosophizes that only those born with native gifts for acquisition will become successful; his own success as one father of a new society in a wilderness seemed for a moment to dissolve. But his perseverance, if it gave him no reward, reveals the courage of the true maker of a culture who inevitably works against the grain of the meretricious and common—for him and his generation, the acquisition of visible success in acres, houses, and barns.

Trapped by the materialism of their society, homesteaders and their families came to give direct expression to their anger. "A New National Anthem," a Populist campaign song of the 1890s, illustrates the sentiment of rising agrarian dissidence: "My country 'tis of thee / Once land of liberty, / Of thee I sing, / Land of the millionaire; / Farmers with pockets bare; / Caused by the cursed snare— / The Money Ring." The concluding lines of the third verse show a Populist focus, the anathema of interest rates: "Yet still I love thy rills, / But hate thy usury mills, / That fill the bankers' tills / Till they overflow."[3] Other songs in *The People's Party Campaign Book* (1892) amply demonstrate the volcanic emotion generated by the disillusioned group of settlers and farmers. In such parodic material, as a previous chapter illustrates, both the ideal and its loss are implied. The whole coin of Jeffersonian liberty and fair opportunity and the gross materialism of an era shine through this song.

Garland's preface to *Jason Edwards* conclusively states the painful sense of loss a culture in rapid transition had experienced. Once, he recalls, the West was

> "the El Dorado of the homeseeker. Free land, free homes, were the alluring words whose music made the heart of the toil-worn artisan leap like a child's and his breast expand with a nameless exaltation and longing. But today this dream—this most characteristic American emotion—has almost gone. Free land is gone. The last acres of available farmland has passed into private or corporate hands. The nation has squandered the inheritance of the unborn as well as the living, and henceforward the stream of emigration must run athwart the speculator's barriers or rise to the level of his greed."[4]

Garland's passion reflects the several elements of the countermyth of dispossession analyzed in the preceding chapters. Note his contrast between "El Dorado" (literally, the gold mountain, a symbol of paradise; in context, the ideal or weedless garden) and the deprivation caused by the "speculator's barriers" where farmers have little alternative but to "rise to the level of his greed." This dramatic conflict—melodramatic in its passion—is implied or stated in most songs and narratives on the theme of cultural dispossession, the unweeded garden. Garland's moving eloquence, with sources in the long-witheld anger of Populist thought, is to be clearly distinguished from the "hard" colloquial idiom of "Starving to Death on a Government Claim" or the now forgotten "The Mortgage Worked the Hardest of Them All," in which the narrative persona recalls his wife's death: like that of Delia Morse, it was a "mystery—the doctors never knew; / But I knew she died of mortgage just as well as I wanted to."[5] The tangible home is the settler's ideal, but obviously, in such a song the home serves as the symbol of the parodic garden.

The following elements appear with a frequency that distinguishes a cultural theme or "set" of attitudes: (1) the figure of a suffering plowman (or comparable pioneer) whose loss implies the irony of his predicament in the context of his stated or understood expectations of freedom and opportunity; (2) the loss of the plowman's innocence to a lurking tempter/land speculator who offers permanence and democracy on the land (symbolically fertile, egalitarian, conferring virtue) but whose deceptions cause a homestead variation of the Fall; (3) the resulting post-lapsarian barren land, which "The Arkansas Traveler" and "The Old Settler's Song" both illustrate though in somewhat different ways. The nineteenth-century western novelists obviously complicate these variations of the dispossession theme by adding a dimension of human character and its intangibles. Their realism, of course, was an organic element of their social vision.

The heir to an evolving folk and literary tradition, Garland's early work, however flawed at times by poor writing, clearly demonstrates the darkening clouds of tragic loss inherent in the earliest songs and satire. The excessive idealism of young love in *A Spoil of Office*, for example, shrugs off the clumsy locutions of genteel refinement when the lovers meet with tough, bitter Kansans to involve them in Populism. Here is the barren land aroused by the loss of its "El Dorado," where, as the suffering people indicate, homestead hope had shriveled. The suffering plowman is now a suffering people. Such moments justify reading Garland's earlier realism analytically. The raw land and its weary, strangely eloquent people inspire a despondent Bradley Talcott and Ida Wilbur, the idealistic young lovers whose experience in Congress has led to spiritual paralysis. The driver who takes them to the Kansas Alliance meeting seems a historian of dispossession, so to speak, and thus Garland's spokesman. Once a hopeful farmer in the next county, he remarks that he had "sunk nine hundred and fifty dollars" in land, home, and tools before mortgage debt dispossessed him; he explains that "they're all mortgaged out there." A second element is here evident: the innocent victim. Talcott, thoroughly disillusioned by his tenure in Congress, broods on the driver's remark as they pass through a barren land. The driver's predicament seems the common fate of the homesteaders—their "pitiful tragic life—a life of incessant toil."[6] The theme of *Main-Traveled Roads* is repeated with remorseless clarity of focus in this scene from the novel. The setting, the district schoolhouse on the "illimitable prairie," seems as indifferent to human suffering as the frontier land speculation that caused that suffering. It is the third element of the unweeded garden of dispossession.

At first, the assembled farmers appear to be an unpromising audience for Ida to rally to heights of political action; they are unkempt, drab, the men with hands like "bludgeons" and still wearing their wool "Kansas" hats. Talcott finds himself seated next to a young farmer whose hands seem raw in contrast to his sensitive eyes and "low, soft voice." He is Garland's natural gentleman, uneducated but intuitive. Brother Williams, the older generation of pioneer exemplified, is similar in appearance. When he rises to speak, however, the classic simplicity of his noble eloquence tells of lost communal ideals. Garland suggests this through Williams's manner: "His words were well chosen and his gestures almost majestic. He spoke in a conversational way, but with great power and sincerity."[7] For Garland, nature speaks through these inspired plowmen and speaks with true spiritual force; moreover, these representative New World democrats are in themselves true models of the potential of the agrarian ideal, however eroded by the neglect of an indifferent Congress. The forces represented by the land speculator have all but choked out these healthy organisms in an unweeded garden of dispossession. Through Garland's art, such representative characters are given the dignity of protest, a literary act implying their membership in the human community.

The Morse narrative, viewed in this cultural context, recovers hope through communal values awakened in memory as the narrator writes of failures so desperate he could only walk away. Exile and social outcast that he became in old age, Morse yet stood apart from the materialism of blind upward mobility. Here, he found, he was free, inwardly as well as objectively, from the demands of an expansionist period. Like Frost's lone striker, he could choose freedom from harsh employment—"the toots of the master's whistle." Like other homesteaders, he came to understand that society—more specifically, a prevailing laissez-faire attitude among those in power—had been responsible for his economic dilemma: persistent failure. But the process of enlightenment was gradual, emerging in the later century with the rising sentiment among western and southern farmers, who came to favor the previously unpopular Populists. The government continued to be industriously ineffectual. The Homestead Acts came too late and too often compromised by legislators to benefit the dispossessed thousands like the Morses, whose voices have now been silent for a century.

Morse's recognition of his losses is the result of his painfully acquired experience; it seems a tragic knowledge. We find him reflecting the bitter wisdom of losses, which often parallels the communicated wisdom of songs and tales, of political speeches by Populists, and of other materials which I have described as evidence of a cultural theme of dispossession. For those who desired permanence on the land, there seemed little or no promise of future economic viability; arid plains or rain-soaked forests proved less rewarding than a drifter's life (with his "acres of clams"). Indeed, even potentially fertile plains, as the Morse family found, lost their viability in the harsh economic climate. The defeat of the Populists in the election of 1896 closed off hope of needed social reform. (Many of their reforms were later adapted by Franklin Roosevelt's administration to mitigate the disasters of the 1930s.) In such loss as the prairie farmers' futility reveals, what of significance remains? If Morse is representative—and I am certain that he is—we find a power of acceptance and ability to adjust to loss and to survive, emotionally and economically, among the resilient people who homesteaded the United States. This wisdom—an ability to remain independent in poverty, logical in failure, perseverant in direction—forms a heritage too ample to waste in the silence of ravaging years and too significant in the context of modern culture and literature to let lie fallow in the archives of research libraries. Other scholars will find a lode of material with which to structure their illumination of the yet unknown frontier wilderness and its dark valleys.

Appendix A: Letters to Manly and Anna Morse (1895-1900)

These letters were written by Omar Morse to his son Manly and daughter-in-law Anna—whom he addressed affectionately as "Dear Lad and Lassic," signing himself "Your Pop"—when Manly had become a skilled railroad blacksmith in Burlington, Iowa. The excerpts were selected for Morse's comments on the end of the century, for the homely details of farm and domestic life, for their amplification of the narrative voice of the autobiography, and for the surprising attacks on "money-power," the Populist response to (and term for) the economic ills of frontier and subsequent homestead life.

The dates and postmarks indicate that he began to write family news to Manly and Anna on his return to the remaining twenty acres of his last homestead in 1895, and possibly before this date. He headed these letters variously "The Old Home" and "The Cabin under the hill" in a symbolic gesture of ownership. This pocket-sized homestead was free and clear of mortgage, his long search ended. For him it was a triumph and a wise decision for later years; he could enjoy a taste of leisure while his son, Omar H. Morse, Jr., offered companionship and the aid of his labor. Morse could no longer work as he had, and the still relatively unchanged pine and oak woodland of Roscoe Township in Goodhue County, Minnesota, offered a sanctuary for his old age and fulfilled his lifelong dream of independence on his own land. But it was a hardscrabble existence; they "batched it" in such independence as they could manage on twenty acres, some yet uncleared, of backwoods land. Both father and son, as in the past, worked as hired hands when their time was not occupied on their symbolic homestead-garden of the West. The excerpts suggest Morse's continued resistance to the economy of dispossession in his distrust of an increasingly technological period that again promised the common man progress and a distribution of wealth in return for his labor. "The whole country is being improved in everything but morals," the aging homesteader writes. Historians have verified his epitaph to a post-Civil War era of perverse, corrupt vitality and incompetant political leadership.

Morse's pioneer strength in old age (he was seventy-seven in 1901, the year of his death) appears in the courage of his acceptance. He had learned to exchange his great losses for small triumphs: he writes of his promising garden twelve rods in length (until the drought years of 1896-1900); of a sleek plowhorse named Elick, which his visiting grandson rode to the "seeder" (a planting drill); and of the corrupt politics of the Spanish-American war. Young Omar told Manly in 1900 that the summer's heat had caused serious weight loss for them both: "Poor Pap looks starved out," he writes, reflecting the experience of a lifetime on the homestead farm. Morse himself did not mention this, although his narrative and letters both refute the frontier stereotype of uncomplaining stoic silence. With "crops short on both ends" following a three-year drought, he and his son faced a dwindling income; for this reason he laments the scarcity of job opportunities for an aging farmer, stonemason, and plasterer. In one excerpt he takes pride in a chimney finished and a house plastered to his satisfaction, salvaging such dignity as his circumstances allowed; in the same letter he had been forced to ask his daughter-in-law for an additional supply of old clothes. For one whose life was spent in homesteading on unbroken prairie sod and uncleared forest land, continued poverty was an indignity that a lifetime had taught him to accommodate. His son's reference to another acre cleared and burned off on "The Old Home," protesting a fall chore of grubbing roots ahead, demonstrates the pioneer farmer's economy with an image more memorable than a comprehensive frontier history. A second generation continued to clear the land and to face the hardship of poverty. Obviously, hired help was out of the question.

Two of Morse's letters to Manly and Anna require a note of further explanation because they reflect the political tensions of an era that was a national disgrace. The history of farmer's politics during the gilded age of 1870 to 1900 began with the organization of the Grange and the Farmers' Alliance, and ended with the defeat of William Jennings Bryan and free silver in 1896. The central issues during this period were the control of government for the people as a whole versus existing control by industry and business (a continuation of Jefferson's agrarianism versus Hamilton's capitalism and Jackson's fight with the U.S. banks); and government regulation of industry and business to decentralize monopoly and control international business. The farmers' interests were served by the Farmers' Alliance after 1870, and in the elections of 1892 and 1896 by the Populists (or People's Party), who gave their support to Bryan. They were defeated in both elections, but their principles and platforms later became a heritage instrumental to Theodore Roosevelt's trust-busting administration (1901-08) and Franklin Roosevelt's New Deal (1932-38), as well as other twentieth-century reforms. Such writers as Richard Hofstadter, C. Vann Woodward in "The Populist Heritage and the Intellectual,"[1] and Vernon Carstenson in *Farmer Discontent* amplify the intellectual resources that the farmers' party brought to American society and government. As these writers have pointed out, such now uncontroversial legislation as antimonopoly laws, equal employment rights, farm bureaus, and low-interest loans to farmers originated in the political platforms of this dissident party of grassroots liberals. They were true progressives.

Yet scholarly suspicion of jingoism, racism, and ignorance among these early liberals remains entrenched. The disgrace of the 1950s "witch hunts" conducted by Senator Joseph McCarthy has poisoned the wellsprings of early liberalism, generated in the disillusion of the early West. McCarthy, from the rural Midwest, became the representative *bête noir*, a political anathema. The narrow conservatism of Grant Wood's

American Gothic seems yet to characterize the region. I point this out to make clear the history of dissent which Morse's loosely Populist liberal thinking, evident in his letters to his son, clearly illustrates. He could find an identity in a community of meaningful dissent. He became a Populist late in life (most probably he had originally been a Republican in the Lincoln tradition); several lengthy letters echo Populist idiom, but they and his only writings are neither racist nor jingoistic. They suggest that his homestead losses were the source of his anger at himself—Populism later gave him the creative language to direct his anger also at organized sources of oppressive control.

Morse felt as the Populists did that "money-power" supplanted the individual's rights—in one instance, that employers in the then new factories controlled his son's economic independence. Yet the unusually strident tone of this letter indicates his exposure to Populist politics which, to the party's disadvantage, too strenuously advocated a government that would control industry (chiefly the railroads, whose high shipping costs caused distress among farmers), advocated unionist philosophies to unite urban and rural labor, and sought redress of old and persistent wrongs created by inadequate land laws. Research in the politically active north central states where the Morses lived has not uncovered other materials written by the farmers themselves that illustrate with such clarity the consequences of the government's failure to control western settlement. The farmers' economic disadvantage had begun with land speculation and the corporate interests of railroads, large flouring mills, and grain elevators, to which cooperatives were the only answer. The histories of other areas of the expanding frontier west of the Appalachians indicate that this problem was not confined to one region. Because his experiences spanned most of the century, Morse's letters illustrate an invaluable synthesis of early nineteenth-century aspirations and the ordinary man's outrage when he at last could see, if he had not seen previously, the supremacy of money interests that had long controlled western expansion.

The following excerpts have been arranged by topic to suggest the spectrum of Morse's opinions: (1) change made by technological progress, (2) reading, (3) rural life, (4) political views, (5) parental advice, (6) old age and retirement, (7) humor, (8) his statement of purpose and method for his autobiography. Information has been interpolated as seemed necessary to provide a historical perspective on an almost unknown figure, the ordinary family homesteader.

In most instances either Morse recorded the date or the envelope was clearly postmarked. (All letters were mailed at Pine Island, the post office nearest Roscoe.) Otherwise, dates have been supplied from evidence in the letters or omitted.

Those errors that seriously obscure the intent of a passage have been silently edited, but never if doing so might destroy the character and tone of the excerpt. The emphases throughout represent Morse's own underlining.

Progress

Pine Island is growing the mill on Main St South is being enlarged—Brick front—35 × 60—3 stories

Electric lights—water works—Zumbrota [a nearby small town also in Goodhue County] is booming

The whole Country is being improved in every possible way except in morals

[?] There is considerable talk of building Several brick buildings this coming season in P.I. [Pine Island] also a System of water works streetcars etc etc etc

August 8, 1896. Haying Harvest and Stacking has all been *done up* without a sprinkle Threshing has commenced

Horse Power Threshing is all done away *with* and Streamers *are all the go* Corn will be a failure if it dont rain soon—

[?] Pine Island has a new Creamery Cost $3000—just completed. Electric Lights & a System of Water Works goes in this season—and several other Buildings—

I feel like a fish out of water to think I can't have any hand in the improvements—Every dog has his day & Mine is past so it is no use to whine [Morse had also been a builder and stonemason. His interest in progress in Pine Island was that of an aged man in need of income.]

Reading

1898. We get the war news three times a week in the New York World—there seems to be a good deal of Debate but, little done [Morse's reference is to the Spanish American War in Cuba.]

1898. I am taking a paper which is published by J.R. Francis—Chicago called the Progressive *Thinker* the best paper I ever read [Morse makes no other reference to his reading. The *Progressive Thinker* was a spiritualist paper.]

Rural Life

[?] We have the finest garden in town Roscoe [a township], and I have put hours in to keep it in good *shape* We have about [word illegible] here and have got a good start with Small fruit. Next year we will have Black Beans, Black-Cap Strawberries, grapes—currents, and On the next and last page I will give you a rough Sketch of our garden as it now Stands [Morse's sketch locates the garden behind a grove of trees planted as a windbreak. In addition to the fruit and vegetables mentioned, he records areas designated for melons, cabbages, gooseberries, tomatoes, sweet corn, beets, onions, early potatoes, and cucumbers. The plot was twelve rods long; he did not record the width.]

[?] We keep old Elick and he is fat and sleek and full of *kinks* Omar [Jr.] is going to put him onto the seeder for little Sammy T [Thomas, his daughter Lydia's son] to ride where he will get his fill of Exersize for a couple of weeks Sid Barteau is in Red Wing [county seat of Goodhue County] awaiting a hearing for Shooting a *Sweed* [Melting-pot rural United States was undergoing a process of assimilation that reflected, and still reflects, the violence of American life.]

May 15, 1900. Our Berries are nearly all *froze* out I feel very much dissaappointed Over it as it was my only chance for raising pin money. Omar has nearly 100 new hens and about 40 or so Laying— We sell some Butter and eat much (Our neighbors are [now just] planting) Our Corn is up. (Well nearly dry.)

[?] Our fruit that Mrs. Coon [a housekeeper] put up come out in good shape. Have quite a lot of [word illegible] Eggs—Pork—Potatoes—Milk and Butter and all of us a good *appetite*—What more can we conscientiously [truly?] ask for— We have the Biggest Woodpile of any poor man in town all cut and piled up in *good shape* and quite a lot of last years *wood*

August 8, 1896. I have a few times in my life been done up with the heat and probably that is a very good reason *why* I cant Stand it now—90—4 5 and 8 for two weeks and not a drop of rain for 6 *weeks* [Morse then mentions his dislike of housework when he believes he should be working in his garden or helping his son in the fields].

[However] We shall have enough to eat drink and plenty of *old clothes* and the high *flyer to ride us around*

the 4 [Fourth of July]. We went to Wasioja [either the village of Wasioja (from Sioux meaning "pine clad" or "pine river"), which no longer exists, or the township that borders Roscoe Township[2]] to a Populists *Picknick* with Lydia and the kids [his daughter and grandchildren] Jim saw us coming in time to skip and we were all glad we did. [Perhaps it was the windy rhetoric common to the Bryan Free Silver campaign that seems to have afforded Morse an excuse "to skip" this picnic.

His decision to be a Populist may or may not predate this letter, which indicates no year.]

[?] I used to go to Mantorville [county seat of Dodge County, nearest the Morse's homestead from 1856 until 1878] and saw wood to get Money to buy drugs and pay $8/per gallon for *Brandy to mix it up*

a little package of poison in the sahpe of *drugs that never cost* the druggist $1-1-1 [?] cost me $14 of hired Money at 25 *pr ct*

$100 at Philadelphia in One summer the same another season to the Grapenberg Co—N York and so on year after year—slow poison but sure—

The less you have to do with Drs. the safer and Healthier [Morse here recalls earlier homestead years in Dodge County when his wife's illness increased his debts, already burdensome. The cost of prescribed medicines and borrowed money had to be earned by sawing wood and other jobs because cash was in short supply on the homestead.]

Political Views

Oct 14.—a big Crop of everything this season but the *prices* of products is *down down* to nothing—Oats 15—Potatoes—12—Corn 20—Rye 27—Wheat 40—a bushel of Barley will buy [only] 5 glasses of BEER good Democratic times and the Republicans *are* no *better* There is no salvation for this boasted Land of Liberty unless the People's Party or Pops [Populists] get into power and maybe not then it can't be any worse—try them in [two illegible letters, possibly an abbreviation] and dont for Gods Sake vote for either of the Old Parties any longer— [This letter likely predates the November, 1892, election when the Populists were virtually eliminated at the polls.]

we keep the *high flyer* yet she is slick as a mould and fleet as the *wind* and gentle as a Schoolmom. [Morse's horse-of-all-work]

29th April 1896. Grover [Cleveland] fishes and hunts *ducks* and at the same time *drains* $150/ per Day—I hope you will have better luck fishing than he *does*—he never was known to get a bite

October 14. [1880s?]We are Republicans in principle just the same as ever *but* prepared to shoulder your Fuzee [fusee] at call—[The imprint of the Republican Party on Morse probably shaped the views of independence he evidences in the autobiography. He refers here to the Spanish-American War. In the following sentence he rejects this party and reflects Populist sentiment.] Fun for the big Heads in Washington but *Death To the Toads* the administration is all right they are on the top now—but look out there is a day of Reckoning Coming

1898. If Dewey—Sampson and Co had orders to go ahead and smash and sink the whole concern and not interfere with the business [not be harrassed by the McKinley administration] they would accomplish Something

McKinley is no warrior and his advisors are money Sharks and speculators ["Money sharks" (banks and other lenders) and "speculators" (large landowners) are Populist terms common in campaign materials.]

Starving Cubans—O my—look at the starving Miners here at home—helpless women and children without a crust of bread—whole families right in St. Paul Starving to death

On to Cuba with shiploads of provisions—Millions of money squandered already and the farce is only just commenced—makes me tired the whole thing is speculation

[?] Our Republican Government had So Much Synmpathy for the Poor Cubans. They knock out the Spanish Fleet and have assumed the responsibility of Seducing the Philipine Islands—Big job two they have got on their hands *McKinly's last Order More Troops*—More Canned Mule Meat—More Ships More Murder

[?] Money matters seem to have closed up business and left the country *intoto* [probably stranded, i.e., in a depression or recession]

May 29, 1899. the whole world is all ablaze making preparations to celebrate the Homecoming of Admiral Dewey—

Several millions will be spent—I call it foolish—while Starvation and want for the very bread of life is to be seen on every Corner—(*shame on such patriotism*)

Dewey no doubt is a great man and a Hero and a proper respect Shown him on his return is all right—but I think it *all wrong* to squander so much money that might and should be used for better purposes

[Morse's liberal humanism underlies his political views toward the war even though like most of the nation when war began he hoped that "Dewey—Sampson and Co" would finish their "business" quickly. His isolationism is apparent in his concern for the starving unemployed at home rather than Cuban refugees, but his humanitarianism becomes evident in his shock at the inhumanity of war and American imperialism in the Philippines. Mark Twain's "To a Person Sitting in Darkness" holds a similar view of Philippine independence. Morse's humanism may also have had its source in the agrarian idealism of his own generation, stimulated first by the Republican and then by the Populist party.]

Parental Advice

[?] Omar was 25 the first of March I had a nice *Album* laid away for a month *or more which* I presented to him in the Evening with a few words of *Parental Advice—*

[?] I promised to tell you Sometime what my ideas of [the] Life that is to be were Or is [are] but I shall have to postpone a little time for various reasons—it will come in due time and will keep for the present

[?] You are nearly 40—about One half of your life has been spent in the hardest kind of Servitude for an Aristocratic Corporation that cares less for your interest or well being than we do for Our Stock—while your Labor and sweat holds Out to help build them up and enrich them *you are all right*—if you vote right [Morse refers to his son's employment in the railroad shops at Burlington, Iowa.]

But you understand this state of things can't last always—The Strongest Constitution[s] fail up in time and Old Age comes on—the knees get weak and the eyes *grow dim* and many other Symptoms of debility I might enumerate—having experienced all this in my short Life— When this time comes as it surely will if you live long enough—a little Spot of God's green Earth to fall back on will help Materially to tide you Over the pinch [even] if it be but a few acres with a comfortable Shanty to shield the wife and little ones from the pelting blasts of winter and the Scorching rays of the Summer Sun—

I believe you advised us in days gone by to get rid of this little Homestead— It is true that it is not as desireable a place as we would like but we have it free and clear— It makes us a home and by being Saving and Equinomical [economical] we live and are independent asking no Odds of Corporations *trusts* or Combines [? word partially illegible]

I say we are independent—in this sense[:] if we want a holiday—Or if we feel inclined we can sleep in the Morning regardless of the toots of the Masters Whistles [probably factory whistles] and the grass grows just the same—the corn Beans Cabbage and other products thrive and the Chickens tend to their business just the Same— We are [our] Own masters as well as servants This I call *Independence what would you call it*

Dont tell me as you did at One time that you would not take a farm as a gift and be obliged to live on it this is all idle talk or will be when you have spent all your strength and even your *Health* in those ill ventilated Smoke houses [Morse's metaphor for the railroad shops] and long for a breath of fresh air—

Think of these suggestions seriously—Candidly and you will say I am right Once *in your Life*! NB I have broken off from writing several times and it is not very Gramatical but I think you will get hold of what I am at if you can read it at all I will wrote you again Sometime

[?] We suppose in the first place your home in Burlington probably cost you $2,000 may more— may be less

The interest on that Sum—Taxes—Repairs can amount to no small Sum every year—and as the property wastes in use and the wear and tare—Repairs are more and more Expensive— There is also a probability and a great liability for such property to decrease in value

A Spark of fire—a flash of *Lightnin*—the breath of a Cyclone might *wipe* out the savings of years in less time than it takes to write it up Then where are you— This one phase of the Situation—you may call it a *Bugbear*—but it is worth Consideration all the same

The East and West are antagonistic Socially as well as politically. The great Money power Centers in the East— there's where we find our *Million'heirs*—great Contractors in Ship building—Manufactories in Every Thing the World Needs and in Somethings the world would be the better without these Death Dealing implements they are now using in the Philipines—for Conquest—against the poor Devils that have got rid of the Spaniards and have now a more relentless foe than Spain ever was—

Shame on this Government sending poor Soldiers 10,000 miles to fight for a country that is not worth the *Powder* a country that a white man cant live in isn't worth fighting for— But I am getting a little off my subject you will say [Morse's racism here is unusual.]

These enormous Manufactories are Supplying these huge Contractors with Material which in turn is to be turned Over to the government nearly and in Many instances doubling their investments and of course they can afford more pay for what they bring—

This you see narrows down the supply to these minor Establishments but the poor Laboring Class gets a mighty small share of the profits—just barely enough to keep Soul and body together. This Money power controls the Elections to a great extent—you know this to be a fact and a man situated as you are and thousands of others has got to stand in with the powers that be in Order to hold his job.

Now what we propose or advise *if you please* is this—when

your Burlington property will sell for a good fair price—close the contract *before you sleep* and Either invest in a little real estate wherever you can find a desirable and healthy Location Or put the proceeds out on interest Secured Fully On real estate to have and to hold till such time as your *unable* to fill the position you now Occupy— *Hows That*—sensible you will say

[In the preceding pair of letters, Populist views have been fused into Morse's agrarian sense of independence and individualism, which of course dates from his early democratic faith in the country. We also see a strong proletarian and unionist view, which is in paradoxical opposition to his rural belief in land as a source of the working man's individualism. The next excerpt illustrates his contempt for politics and most politicians.]

[?] Vick [Victor W. Sterling, Omar's son-in-law and a minor official in the People's Party] is very much interested in politics and it seems he is a Sort of Stool Pigeon for the Party—I'll bet he'l weigh 400. [Morse misuses the term "stool pigeon" to express contempt for political officials in general.]

November 25, 1900. I sometimes wish Omar [Jr.] had got into the shop or some other Business about the time he was at Burlington [Iowa, then the location of the C.B&Q. Railroad Repair Shop where Manly was working. Morse concedes the economic advantage of skilled industrial labor in this letter of 1900.]

Old Age and Retirement

July 23, 1895. Old age and debility have come upon me *all at once* and if I continue to *fail up* as I have for the last year or two it won't take very long *to* do me *up* entirely— I hope to have done the best I knew under the circumstances and why should I *fear* the future— I believe I do not still life is preferable for a time *at least*

I am *thankful* for the continued *Health* and comforts of this life and that through some mysterious *providence* [I have] run clear of a thousand ills and temptations *which seem* to be [the] *lot of* Mankind generally

[1896] Last week I was away 10 or 12 miles put up a long chimney and lathed a new house and am going down about Sunday to plaster the same [Morse points out his independence in old age, but a later paragraph indicates that poverty reduced him to again requesting that his daughter-in-law send old clothes.]

May 5, 1895. Omar says he thinks I must have been born tired He don't know that when I was his age I was worth two *like him* for hard service and if I had saved myself a little in them days I might *have been better today* [Omar, Jr.'s letter of August 19, 1900, explains his father's weariness five years earlier: "I am reduced to 143 pounds and Pap weighs 120. Poor man he is almost starved out can't hardly eat a thing." Apparently the debility of old age had begun, though with less marked symptoms, earlier in 1895. Summer heat and drought seem to have had their effect on both Morses, father and son.]

[?] You will expect to hear how we are getting on in our household *affairs*— Everything is in order and on time. It is a wonderful improvement on the old plan [before Lydia, his daughter, came as a housekeeper]—*but* it is not what Home used to be in the years *ago* when the family were all together and a Mother to look *after us*

—no no—not much [Morse's devotion to Delia and to her memory illuminates a strong homesteader's family sense and his pioneer respect for the women, usually in smaller numbers than men, who shared their fortunes. Women, of course, suffered keenly the deprivations of poverty, rural childbirth, and isolation that were a homesteader's lot. The autobiography emphasizes his high regard for his wife as the center of family life.]

Humor

[1899] our garden took a powerful sweat last Sunday and some of it went down the stream [when the stream nearby flooded after a long drought].

[?] Crops are short at both ends and ready money is nil.

[May 5, 1895] the strongest constitutions fail up in time and old age comes on. [The *Dictionary of American English on Historical Principles*, 1938, defines *fail up* as a New England expression meaning "to become bankrupt, to fail." Morse's usage implies the homesteaders' experience of disaster when either husband or wife was ill or died.]

Harry must be quite a lubber by now and the girls o my [The same Dictionary gives the "lubber" grasshopper, or big clumsy locust, of the plains; Morse more likely intended grown taller, and/or plump or boyishly clumsy and awkward.]

Purpose and Method of His Narrative

[?] —away back several years ago I took a notion to *write* some of my Earthly Career—or make a record of some of the most important incidents of my life to leave for the Childrens perusal after I have *passed away* thinking it might possibly interest them in some way

It was a task of no small proportions as 50 years had already gone *into the past* and in order to make anything of a Systematic record I must go back to the beginning—not of the Creation exactly but to the Commencement of my Existence and pick up from *Memory* each item as it transpired and follow up step by step through all the long years and get it in shape to make One continued Chain of *events* from the beginning to End— I thought I realized what an undertaking *I had on hand* but I really did not as I have discovered later on

Still I had the Cheeck or grit call it what you will to make the trail—Please Bear in mind that I never was so given over to vanity as to suppose that my production would reflect any great amount of tact or skill as a story writer [*Webster's New Collegiate Dictionary*, 1973: "tact—sensitive mental or aesthetic perception (converted novel into play with remarkable skill and tact)."]

My object was merely to show to my family when on Earth I had a personality—did really Exist and that I tried to lead a sober and industrious life such as becomes a *true American Citizen* and that in all the transactions of *life* I had for my Object the betterment of mankind *generally*.

I have spent some little time on what I call my narrative as I had Opportunity and of course laid it away as often as taking it up. Sometimes I thought never to bother my head more with it but I intend now to complete it as best I can sometime in the future providing I have time. I fully realize that what I have yet to do can not be accomplished too soon. [This statement of purpose echoes those made in the narrative itself. In spite of his apology for vanity, Morse was justifiably proud of his achievement. His apparently needless justification of a "sober and industrious life" as a "true American citizen" who intends only the betterment of mankind reflects the nineteenth-century common man's work ethic. But his small reward for herculean labors must have caused doubt and guilt.]

[The following essay indicates Morse's intellectual capacities, with its level of prose and its apparent Emersonian conclusion. He wrote on a continuous strip of letter sheets pasted together as if to suggest an essayist's unity of focus. At the end, he adds a note to Anna Morse.]

Where is Heaven

I have been in the habit of spending an hour or so in Our Cemetery. Occasionally as it seemed a [illegible word] place for reflection and study.

Everything is so quiet and still and so unlike the Outside world of care and strife—Bustle and worry anxieties disappointments and the ills and evils of a wicked World.

There are a great Many designs and various inscriptions with much Ornamental skill and taste displayed by the artists in getting up something Showy and Expensive yet some are very neat and Simple in Construction and to my mind far more appropriate.

One very plain and inexpensive Slab broken and almost hidden in the *grass* arrested my attention or more properly—my curiosity—to know what might be inscribed thereon—in turning it up to the light I noticed a panel sunk in the Marble with a beautiful hand in high relief the index finger pointing upward towards what was evidently designed as a representation of an arched *ribbon* with streaming ends.

On the Arch in raised Letters appeared the simple Legend There is rest *in Heaven* [From colonial times, such emblems were common in settlers' cemeteries, although the newer emblem Morse observes became increasingly popular after the 1830s in the eastern United States, and of course about thirty to forty years later in the West.]

It really seemed to give me some consolation to believe there was rest somewhere from the turmoil *of Life* Its *Cares* and Anxieties its hopes and ambitions.

With the accumulations of years the burdened they [reference vague] have brought the weary of ages and anxious sleepless nights from a multiplicity of business Duties a quiet peaceful tranquil rest—[this] has suggested more real enjoyment than Earth with its griefs and separations *has ever brought*

But mind—the Legend says that Rest is in Heaven—now follows the question

Where is Heaven—

Is it above—around—or beneath—Is it some place in the Natural universe—a location on some distant orb—its capitol the New Jerusalem with Streets paved with Gold and its Mansions the homes of the blest?

Does God dwell there? Sitting On an *ivory* throne in Stately pomp—and Does He from this lofty eminence send out his Mandates after the Manner of an earthly *Potentate* to his Subordinates directing the movements of the elements—the course of the winds—the fall of rains and Overflow of Rivers—the ebb and flow of tides—the Cause of Lightning—*Earthquakes* and all the varied *Pnenomena of nature*

This seems to be the Christian conception of Heaven but it is not mine. no—no! If not *where* is it?

The Grave brings repose to the Body—Ambition ends at its portals—Hope has fled—Cares and toils have ended,—Smiles at meeting and griefs at parting are unknown and yet this is not the rest to which the finger pointed nor is it the Heaven to which the human Soul aspires but on the contrary it covets a conscious individual Existence where pain and sorrow can *never come* where ignorance gives place to knowledge where Friendships ever abide and partings are unknown

My theory then is—Heaven is not a location but is a condition following Earth life and is an inheritance *from it*—It has no Central City—Is not divided into districts but is immensity itself *Its presence everywhere—Its Center nowhere* Like imagination—it is anywhere and everywhere at [its own?] will

This to me is a very rational idea Even more a happy one

[Morse's life ended as it had been lived, with the simple dignity of a son's care, in an isolated cabin near Pine Island, Minnesota. Two of Omar, Jr.'s letters to Manly describe his death; they serve as an appropriate conclusion to this section. The letters, addressed to "Bro Manly & Wyf" and signed "Your bro O.H.M.," are dated April 14 and 15, 1901.]

Yours Recd Friday. The past three days pop has failed rapidly. has been in some pain. is now entirely helpless. for two days has had no control over water so it keeps me changing his clothes & bed as fast as I can dry them bowels not moved for 5 days. he has laid stupid all day. dont talk. Cant see mutch dont seem to know any thing. unless he rallys again it surely wont be long now. I have been up a good share of the last three nights—shall try to have someone to night. [Omar, Jr. here discusses his problem with household help—he was unmarried—and his habitual shortage of money, concluding with a plea for cash to pay his father's doctor bill of twenty dollars.]

—its an awful thing to be so eternally strapped always—but it has always been so & and will be to the end of the Chapter. I dont feel very [illegible word] this spring & will not be more than ½ a hand for a while at that. I dont know what the devil I'll do when I am left here alone. I shall be just about living. this is such a cussed neighborhood one might as well be on Cruso's Island. I shall try and get this mailed tomorrow.

Our poor old father has Just passed away only Rena a friend and I present
will write more fully later

[Omar includes two bills for his brother's assistance: the first, from W.L. Craddock, M.D., for "Medical Services to date: $18"; and the second, his promise to pay T.S. Mellinger for "one casket and hearse (the rest is illegible) $36."]

Appendix B: Morse's Essay on the Philippine Islands

[This essay appears in the manuscript of the autobiography after the main body of the narrative. It is included here because it reflects Morse's attitudes. He embraces the spirit of independence central to the homesteader and farmer he was. Significantly, the humanitarian liberal attitude evident in his letters, which he may have absorbed from the Populists as well as his own cultural background as a homesteader, has not lost its provincial American isolationism. Populists who favored the Spanish-American War because it seemed patriotic to fight a decadent European aristocracy became equally antiimperialistic when the United States (and American corporations) landed in the Philippines. Morse's title is "My Opinion of Our War with the Philipines."]

I regard this war as unjust and absolutely needless—a means of the wanton waste of human life The United States—is less just, and has less cause for the war than had England when she forced the war of the Revolution

And I would say—that were I a Philipino—as I am an American—that while a foreign foe were landed on my Strand, I never would lay down my arms—No Never—

They call them Rebels and insurgents but they are nothing of the kind because they never acknowledge the right of the United States to rule them nor swore fealty to our Government

They are a people fighting for their Independence and Liberty— Consequently the war is unjust unrighteous and unholy[.]

Appendix C: Family Record of O.H. Morse

[This genealogy concludes Morse's autobiography; it serves as a supplemental record of useful information. There was no Bureau of Vital Statistics in the nineteenth century. Family bibles and family histories were accepted as evidence when needed.]

O H Morse was born Nov 12th 1824
Delia Mason was born Jan 14th 1830
Married Nov 6th—1850

Children:
Alredine H. Morse was born Aug 22—1851
Mary M Morse was born April 22nd 18[?]
Lydia A Morse was born May 18 1857
Manly H Morse was born Nov 9th 1861
Omar H Morse was born March 1st 1872

Family Record of Stephan D. Morse, father

Stephen D Morse was born in Otsego County—New York about the year—1780—July
Polly Barnes was born in Otsego County—New York about the year—1784
Were married 1800—

Nine children were *born* to *them* and named as *follows*

1 Mary Morse		1801
2 Stephan R Morse		1803
3 Sanford D Morse		1805
4 Ansil [Ansel] H Morse		1808
5 Louisa Morse		1810
6 Lydia A Morse	Feb 22	1813
7 Myron E Morse	Sept 7	1816
8 Alzina A Morse	Jan 7th	1820
9 Omar H Morse	Nov 12th	1824

Deaths

Mary Allen	Colosse Oswego Co NY	18
Sanford D	Eaton Rapids Mich	18
Louisa Loveridge	Fon Dulac Fon Du Lac Wis—	18
Ansil H Morse	Hastings NY	18
Stephan R Morse	Illinois Knox Co	1889
Alzina A Pierce	at San Diego Cal	Jan 16 1897

[The following names are in another hand.]

Omar H. Morse	Roscoe Minn	Apr 15 1901
Lydia A Thomas	June 1901	New London Wis
Myron E. Morse	Aug 15 1904	San Francisco Call

[In Morse's hand:]

The above record may not be strictly correct but is nearly so as it is made without any notes or authorized records but will show that such persons lived and were born Lived and died—about the dates above recorded April 1897

Notes

Note: For complete bibliographic information, see the list of "Works Consulted," beginning on page 221.

Introduction

1. Horton, *Land*, 56.

2. There are 395 published agrarian narratives listed in Louis Kaplan, *A Bibliography of American Autobiography* (Madison: Univ. of Wisconsin Press, 1961), which may be broken down chronologically as follows: 10 published prior to 1800; 65 between 1800 and 1850; 275 between 1850 and 1900; and 45 between 1900 and 1945. Richard G. Lillard, *American Life in Autobiography*, 42-45, annotates several hundred published agrarian narratives, largely those published between 1880 and 1890. Additional bibliographies—such as *The Subject Bibliography of Wisconsin History* (Madison: State Historical Library of Wisconsin, 1947), 32-34, 40-43—give listings pertinent to specific geographical areas, others to specific historical periods; however, agrarian narratives are not listed separately. Hundreds of others are kept in the archives of various state and national repositories and remain unpublished. Clearly these national treasures of the ordinary man's history deserve their bibliographers and scholars, but no individual research can absorb all of this material. An estimated two hundred were therefore sampled in the Newberry Library in Chicago, the Wisconsin and Minnesota Historical Society Libraries, and the Beineke Library of Yale University, in order to ascertain underlying narrative patterns and purposes. Almost invariably, the pioneer agrarian, published and unpublished, who records his or her harsh struggle with nature and economic circustance has successfully over-

come them. In other words, most of those who wrote of early farming were those who had some success in life,—or concealed their lack of it.

3. *The Narratives of Noah Harris Letts and Thomas Allen Banning*, edited by Paul Angle. Angle is unaware of the economic hazards of the homestead, although he recognizes the hardships of the thousands who remained hired hands. The Banning memoir is another success story. Mr. Banning's advantages as an educated man served his upward mobility as a business man, Judson's memoirs were published by a friend after her death; this pioneer wife had a keen perception of cultural relativism in her observation of white dispossession of Indians and the deracination caused by misunderstanding of their customs. However, she seems unaware of the economic motive of her farmer husband's continued moves westward. In Washington state, his entrance into local government as a county recorder contributed to family permanence.

4. Simpson, *Mexico, Mother of Towns*, 211-313.

5. Donnelly, *Ceasar's Column*, 107-8.

1. The Dispossession of the Morse Family

1. Gates, *Landlords and Tenants*, 12.

2. Ibid.

3. Ibid., 146-47, 318-25.

4. Bogue, *Money at Interest*, esp. 273-74 and conclusion, where Bogue argues the benefits of capitalistic ventures in land speculation but concedes that boom-and-bust cycles starved out midwestern farmers.

5. Swierenga, *Pioneers and Profits*, esp. xii-xiii, 227. Swierenga demonstrates that both local and out-of-state speculators were the first owners of government land in Iowa. However, he concludes that speculators were as beneficial to the area as homestead farmers, since they sold both prime and marginal land, thus broadening the tax base for frontier communities.

6. *New York Tribune*, June 16, 1860, quoted in Gates, *Landlords and Tenants*, 146.

7. Gates, *Landlords and Tenants*, 68. Gates does not mention that Sawyer was a U.S. senator but lists him with other timberland speculators from throughout Wisconsin who actively campaigned against needed mortgage and loan reform, McKenna, however, names him as an important citizen and senator in his early local history, Fond du Lac County, Wisconsin, 1: 276. Fond du Lac County Mort-

gages, Book G, p. 28, records Morse's mortgages from Philetus Sawyer of Winnebago County in 1851 for $267 at 12 percent interest. Morse was able to pay this mortgage when the three-year due period ended. We can safely assume, I believe, that Philetus Sawyer was a prominent citizen in Fond du Lac County and also resided in Winnebago County at a later period. Two Philetus Sawyers, barring a father-son relationship, seem unlikely.

8. Benton, *Thirty Years' View*, 1: 5-6.

9. Andrew Jackson, "Message to Congress Objecting to Senate Land Bill," *Congressional Globe*, Dec. 1833 (Washington, D.C.: Blair and Rivers, 1835), 12.

10. Gates, *Landlords and Tenants*, 59-60.

11. The political situation was complicated by the attempt of the Republican "establishment" of the 1830s to blame the dissatisfaction of the Rock River settlers on the Locofocos (early Democrats). The November 1, 1839, issue of the Galena *Democrat* reported that a Locofoco lawyer had been instrumental in leading the protest and that the settlers had not been dissatisfied until they were told by the lawyer that the Land Office would accept their Springfield and Alton banknotes only if forced to. I have thus assumed (correctly, I believe) that the statement issued by the Rock River settlers at their first meeting reached the Galena party in power, the Republicans, through the press. The Land Office capitulated.

12. Shannon, *The Farmer's Last Frontier: Agriculture, 1860-1875*, vol. 5 of *The Economic History of the United States*, 53-56, 73-76, 307-8.

13. Gates, *Landlords and Tenants*, 114; see also Humphries, *Following the Prairie Frontier*, 83-85.

14. Turner, *The United States, 1830-1850*, 253.

15. Ibid., 277-78.

16. Marshall, *Farmers and Emigrants' Handbook*, 16.

17. Ibid., 15.

18. *Chicago Daily American*, June 4, 1835.

19. Ibid.

20. Ibid.

21. Churchill, *Landmarks of Oswego County*, 563.

22. Franklin B. Hough, Introduction to *Census of the State of New York* (1857), xxvi. Hough gives a review of the census by townships, 1830-1855.

23. Ibid., xxvi.

24. David Burr, "The County of Oswego Map" (Ithaca: Surveyor-General of New York, 1829). Township population figures are recorded on the map.

25. David Burr, "The County of Oswego [1839 map]" (Ithaca: Surveyor-General of New York, 1839).

26. Churchill, *Landmarks of Oswego County*, 550-68, is a Victorian-American summing up of the County's "blessings."

27. Simpson, *Mexico, Mother of Towns*, 211-12.

28. Oswego County Deeds Book P, p. 282.

29. Churchill, *Landmarks of Oswego County*, 137. Churchill mentions entire farms sold for ten dollars during the economic panic.

30. *History of Fond du Lac County*, Butterfied, 351-83; see esp. the memoirs of H.R. Coleman and Gustave Noveau, pp. 358-59 and 374-75.

31. J.B.D. DeBow, *Statistical View of the United States, Being a Compendium of the Seventh Census* (Washington, D.C., 1854), 326.

32. Fond du Lac County Deeds, Book K, p. 622, records that Omar purchased eighty acres from Myron E. Morse, his brother, on April 7, 1849. The land is described as "the North East quarter of the North East quarter, Section Six, Range 16, containing forty acres," and "thirty acres of land off of the North West quarter of the North East quarter of Section Six" in Rosendale Township, It was virgin land, untilled, and, as he found, impractical. Possibly this land was originally owned by the Ceresco Fourierists. Myron charged his brother the government price.

33. *United States Census: State of Wisconsin* (Washington, D.C., 1854), 326.

34. Fond du Lac County Mortgages, Book G, p. 228. The county index records Morse's subsequent quick sale in Deeds, Book W, p. 616, but the index is inaccurate; hence date, price, and encumbrances regretably cannot be located.

35. Fond Du Lac County Deeds. Data inaccurately recorded, thus lost.

36. Abstract of the United States Land Office, *Dodge County*, vol. 496, p. 164. Morse held Warrant 89,226. He also purchased a five-acre woodlot, which is recorded in Dodge County Deeds, Book D, p. 311. Woodlots were at a premium in Mantorville—a prairie township, as local historians have made clear—otherwise, he would not have paid $100 for his.

37. *Fifth Minnesota Decennial Census* (St. Paul: Superintendent of Census, 1905), 56.

38. *Population of the United States in 1870; Compiled from the Original Return of the Eighth Census* (Washington, D.C.: Government Printing Office, 1914), 40.

39. Goodhue County Deeds Book, T2, p. 292. This deed of mortgage

sale records that Morse defaulted on his mortgage of $316.38 to James Halloway on March 16, 1871; see Goodhue Mortgages, Book 21, p. 269.

40. The autobiography of Omar Morse, "MS. lent by Mrs. Grant Peterson for scholarly publication. Subsequent references (by year) are indicated in the text.

41. Dodge County Deeds, Book E, p. 595. The deed description of this property, sold to Dr. H.C. Potter of New York City, tallies with Morse's warrant for the government quarter-section purchased at the St. Peter Land Office (the first half of the northwest quarter of Section 10, Town 107, Range 16). The sale was for half of his 160 acres. His immediate transfer of title, as he states, indicates an adroit manipulation (his need to satisfy Potter's debt may have taken place a year previous to his actual purchase of his legally preempted claim).

42. Dodge County Mortgages, Book F, p. 427.

43. Dodge County Deeds, Book H, p. 212.

44. *The History of Winona, Olmstead, and Dodge Counties* (Chicago: H.H. Hill, 1884), 860.

45. See esp. 59-60, 64-68.

46. See Shannon, *Farmers' Last Frontier*, 7-9.

47. The brief history of Mantorville is from a variety of sources, including my own observations.

48. Eggleston, *The Mystery of Metropolisville*, 11-12.

49. Kirkland, *Zury: The Meanest Man in Spring County*, 50.

50. "Some Recollections of Thomas Pederson," *Wisconsin Magazine of History* 21 (1936-37): 16-34.

51. Haycroft, "Thirty Years on a Farm in Southern Minnesota," TS, Minnesota Historical Society, is cited by permission. Haycroft, a person of integrity, is a representative farmer-author; many homestead autobiographies, journals, diaries, and other memorabilia follow his pattern. My intent is not to attack him as an individual but to illustrate the effect of the success myth on early farmer-authors. Those who recorded their experiences were more or less successful, or appeared to be so in their narratives.

2. The Morse Narrative and a Countermyth of Dispossession

1. Smith, *Virgin Land*, Chs. 18-20. Here as elsewhere, Smith describes the fact of a decaying national myth without concern for the nature of the change. The success of Edwin Markham's poetry illustrates the emergence of the long, silent history of disillusion and

protest; his brutalized peasant is a satirical, inverted gardener of the West.

2. Smith, *Virgin Land*, 194.

3. Ibid., prologue, chs. 1, 2, 4, 5, 11-12, 14, 16. See also Moore, *The Frontier Mind*; Billington, *America's Frontier Heritage*; and Noble, *The Eternal Adam and the New World Garden*. The origin of this marvelous wilderness garden is, loosely stated, in an eighteenth-century primitivist's concept of unspoiled virtue in nature, exemplified by the noble savage and happy farmer as dwellers in a pastoral Eden or Arcadia.

4. Smith, *Virgin Land*, 126-27.

5. Ibid., 53-54.

6. Ibid., 22-33. After a meeting with Jefferson, an elder statesman, Benton felt he had experienced a laying-on of hands.

7. Ibid., 123-24.

8. Ibid., 134-44.

9. Crèvecœur, *Letters from an American Farmer* (London, 1782), n.p., quoted in Smith, *Virgin Land*, 127-28.

10. Filson, *Discovery . . . of Kentucke*, n.p., quoted in Smith, *Virgin Land*, 129.

11. My reference is to research in these materials principally at the Chicago Public Library, the Newberry Library, the Wisconsin State Historical Library, and the Minnesota Historical Society.

12. *Chicago Daily American*, Sept. 23, 1837.

13. As the preceding chapter points out, even the buoyant optimist Horace Greeley recognized the high-risk economic venture of early homesteading.

14. Twain and Warner, *The Gilded Age*, chs. 27-28.

15. Hooper, *The Adventures of Captain Simon Suggs*, 26-37, 65-77. Hooper's *Adventures* also contains a unique tale of Indian dispossession by unscrupulous whites, the only nonhumorous story in a book that reflects journalists' as well as folk themes of this decade. Internal evidence holds this suggestion. The loss of democracy in unscrupulous land speculation, including the dispossession of Indians, was often attributed to squatters (like the Morses) by an educated class. Land speculators, often unscrupulous (and educated), blamed a poverty-ridden underclass. But the people, the homesteaders, held a different view.

16. Robb, *Streaks of Squatter Life*, 117-32.

17. Yates, *William T. Porter and the Spirit of the Times*, 137. Yates also nicely summarizes land speculation (pp. 111-12). See also Oscar Cargill, *Intellectual America*, 399-405, on Suggs's land speculation.

18. Randolph, *Ozark Folk Songs*, 90. Cf. "Little Old Sod Shanty" in Carl Sandburg's *American Songbag*, 91. Some variants conclude with a bachelor's lament for a wife, suggesting the real problem, but I refer to those that ironically conclude with a wish for a wife in town, to there reside.

19. Lomax and Lomax, eds., *Folk Songs, U.S.A.*, 239.

20. Ibid., 128.

21. Greenway, *American Folk Songs*, 50-55.

22. Botkin, *A Treasury of American Folksong*, 878.

23. Ibid., 878.

24. Gates, *Landlords and Tenants*, 283-88.

25. Randolph, *Ozark Folk Songs*, 3: 23-25. Arkansas is a folk song writer's vision of a hell on earth in numerous other songs. The humor is generally a mask for the dark bitterness of disillusionment.

26. Greenway, *American Folk Songs*, 212. Greenway has not recognized the long history of complaint that the hard-times songs represent, but he remains the most insightful scholar of protest songs I have read.

27. *Falls Evening News*, April 13, 1858, n.p. Quoted by permission from the Babcock Transcripts in the Minnesota Historical Society. (I wish to thank Dallas Cheslock and her staff for their assistance.)

28. Ibid.

29. See Gates, *Landlords and Tenants*, and, for an opposing view, Bogue, *Money at Interest*, 273-74.

30. Hicks, *The Farmers' Alliance and the People's Party*, remains a reliable if partisan study of the Populists. Others more recent worth serious consideration include Parsons, *The Populist Context*; Klepper, *The Economic Basis for Agrarian Protest Movements in the United States*; McKenna, *American Populism*; Canovan, *Populism*; Durden, *The Climax of Populism*; and David Emmons's study of boomerism, *Garden in the Grasslands*.

31. Edwin Atwood Papers, Minnesota Historical Society. I wish to thank the society for permission to quote.

32. Atwood Papers.

33. My thanks to the Minnesota Historical Society for permission to quote from Ignatius Donnelly's speech in *Proceedings of the Great Anti-Monopoly Convention Held in the City of Rochester, Minnesota*.

34. Hofstadter, *Age of Reform*, 77-78.

35. Ibid., 80. Donnelly and the Farm Alliance hoped the inclusion of blacks would end the race issue that the Civil War had left in both the South and the North. Hofstadter points out that William Jennings Bryan apologized in a speech to Jewish Democrats in Chicago for his

attacks on the Rothschilds; he had intended no racial criticism. Politically shrewd, Byran voiced a common American view of this banking firm, however, which Donnelly's *Caesar's Column* shared. Such prejudice reveals the tragic flaw of the optimistic young giant that nineteenth-century America had become. Dispossession is a comparable blindness.

36. Theodore L. Mydahl, ed., "The Diaries of Ignatius Donnelly," 50.

37. Ibid.

38. Donnelly, *The American People's Money*, 11.

39. Donnelly, *The Golden Bottle*, 110.

40. Donnelly, "Diaries," entry of Nov. 10, 1892, 6:110.

41. Donnelly, *The Golden Bottle*, 213.

42. Ibid., 311-12.

43. Donnelly, "Diaries," 3:32.

44. Eggleston, *The Mystery of Metropolisville*, 7.

45. Ibid., 11-12.

46. Ibid., 90-91.

47. Ibid., 320.

48. See Henson, *Joseph Kirkland*, for a summation of received opinion of Kirkland's novels and stories.

49. Randolph, *Ozark Folk Songs*, 2:90.

50. Kirkland, *Zury*, 50.

51. Ibid., 65.

52. Ibid., 1.

53. Ibid., 4.

54. Henson, *Joseph Kirkland*, 50-51.

55. Letter of Joseph Kirkland to Hamlin Garland, July 30, 1887, typescript, Joseph Kirkland Papers, Newberry Library, Chicago.

56. Ibid., Sept. 16, 1887.

57. Hensen, *Joseph Kirkland*, 93. To clarify, Howells's source of the historical "evolution of civilization, an ironclad law of mechanistic progress," was Tolstoi, not Herbert Spencer as some critics believe. Kirkland, in following Howells, sought structure in varied antiromantic philosophers and, with his peers, was convinced that civilization as he knew it was far superior to the amoral era of the central Illinois frontier; a scientific law had been operative. Yet he recognized dangers of blind speculation in his own economically turbulent day.

58. Garland, *Main-Travelled Roads*, 67-129. The 1899 Border edition contains Garland's completed work on this book as well as Howells's seldom-read Introduction.

59. Ibid., 97.

60. William Dean Howells, Introduction to *Main-Travelled Roads*, 5.

61. Garland, *Main-Travelled Roads*, 120.

62. The last paragraph of Garland's headnote from which his title is taken, amplifies his pessimism: "Mainly it is long and wearyful, and has a dull little Town and a home of toil at the other [end]. Like the Main-travelled road of life it is traversed by many classes of people, but the poor and weary predominate." Garland dedicated this book to his parents, whose homestead experience brought them, he writes, "only toil and deprivation." Clearly, Garland saw that the American farmer prospered no more and was less advantaged socially than the European peasant.

63. Smith, *Virgin Land*, 244-49. See also Donald Pizer's comprehensive *Hamlin Garland's Early Work and Career*.

64. Garland, *Jason Edwards*, 211-13.

65. See also Maurice Felheim's Introduction to Twain and Warner, *The Gilded Age*, x-xii; note esp. chs. 42-45 of the novel.

66. Ibid., chs. 51-53, 59.

67. Norris's *Octopus*, included for its authenticity, has been freely paraphrased.

68. Ibid., Book II, chs. 6-9, pp. 334-448.

69. Boatwright, *Folk Laughter on the American Frontier*, 161-69. Boatwright sees western optimism concealing loss in stoic acceptance of present misfortune with an anticipation of change that is unlikely to be adverse, and *may* be for the better. Perhaps this is also Morse's attitude.

3. The Repossession: A Creative Recovery of Community

1. Swierenga, *Pioneers and Profits*, 156. Swierenga quotes several interesting newspaper reports of the absurd, tragic circumstances of a land rush as well as the needless complexities of entering a claim.

2. Humphries, *Following the Prairie Frontier*, 229-65. The ridiculous scramble can be summarized by Humphries's remark describing the end of the wild spectacle: "But hundreds of boomers, dilillusioned, landless, now lined the track, waiting for a chance to get out of the Strip. . . . the last of the Prairie Frontier" (p. 265). I find this book of unusual interest in spite of Humphries's Twainian mask of the genteel "rough" who finds a few too many irresponsible and shiftless, greedy characters in the West, his native region.

3. Watson, *The People's Party Campaign Book*, 4.
4. Garland, Preface, to *Jason Edwards*.
5. Lingenfelter et al., eds., *Songs of the American West*, 475. This superb collection of "hardscrabble life" songs demonstrates clearly the ironic realism of the unweeded garden of cultural adjustment to the economic failure of the homestead farm.
6. Garland, *A Spoil of Office, 369*.
7. Ibid.

Appendix A

1. Woodward, "The Populist Heritage and the Intellectual," in *Farmer Discontent*, 155-73. Woodward seems prophetic in viewing Populism as a native liberal voice, countering objections to these nineteenth-century dissidents as well as their Midwest successors after the era of Joseph McCarthy, senator from Wisconsin. The myth of the race-hating bigot from mid-America has not yet vanished: such hatreds have no indigenous region.
2. Upham, *Minnesota Geographic Names*, 174.

Works Consulted

Ade, George. "Prairie Kings of Yesterday." *Saturday Evening Post*, July 4, 1932.

Anderson, David D. *Ignatius Donnelly*. Boston: Twayne, 1980.

Atherton, Lewis. *Main Street on the Middle Border*. Bloomington: Indiana Univ. Press, 1954.

Atwood, Edwin. Letters. Minnesota Historical Research Library, St. Paul.

Bennett, Sanford F. *The Pioneers: An Idyll of the Middle West*. Chicago: R.R. Donnelly and Sons, 1898.

Benton, Thomas H. *Thirty Years View*. Vol. 1. New York: Appleton and Co., 1854.

Billington, Ray A. *America's Frontier Heritage*. New York: Holt, Rinehart, Winston, 1966.

_____. *The Frontier and American Culture*. Berkeley: California Library Associates, 1965.

_____. "The Garden of the World: Fact and Fiction." In *The Heritage of the Middlewest*, ed. John J. Murray. Norman: Univ. of Oklahoma Press, 1958.

_____. *Westward Expansion: A History of the American Frontier*. New York: Macmillan, 1949.

Blair, Walter. *Native American Humor*. San Francisco: Chandler, 1960.

Blegan, Theodore. *The Land Lies Open*. Minneapolis: Univ. of Minnesota Press, 1949.

Boatwright, Mody C. *Folk Laughter on the American Frontier*. New York: Macmillan, 1949.

_____, Robert B. Downs, and John T. Flanagan. *The Family Saga and Other Phases of American Folklore*. Urbana: Univ. of Illinois Press, 1958.

Bogue, Allan. *From Prairie to Corn Belt: Farming on the Illinois and Iowa Prairies in the Nineteenth Century*. Chicago: Univ. of Chicago Press, 1963.

———. *Money at Interest: The Farm Mortgages on the Middle Border*. Ithaca: Cornell Univ. Press, 1955.

Boorstin, Daniel. *The Lost World of Thomas Jefferson*. Boston: Beacon Press, 1969.

Botkin, Benjamin A. *A Treasury of American Folksong*. New York: Crown, 1944.

Bradshaw, Maurine N. *Pioneer Parade*. New York: Vantage, 1966.

Brisbane, Arthur. *The Social Destiny of Man*. 1840. Reprint. New York: Augustus Kelley, 1969.

Butterfield, Counsul, ed. *The History of Fond du Lac County, Wisconsin*. Chicago: Western Historical Society, 1880.

Canovan, Margaret. *Populism*. New York: Harcourt Brace Jovanovich, 1981.

Carley, Kenneth. *The Sioux Uprising of 1862*. St. Paul: Minnesota Historical Society, 1961.

Cohen, Hennig. *The American Experience*. Philadelphia: Univ. of Pennsylvania Press, 1968.

Countryman, Levi. Diaries, 1858-1862. Minnesota Historical Research Library, St. Paul.

Crèvecœur, St. John de. *Letters from an American Farmer*. London, 1782.

Curti, Merle. *The Making of an American Community*. Stanford, Cal.: Stanford Univ. Press, 1959.

DeBow, J.B.D. *Statistical View of the United States*, Being a Compendium of the Seventh Census. Washington, D.C., 1854.

Donnelly, Ignatius. *The American People's Money*. Chicago, 1895. Reprint. Westport, Conn.: Hyperion Press, 1974.

———. *Caesar's Column: A Story of the Twentieth Century*, ed. Walter Rideout. Cambridge: Belknap Press of Harvard Univ. Press, 1960.

———. *The Golden Bottle; or the Story of Ephraim Bednezet*. New York and St. Paul, 1892. Reprint with an introduction by David Noble. New York: Johnson Reprint Co., 1968.

———. Speech. In *Proceedings of the Great Anti-Monopoly Convention Held in the City of Rochester, Minnesota*. Rochester, Minn.: Office of the Federal Union Printing Co., 1871.

Durden, Robert F. *The Climax of Populism*. Lexington: Univ. of Kentucky Press, 1965.

Eggleston, Edward. *The Mystery of Metropolisville*. New York: Orange Judd, 1873.

Elkins, Stanley, and Eric McKitrick. "A Meaning for Turner's Frontier Democracy in the Old Northwest." In *Turner and the Sociology of the Frontier*, ed. Richard Hofstadter and Seymour M. Lipset, 120-52. New York: Basic Books, 1968.

Ellis, Amanda M. *Pioneers*. Colorado Springs: Denton Printing Co., 1955.

Emmons, David. *Garden in the Grasslands: Boomer Literature of the Central Great Plains*. Lincoln: Univ. of Nebraska Press, 1971.

Felheim, Melvin. "Introduction." In *The Gilded Age: A Tale of Today*. Reprint. New York: New American Library, 1969.

Fussell, Edwin. *Frontier: American Literature and the American West*. Princeton: Princeton Univ. Press, 1966.

Gara, Larry. *A Short History of Wisconsin*. Madison: State Historical Society of Wisconsin, 1962.

Garland, Hamlin. *Jason Edwards: An Average Man*. Boston: Arena, 1892.

_____. *Main-Travelled Roads*. Border Ed. Introduction by William Dean Howells. New York: Harper, 1899.

_____. *A Member of the Third House: A Dramatic Story*. Reprint. Upper Saddle River, N.J.: Gregg Press, 1968.

_____. *Prairie Folks*. 2nd ed. Chicago: Stone and Kimbal, 1892.

_____. *A Spoil of Office*. Introduction by Eberhard Alsen, 1892. Reprint. New York: Johnson Reprint Co., 1969.

_____. *A Son of the Middle Border*. London: John Lane, 1917.

_____. *Trail Makers of the Middle Border*. New York: Macmillan, 1926.

Gates, Paul. *The Farmers' Age: Agriculture, 1815-1860*. Vol. 3 of *The Economic History of the United States*, ed. Henry Davis et al. New York: Holt, Rinehart, and Winston, 1960.

_____. *Landlords and Tenants on the Prairie Frontier*. Ithaca: Cornell Univ. Press, 1973.

Greenberg, David B., ed. *Land That Our Fathers Plowed*. Norman: Univ. of Oklahoma Press, 1969.

Greenway, John. *American Songs of Protest*. Philadelphia: Univ. of Pennsylvania Press, 1953.

Ham, Gerald (Archivist, Wisconsin Historical Society Library). "The Fourierists of Ceresco." Unpublished.

Harkness, Edward. Diary, 1869-79. Family Papers. Minnesota Historical Research Library, St. Paul.

Havighurst, Walter. *Land of Promise: Story of the Northwest Territory*. New York: Macmillan, 1946.
Haycroft, Isaac. "Thirty Years on a Farm in Southern Minnesota." Papers. Minnesota Historical Research Library, St. Paul.
Hazard, Lucy H. *The Frontier in American Literature*. 1927. Reprint. New York: Frederick Ungar, 1961.
Henson, Clyde. *Joseph Kirkland*. New York: Twayne, 1962.
Hicks, John. *The Populist Revolt: A History of the Farmers' Alliance and the People's Party*. Minneapolis: Univ. of Minnesota Press, 1931.
Hofstadter, Richard. *The Age of Reform*. New York: Alfred A. Knopf, 1955.
——and Seymour M. Lipset, eds., *Turner and the Sociology of the Frontier*. New York: Basic Books, 1968.
Hooper, Johnson J. *The Adventures of Captain Simon Suggs, Late of the Lallapoosa Volunteers*. Introduction by Manley W. Wellman. 1848. Reprint. Chapel Hill: Univ. of North Carolina Press, 1969.
Hough, Franklin B. *Census of the State of New York*. Albany: Charles Van Benthuysen, 1857.
Humphries, Seth. *Following the Prairie Frontier*. St. Paul: Univ. of Minnesota Press, 1931.
Hunt, John W. *Wisconsin Gazeteer, Containing the Names, Locations, and Advantages of the State of Wisconsin*. Madison: Beriah Brown, 1853.
Imlay, Gilbert. *A Topographical Description of the Western Territory*. London, 1792.
Jeffrey, Julie Roy. *Frontier Women: The Transmississippi West, 1840-80*. New York: Hill and Wang, 1979.
Jenkins, Jeff. *The Northern Tier; or, Life Among the Homestead Settlers*. Topeka, Kans.: George W. Martin, Kansas Publishing House, 1880.
Johnson, Oscar B. *The Homesteaders: The Experiences of Early Settlers in Pine County, Minnesota*. Staples, Minn.: Nordell Graphic Communications, 1971.
Judson, Phoebe G. *A Pioneer's Search for an Ideal Home*. Tacoma, Wash.: n.p., 1966.
Kaplan, Louis. *A Bibliography of American Autobiography*. Madison: Univ. of Wisconsin Press, 1961.
Kirkland, Joseph. Letters to Hamlin Garland. TS in Newberry Library, Chicago.
——. *Zury: The Meanest Man in Spring County*. Boston: Houghton Mifflin, 1887.

Klepper, Robert. *The Economic Basis for Agrarian Protest Movements in the United States*, 1870-1900. New York: Arno Press, 1978.
Kramer, Dale. *The Wild Jackasses: The American Farmer in Revolt.* New York: Hastings House, 1956.
Leyburn, James. *Frontier Folkways.* New Haven: Yale Univ. Press, 1935.
Lillard, Richard G. *American Life in Autobiography.* Stanford: Stanford Univ. Press, 1956.
Lingenfelter, Richard E., Richard Dwyer, and David Cohen, eds. *Songs of the American West.* Berkeley and Los Angeles: Univ. of California Press, 1968.
Litwack, Leon. *Been in the Storm So Long.* New York: Alfred A. Knopf, 1979.
McKenna, George. *American Populism.* New York: Putnam, 1974.
McKenna, Maurice, ed. *Fond du Lac County, Wisconsin: Past and Present.* Vol. 1. Chicago: S.J. Clarke, 1912.
Marshall, James. "A Homestead Countermyth and the Prairie Realists." *MidAmerica* 10 (1983), 54-68.
_____. "Twenty Acres of Independence: The Letters of Omar Morse, 1885-1900." *MidAmerica* 9, (1982), 38-52.
_____. "An Unheard Voice: The Autobiography of a Dispossessed Homesteader and a Nineteenth-Century Theme of Dispossession." *Old Northwest: Journal of History and Culture* (Winter 1981), 303-29.
Marshall, Josiah. *Farmers' and Emigrants' Handbook.* Hartford: O.D. Case, 1851.
Merk, Frederick. *Manifest Destiny and Mission in American History.* New York: Alfred A. Knopf, 1963.
Meyer, Roy W. *The Middle Western Farm Novel in the Twentieth Century.* Lincoln: Univ. of Nebraska Press, 1965.
Miller, George F. *The Academy System of the State of New York.* Albany: J.B. Lyon, 1922.
Minter, David. *The Interpreted Design in American Prose.* New Haven: Yale Univ. Press, 1969.
Mitchell, H.H., and V. Curtis. *An Historical Sketch of Dodge County, Minnesota.* Rochester, Minn. Federal Union Book and Job Printing, 1870.
Moore, Arthur. *The Frontier Mind: A Cultural Analysis of the Kentucky Frontiersman.* Lexington: Univ. of Kentucky Press, 1957.
Moore, Ethel and Chauncey O. *Ballads and Folk Songs of the Southwest.* Norman: Univ. of Oklahoma Press, 1964.

Morse, Abner. *Memorial of the Morses: Containing the History of Seven Persons of that Name*. Boston: William Veazier, 1850.

Muir, John. *The Story of My Boyhood and Youth*. New York: Houghton Mifflin, 1913.

Murray, John J., ed. *The Heritage of the Midwest*. Norman: Univ. of Oklahoma Press, 1958.

Mydahl, Theodore L. "The Diaries of Ignatius Donnelly." Ph.D. diss., Univ. of Minnesota, 1942.

Myers, Marvin. "The Jacksonian Persuasion." In *The American Culture: Approaches to the Study of the United States*, 49-61. Boston: Houghton Mifflin, 1968.

Noble, David. *The Eternal Adam and the New World Garden: The Central Myth in the American Novel since 1830*. New York: Braziller, 1968.

———. *Historians against History: the Frontier Thesis and the National Covenant in American Historical Writing since 1830*. Minneapolis: Univ. of Minnesota Press, 1965.

Norris, Frank. *The Octopus*, ed. Kenneth Lynn. Cambridge: Riverside Press, 1958.

Nugent, Walter T.K. *The Tolerant Populists: Kansas Populism and Nativism*. Chicago: Univ. of Chicago Press, 1963.

Parsons, Stanley B. *The Populist Context: Rural versus Urban Power on a Great Plains Frontier*. Westport, Conn.: Greenwood Press, 1973.

Pascal, Roy. *Design and Truth in Autobiography*. Cambridge: Harvard Univ. Press, 1960.

Pederson, Thomas. "Some Recollections of Thomas Pederson." *Wisconsin Magazine of History* 21 (1937-38): 14-34.

Pizer, Donald. *Hamlin Garland's Early Work and Career*. Berkeley: Univ. of California Press, 1960.

Pollock, Norman. "Hofstadter on Populism: A Critique of *The Age of Reform*." *Journal of Southern History* 26 (Nov. 1960), 478-500.

———. *The Populist Response to Industrial America*. Cambridge: Harvard Univ. Press, 1962.

Prosser, Richard. *Rails to the North Star*. Minneapolis, Minn.: Dillon Press, 1966.

Randolph, Vance. *Ozark Folk Songs*. Vols. 2 and 3. Columbia: State Historical Society of Missouri, 1949.

Robb, John S. *Streaks of Squatter Life*. 1847. Reprint, edited with an introduction by John F. McDermott. Gainesville: Scholars' Facsimiles and Reprints, 1962.

Rourke, Constance M. *American Humour: A Study of the American Character*. Garden City, N.Y.: Harcourt Brace Javronovich, 1959.

Sandburg, Carl. *The American Songbag*. New York: Harcourt Brace, 1927.
Sandford, Charles. "An American Pilgrim's Progress." In *The American Culture: Approaches to the Study of the United States*, ed. Hennig Cohen, 77-91. Boston: Houghton Mifflin, 1968.
Sayre, Robert. *The Examined Self*. Princeton: Princeton Univ. Press, 1964.
Schlissel, Lillian, ed. *Women's Diaries of the Westward Journey*. New York: Schocken Books, 1982.
Shannon, Fred A. *The Farmers' Last Frontier: Agriculture, 1860-1897*. In *The Economic History of the United States*, ed. Henry David et al. New York: Farrar and Rinehart, 1945.
Shaw, Barton. *The Wool-Hat Boys: Georgia's Populist Party*. Baton Rouge: Louisiana State Univ. Press, 1984.
Simpson, Elizabeth L. *Mexico, Mother of Towns*. Buffalo, N.Y.: J.W. Clement, 1949.
Simpson, Lewis. *The Dispossessed Garden*. Athens: Univ. of Georgia Press, 1975.
Slotkin, Richard. *Regeneration through Violence: The Mythology of the American Frontier, 1600-1860*. Middletown, Conn.: Wesleyan Univ. Press, 1973.
Smith, Henry N. *Virgin Land: The American West as Symbol and Myth*. Cambridge: Harvard Univ. Press, 1950.
Spengeman, William C. "Autobiography and the American Myth." In *The American Culture: Approaches to the Study of the United States*, ed. Hennig Cohen, 92-110. Boston: Houghton Mifflin, 1968.
State Historical Society of Wisconsin. *Subject Bibliography of Wisconsin History*. Madison: State Historical Society of Wisconsin, 1947.
Sterrett, Andrew Jackson. Diaries, 1853-60. Minnesota Historical Research Library, St. Paul.
Stewart, Elinore Pruitt. *Letters of a Woman Homesteader*. Lincoln: Univ. of Nebraska Press, 1961.
Stratton, Joanna L., ed. *Pioneer Women: Voices from the Kansas Frontier*. Introduction by Arthur M. Schlesinger. New York: Simon and Schuster, 1982.
Stuart, Granville. *Forty Years on the Frontier*. Vol. 2. Glendale, Ill.: Arthur W. Clark, 1957.
Swierenga, Robert P. *Acres for Cents: Delinquent Tax Auctions in Frontier Iowa*. Westport, Conn.: Greenwood Press, 1976.
_____. *Pioneers and Profits: Land Speculation on the Iowa Frontier*. Ames: Iowa State Univ. Press, 1968.

Thompson, Stith. *The Folk Tale*. Berkeley, Cal.: Univ. of California Press, 1977.

Turner, Frederick J. *The United States, 1830-50*. New York: Henry Holt, 1935.

Twain, Mark (Samuel Clemens), and Charles Dudley Warner. *The Gilded Age: A Tale of Today*. 1873. Reprint: New York: New American Libary, 1969.

Upham, Warren. *Minnesota Geographic Names: Their Origin and Historic Significance*. Introduction by James T. Dunn. Minneapolis: Minnesota Historical Society, 1969.

Watson, Thomas E., ed. *The People's Party Campaign Book*. In *American Farmers and the Rise of Agribusiness*, ed. Dan C. McCurry and Richard Rubenstein. New York: Arno Press, 1975.

Woodward, C. Vann. "The Populist Heritage and the Intellectual," in *Farmer Discontent, 1865-1900*, ed. Vernon Carstenson. New York: John Wiley and Son, 1974.

Yates, Norris. *William T. Porter and the Spirit of the Times: A Study of the Big Bear School of Humour*. Baton Rouge: Louisiana State Univ. Press, 1957.

Index

Abasalom! Absalom! (Faulkner), 163
Academy System of the State of New York (Miller), 27 n 8
Adventures of Captain Simon Suggs: Late of the Lollapoosa Volunteers (Hooper), 6, 134-35, 177, 216 n 15
Age of Reform: From Bryant to FDR (Hofstadter), 12, 95
agrarianism, 128, 191, 211 n 2. *See also* Jeffersonian ideals
Albion, N.Y., 32
Algoma Township, Wisc., 44 n 36
Allen, Mary Morse (sister of Omar Morse), 210
American Dream, 18, 109
American Gothic (Wood), 192
American People's Money, The (Donnelly), 148
Anderson, Sherwood, 8
anti-Semitism, 144, 146-47, 217 n 35
"Arkansas Traveler" (folk song), 141, 154, 167, 186
Atala and René (Chateaubriand), 129
Atwood, Edwin H., 144-45

Babbitt (Lewis), 152
Backus, Harry, 42, 127, 141
Backwoodsman, The (Paulding), 129
banking, 98-99. *See also* specie
Bardwell, Mr., 58
Barker, Captain, 40
Barlow, Augustus, 66 n 79, 116
Barnes, Ansel, 26
Barnes, Mr., 71
Barnes, Rev. Gamaliel (father-in-law of Stephan D. Morse), 16, 23 n 1, 37 n 26, 106, 174
Barnum, Rev., 50
Barteau, Sid, 195
Batson, Mr., 80
Bellamy, Edward, 148
Benton, Thomas Hart, 96, 97, 128, 216 n 6
Boatwright, Mody, 174, 219 n 69
Bogue, Alan, 12, 93
"Boomtown: A Social Study" (Garland), 158
Bowie, Jim, 136
Brainerd, Minn., 77, 78, 111
"Branch Roads" (Garland,) 165
"Bride Comes to Yellow Sky" (Crane), 125
Brockport, N.Y., 32, 39, 42
Brook Farm, 33 n 20, 147
Bryan, William Jennings, 191, 217 n 35
Buffalo, N.Y., 34, 35, 39
Burlington Railroad, 94. *See also* Morse, Manly: as railroad employee

Caesar's Column (Donnelly,) 22, 146, 217 n 35
Campbell, Thomas, 129
Canfield, E.V., 68
Canovan, Margaret, 94
Carey, D., 30
Carley's Mill, 23 n 1, 25 n 5
Carpenter, William D., 52 n 51
Carstenson, Vernon, 191
Catlin, Hank, 79
Cerescans. *See* Fourierist Phalanx
Ceresco, Wisc., 43-44, 46, 109
Chateaubriand, François René, Vicomte de, 129
Cherokee Indians, 181
Cherokee Strip land rush, 180-81
Chicago Daily American, 99, 104
civilization: Donnelly's view of, 150; Kirkland's view of, 157-58, 160, 161-62; Garland's view of, 167; Twain's view of, 169, 170
Civil War, 60-61, 114
Clare, John, 34 n 22
Clarendon, N.Y., 39, 40
Clarkson, N.Y., 41
Cleveland, Grover, 196
commercialism, of western expansion, 9
Conestoga wagon, symbolic value of, 157
Coon, Mr. and Mrs., 83, 88, 89, 195
Cooper, James Fenimore, 104, 124
corporation, as usurper, 146
Countryman, Levi, 14
Craddock, W.L., 207
Crandel, W., 53
Crane, Stephen, 121, 125, 165
Crèvecoeur, J. Hector St. John, 101, 128, 129-30
Croffut, W.A., 142-43

debt, as common problem of homesteaders, 7-8. *See also* mortgages
Derwent, Colonel, 99
Detroit, Mich., 35, 39
Dewey, Adm. George, 197-98
Dickinson, Norm, 68, 69, 74, 75
diminishing returns, law of, 116
Discovery, Settlement and Present State of Kentucke, The (Filson), 128
disease, frontier, 39 n 27. *See also* medicine, frontier
dispossession, of land: faith in frontier myth despite, 5, 18, 66, 81, 84-85, 122, 126, 174-75, 187; disillusion due to, 7, 12, 87; of Omar Morse, 8, 14-15, 52, 63 n 71, 64-65, 66, 78, 94, 95-96, 109, 110-11, 112-16, 123, 179; rate of, 11-12, 96, 107, 112; descriptions of, 14; and relocation, 56 n 59; causes of, 93-94, 104, 110, 134, 166, 179, 181; and land reform, 101; inevitability of, 103, 177; of Stephan D. Morse, 106-9; as countermyth, 126, 137, 138-39, 165, 185-86; of Ignatius Donnelly, 147; in Kirkland's *Zury*, 155; evidence of, 178, 179; protest against (*see* Farmer's Alliance; People's Party)
dispossession, of values, 124, 185
"divine average," 7, 127
Donnelly, Ignatius, 7, 22, 70 n 84, 75 n 90, 146-50, 217 n 35
Dreiser, Theodore, 121, 175
Dresback, Sim, 71
Dwight, Timothy, 129

Eaton Rapids, Mich., 36, 38
Economic Basis for Protest Movements in the United States, 1870-1900, The (Klepper), 94
education: nineteenth-century attitude toward, 27 n 8; schoolhouses built by Omar Morse, 70, 79
Eggleston, Edward, 120, 151-54, 162

Egliston, D., 46
Elsie Venner (Holmes), 156
"Emigrant's Farewell" (poem), 10-11
Erskine, E., 26
experience: vs. innocence, as theme, 34 n 22, 63 n 71; need to learn from, 70, 75, 90, 188

"fail up," 203
Fairwater, Wisc., 46
Falls Evening News (Little Falls, Minn.), 142, 217 n 27
Farmer Discontent (Carstenson), 191, 220 n 1
"Farmer Is the Man" (folk song), 137-38
Farmers' Alliance, and political resistance, 18, 94, 97, 114, 143-46, 191
Farmers' and Emigrants' Handbook, The (Marshall), 103
Farmer's Last Frontier, 1860-1897, The (Shannon), 11
Faulkner, William, 8, 139, 163, 175
Filson, John, 128, 130
Financier, The (Dreiser), 121, 155
Fitzgerald, F. Scott, 18
folk songs, protest in, 136-42, 155, 177, 184, 217 nn 18, 25, 26, 220 n 5
Following the Prairie Frontier (Humphries), 180
Fond du Lac, city of: appearance of, in 1846, 43, 132-33; history of, 43 n 34, *See also* Morse, Omar: farms of
Fond du Lac, county of: population of, 109; Omar Morse claim in (*see* Morse, Omar: farms of)
foreclosure: of Morse family home (1840), 28; problem of, 28 n 9, 93; stop and replevin laws for, 97; avoidance of, 114
Forsythe, Mrs., 79
Fourier association, 33. *See also* Fourierist Phalanx
Fourierist Phalanx, 33 n 20, 43 n 35
Francis, J.R., 194
Freeman, R., 66
From Prairie to Corn Belt (Bogue), 12
frontier: disappearance of, 124-25; as garden, 125, 126, 127-31, 147, 150, 156-57, 159, 163, 171, 174, 176, 182, 216 n 3
Frontier Women (Jeffrey), 19

Galena, Ill., fraudulent land speculation in, 99-100
Galena *Democrat*, 99
garden: as metaphor for wilderness, 125, 126, 127-31, 147, 150, 156-57, 159, 163, 171, 174, 182; as metaphor in *Richard II*, 176
Garden of Earthly Delights, A (Oates), 139
Garland, Hamlin: "peasant among peasants," 6; as Populist voice, 7, 101, 121, 126, 139, 166-67; parents of, 13; nostalgia in, 121; correspondence with Kirkland, 158-59; on loss of culture, 185, 186-87, 219 n 62
Gates, Paul: on dispossession, 11, 13, 14, 141, 180; on "gilded age," 49 n 42; on numbers of public farms, 93; historical correctiveness of, 117, 123
George, Henry, 97, 140
Gertrude of Wyoming (Campbell), 129
Giants in the Earth (Rölvaag), 21
Gilbert, Grandmother, 65
Gilbert, Mr., 57
Gilded Age, The (Twain and Warner), 43 n 34, 49 n 42, 120, 133, 151, 154, 168-71
Gillet, Mr., 56
Golden Bottle, The (Donnelly), 148-50
gold rush, in California, 47-49, 137

Goodrich, Darius, 52
Goodrich, W., 52
Gopher Prairie, as example of homesteaded town, 10
Grange, emergence of, 191
Greeley, Horace, 93-94, 97, 102, 216 n 13
Greenfield Hill (Dwight), 129
Greenway, John, 138, 141

Hackleton, Major, 99
Hall, James, 70 n 85
Halloway, James, 111
Ham, Gerald, 33 n 20
Hamiltonian capitalism, vs. Jeffersonian agrarianism, 191
Hamiston, Mr., 79
hardpan, 86
Harrison, Alban, 55
Harvey, Coin, 146
Hasbrook, Mr., 80
Hastings Township, N.Y., 23, 39, 41, 105-6, 117. *See also* Morse, Omar: childhood homes of
Haycroft, Isaac G., 121, 215 n 51
Hayward (or Heyward), Geo, 68
Hill, Dr., 71
Hofstadter, Richard, 12, 95, 191
Holley, G.W., 131
Holley, N.Y., 32
Holmes, Dr. Oliver Wendell, 156
Homestead Act of 1862, 97, 100, 188
homesteaders: disillusionment of, 7, 12, 13, 142, 144; poverty of, 7-8, 100, 104, 106, 109, 110, 146; liberalism of, 8; victimization of, 11, 18, 110, 125-26, 178, 182; exploitation of, 12, 99, 100, 105, 132; characterization of, 19, 93, 101-2, 117; burden on women, 20-21; and love of family and community, 37 n 25, 181; high cost of provisions for, 59, 63; Indian hostilities against, 61; cash supply of, 67 n 80, 75 n 90, 132; numbers of, 93; Jacksonian view of, 98; cost of, 102-3; cautions for, 103-5; and population expansion, 105-6; lost viability of, 107-8; risks of, 118; silence of, 121; countermyth of, 126, 137, 138-39, 165, 185-86; independence of, 128, 130, 132, 141, 163, 183; alienation of, 139, 140, 175, 187-88; futility of, 164-65; perseverance of, 184; problems of assimilation for, 195. *See also* dispossession, of land; Farmers' Alliance; myth, of frontier promise; People's Party
Hooper, Johnson, 6, 134-35, 153, 170, 216 n 15
Hoosier Schoolmaster, The (Eggleston), 152
Horton, Walter, 9
Howard, Jim, 80
Howells, William Dean, 159, 164
Humphries, Seth, 180-81
Hunts Corners (Hastings Center), 28
Hurlbutts brothers, 57

illusion, of pioneer myth: characterized, 4, 18; and disillusionment, 7, 12, 87, 137, 142, 166; vs. reality, 63 n 71, 103, 125, 136-37
Indians: displacement of, 10, 114, 216 n 15; hostilities against homesteaders by, 61. *See also* Cherokee Indians; Sioux Indians
Industrial Revolution: effect of on pioneers, 5-6, 12, 21, 124, 138, 190; and viability of farming, 100-101
Ingram, D.F., 67
Inkpaduta, Chief, 61 n 66
innocence vs. experience, as theme, 34 n 22, 63 n 71
Irondequoit Bay, 41

Jackson, Andrew, 97, 98, 100
Jackson, Mich., 35, 36, 39
Jason Edwards (Garland), 101, 163, 165-66, 167-68, 185
Jeffersonian ideals: reversal of, 4; "divine average" and, 7; and Populists, 12, 125; independent farmer and, 42 n 33, 93, 98, 108, 128; legislation informed by, 97-98; vs. Hamiltonian capitalism, 191. *See also* Benton, Thomas Hart; Jackson, Andrew
Jeffrey, Julie Roy, 19
Johnson, Samuel, 131
Judson, Phoebe Goodall, 14

Kane, Jim, 75
Kassoon, Minn., 119
King Ranch, Tex., 93
Kirkland, Caroline, 162
Kirkland, Joseph, 120-21, 139, 154-62
Klepper, Robert, 94
Knights of Labor, 101

La Crosse, Wisc., 55-56
Lake Erie, 34, 35
land: availability of, 5; cost of, 5; struggle for ownership of, 7, 13, 14, 54 n 54, 109, 123, 133, 175 (*see also* homesteaders); advertisement for, 9-10; reform policies, 11; demand for, 106, 108; productivity of, 117-18, 137; auction for, 180-81; rush for, 180-81, 219 nn 1, 2; right to ownership of, 128. *See also* dispossession, of land; land fever; land speculators
Land: Buyers', Homesteaders', and Locators' Guide to Minnesota (Horton), 9
land fever: exploitation of, 12; and pioneer movement, 54 n 54; pervasiveness of, 135, 136
Landlords and Tenants on the Prairie Frontier (Gates), 11, 49 n 42, 117, 141, 180
land speculators: as demons of the frontier, 6, 8, 11, 12, 99, 104, 126-27, 147, 164; dishonesty of, 13, 96, 100, 114, 136; Morse brothers as, 47 n 41, 59 n 64, 109; "speculation fever," 49 n 42, 151; power of, 97, 105, 115, 160; opportunism of, 105; distrust of, 119; instability of, 120; wealth of, 131; satire of, 134; Jim Bowie as, 136; in Eggleston's *Mystery of Metropolisville*, 151, 152-54; in Garland's *Jason Edwards*, 166; benefits of, 212 nn 1.4, 1.5
Last of the Mohicans, The (Cooper), 124
Leavitt, Emily, 16
legislative apathy, as cause of homestead failure, 166, 188
Letters from an American Farmer (Crèvecoeur), 128
Letters from the Earth (Twain), 170
Lewis, Sinclair, 8, 10, 140, 153
liberalism: emergence of, 8, 14, 94, 125, 191; suspicion of, 191-92. *See also* People's Party
Liberty Pole, as Revolutionary symbol, 29
Life of Thaddeus Stevens (Woodwards), 146
Light in August (Faulkner), 163
Lincoln, Abraham, 60, 61 n 66, 125
log cabin, symbolic value of, 29 n 13, 125
Looking Backward (Bellamy), 148
Loveridge, C.B. (brother-in-law of Omar Morse), 33
Loveridge, Louisa Morse (sister of Omar Morse), 33 n 19, 210
"lubber," 203

MacBane, F., 40
McCarthy, Joseph, 191, 220 n 1

McHinstry, R., 71
McKinley, William, 197
Magee, Win, 55
Maggie: A Girl of the Streets (Crane), 121, 165
Main Street (Lewis), 10, 140
Main-Travelled Roads (Garland), 126, 163-65, 187, 218 n 58
Man That Corrupted Hadleyburg, The (Twain), 183
Mantorville, Minn., 57, 58, 110, 117, 119-20, 196, 215 n 47
"Man with the Hoe, The" (Markham), 126
Man with the Hoe, The (Millet), 126, 165
Markham, Edwin, 126, 139, 165, 215 n 1
Marshall, James M. (great-grandson of Omar Morse), 17
Marshall, Josiah T., 103
"Mary's Little Lot" (folk song), 140-41
Mason, Delia. *See* Morse, Delia Mason
Mason, George W. (brother of Delia), 54, 64, 65, 67, 68
Mason, J., 50
Mason family: as homesteaders, 20, 53-54, 56; Omar's acquaintance with, 47, 49, 54; Delia's visit to, 64, 65
Masters, Edgar Lee, 8
materialism: development of, 15, 86 n 101, 126, 185; in Kirkland's *Zury*, 161
medicine, frontier, 66 n 77, 71, 116-17, 196. *See also* disease, frontier
Mellinger, T.S., 207
Member of the Third House (Garland), 166
Mexico Academy, 27 n 8
Mexico, Mother of Towns (Simpson), 16, 24 n 3
Miller, George F., 27 n 8
Miller, Robert, 46
Millet, Jean François, 126, 165
mineral trusts, exploitation of land fever by, 12
Minnesota Territory: settlement of, 54, 110-11; Indian hostilities in, 61
Money at Interest (Bogue), 12
moneylenders: as demons of the frontier, 6, 8, 11, 12, 99, 104, 126-27, 147, 164; farmers as, 148; profitability of, 148. *See also* land speculators
"money-power," evil of, 192
Monroe, Lila Day, 19
Morse, Allen (son of Sanford), 38
Morse, Alzina (daughter of Sanford), 38
Morse, Alzina A. (sister), 49, 210
Morse, Anna Schaeffer (wife of Manly): as maternal grandmother of J.M. Marshall, 17; as wife of Manly, 83; letters from Omar to, 189, 193-206; advice of Omar to, 198-201
Morse, Ansel (friend), 59
Morse, Ansel H. (brother), 28, 47 n 41, 59 n 64, 210
Morse, Anthony, 16
Morse, Daniel (distant relative), 32
Morse, Delia Mason (wife): as Omar's wife, 5, 14, 19-21, 58; appearance of, 15, 20; Omar's portrayal of, 19, 21; courtship of, 19-20, 47, 49; death of, 20, 72-73, 185; marriage to Omar, 49-50; illness of, 61, 65-66, 71-72; trip to Waseca, 64, 65; medical expenses for, 116-17; birth of, 209
Morse, Jedidiah, 16
Morse, J. Howard, 16
Morse, Lulu (wife of Omar, Jr.), 16
Morse, Lydia A. (daughter), 60, 64, 65, 74, 75, 76, 195, 202, 209

Morse, Manly (son): as railroad employee, 5, 77, 79-80, 88, 199-201; birth of, 62, 209; childhood of, 65; illness of, 66-67; and news of Delia's death, 72; young manhood of, 73-74, 75, 76-77; assistance to Lydia Thomas, 78; as source of family income, 81 n 97; marriage of, 83; visit to Omar by, 88; letters from Omar to, 189, 193-206; advice of Omar to, 198-201
Morse, Mary (daughter of Sanford), 38
Morse, Mary (second wife of Sanford), 38
Morse, Mary E. Thomas (first wife of Sanford), 38
Morse, Myron E. (brother): farms of, 28, 44; jobs with Omar, 29; in Fourierist Phalanx, 33 n 20; land sale to Omar, 47 n 41, 109; birth and death of, 210
Morse, Omar: belief in frontier myth, 4-5, 7; disillusionment of, 7, 14-15; universality of experience of, 7, 13-14, 17-18, 95, 180, 188; defenses of, 8; dispossession of, 8, 14-15, 52, 63 n 71, 64-65, 66, 78, 94, 95-96, 109, 110-11, 112-16, 123, 179; political views of, 8, 14, 21-22, 31 n 14, 94, 182, 192, 196-98, 208; appearance of, 15, 26; relation to other Morses, 16, 17, 209-10; courtship of Delia by, 19-20, 47, 49; effect of death of Delia on, 20, 73, 202; birth of, 23, 209; education of, 24, 26-27, 27-28, 30; work experience of, 26, 27, 29, 30-33, 40-42, 44-46, 52, 53, 59, 60, 62-63, 67, 68, 70, 71, 72, 73, 74, 76, 78-79, 80, 81 n 97, 84; trip to Michigan by, 34-39; homesickness of, 36-37; illness of, 38, 39-40; antislavery sentiment of, 42 n 33; move to Wisconsin by, 43-46, 102; near drowning of, 45; marriage to Delia, 49-50; economic problems of, 50-51, 61, 64, 65-66, 67, 69, 70, 76, 95, 102, 109-10, 190; move to Minnesota by, 55-57; stoicism of, 55 n 57, 64 n 74, 88, 190; in Brainerd, Minn., 77-80, 111; old age of, 82, 87-88, 90, 190, 201-2; trip to Iowa and Illinois by, 82-83; views on Spanish-American War, 101, 190, 194, 197, 208; idealism of, 127, 177; independence of, 183, 199, 201; perseverance of, 184; letters to Manly and Anna, 189, 193-206; views on progress, 193-94; reading by, 194; views on rural life, 194-96; parental advice of, 198-201; essay on Heaven by, 204-6; death of, 206, 210. *See also* mortgages: of Omar Morse
—autobiography of: tone of, 13, 174; original manuscript of, 15; title of, 15, 23; editing of, 16-17; authenticity of, 17; portrayal of Delia in, 19; candor in, 21, 182; reasons for, 121-23, 183, 203-6; structure of, 163, 178-79
—childhood homes of: birthplace of (town line farm), 23 n 1, 24-25, 106, 107; second home of (Mexico or Parish Township), 26, 28, 109; move to Hunts Corners (1840), 28; move to one-acre farm (1841), 28-29, 30
—farms of: in Fond du Lac County, Wisc., 4, 7, 46, 47, 49-52, 102, 214 n 32; on Liberty Street, Ceresco, Wisc., 53, 109; in Winona County, Minn., 56-57; in Mantorville Township, Dodge County, Minn., 58-60, 61, 63-66, 110, 112-16, 119, 214 n 36, 215 n 41; at Sam Denton farm,

66-67, 111; in Pine Island, Goodhue County, Minn., 66, 67, 111; in Roscoe Township, Goodhue County, Minn., 5, 6, 7, 68-69, 74, 75-77, 80, 81, 84, 88-89, 111, 116, 189, 194, 199
Morse, Omar, Jr. (son): inheritance to, 5, 6, 16; birth of, 70, 209; boyhood of, 74, 75, 77, 78, 79, 80-81; trip to Iowa and Illinois by, 82; at Roscoe farm, 84, 190, 195; as companion to Omar, Sr., 189; advice from Omar, Sr., to, 198, 201; letters to Manly, 206-7
Morse, Polly Barnes (mother), 7, 16, 26 n 6, 49, 52, 209
Morse, Samuel F.B., 16
Morse, Sanford D. (brother), 34, 36-39, 107, 210
Morse, Stephan D. (father), 7, 16, 23 n 1, 49, 51-52, 106-9, 209
Morse, Stephan R. (brother), 83, 210
mortgages: and homesteaders, 93-94, 96, 103, 178; stop and replevin laws, 97; Jacksonian reform for, 98; reform of, 114, 143; in Donnelly's *Golden Bottle*, 148; in Garland's "Up the Coulee," 163
—of Omar Morse: on Fond du Lac farm, 50-51, 102; on Dodge County farm, 61 n 67, 66 n 79, 111, 115-16; on Roscoe Township farm, 69-70, 79, 81, 189; in Pine Island, 214 n 39
"Mortgage Worked the Hardest of Them All, The" 185
Moses, P.H., 59
Muir, John, 40 n 30, 121
Mystery of Metropolisville, The (Eggleston), 120, 151-54
myth, of frontier promise: characterized, 4; plowman as hero of, 4, 7, 10, 19, 95, 121, 122, 128, 129, 130, 137, 138, 186; persistence of, 5; land speculator/moneylender as demon of, 6, 8, 11, 12, 99, 104, 126-27, 147, 164; disillusionment from, 7, 12, 145, 166; paradox of, 9, 95; and perception of fact, 13; materialism of, 15; and American Dream, 18, 109; loss of, 63 n 71; Turner as spokesman of, 101-2; vs. reality, 103; in Cooper's works, 124; Populist revival of, 125; dispossession as countermyth, 126, 137, 138-39, 165, 185-86; patriotism of, 128

Narratives of Noah Harris Letts and Thomas Allen Banning, The, 14, 212 n 3
"New National Anthem," 184
newspapers, satires of frontier myth in, 142-43
Nininger, Minn., 147
nonconformism, on frontier, 37 n 26
Norris, Frank, 93, 171-74, 177
Northern Pacific Railroad, 77

Oates, Joyce Carol, 139
Octopus, The (Norris), 93, 171-74
"Old Settler's Song" (folk song), 137, 141, 167, 186
Oneida, N.Y., 147
Osborn, Almond, 44
O'Tuck, Shay, 62
Owatonna, Minn., 65

Paddock, Elbridge, 66, 116
Paddock, Martha, 66, 116
Page, O.N., 65, 66, 67, 79, 80
Parish Township, pioneering of, 16
Parker, James, 69
Parkman, Francis, 101
pastoralism, 128
Paulding, James K., 129
Penney, Frank, 80

Penney, Minnie Morse (Mary M.; daughter of Omar Morse), 65, 71, 80 n 96, 209
People's Party: emergence of, 7, 12, 14, 94, 178; agrarian policies of, 14, 95, 114, 191; political resistance of, 18, 126, 143-44; Morse as advocate of, 21-22, 94, 182, 192; V.W. Sterling as secretary of, 70 n 84, 174, 177, 201; political platform of, 97; and revival of frontier myth, 125; protest songs of, 138, 184; anti-Semitism of, 146-47; defeat of, 188. *See also* Donnelly, Ignatius; liberalism
People's Party Campaign Book, 184
Perkins, Mr., 80
Peterson, Evelyn Morse (granddaughter of Omar Morse), 16, 215 n 40
Philippine Islands, 197, 198, 200, 208
Philosophical and Political History of the Settlements and Trade of the Europeans in the East and West Indies (Raynal), 128
Pierce, Alzina Morse (sister of Omar Morse), 39, 49, 50, 52 n 50, 210
Pine Island, Minn., 193
Pioneers, The (Cooper), 124
Pioneer's Search for an Ideal Home, A (Judson), 14
Pioneer Women: Voices from the Kansas Frontier (Stratton), 19
Populism (Canovan), 94
Populism (Youngdale), 95
"Populist Heritage and the Intellectual" (Woodward), 191
Populists. *See* People's Party
Porter, Mr., 70
Potter, Dr. Horace C., 61-62, 97, 115, 119, 215 n 41
Pound, Ezra, 146
Poverty and Progress (George), 140
Prairie, The (Cooper), 124, 130
progress: scientific law of, 160, 218 n 57; Omar Morse's views on, 193-94
Progressive Thinker, 194

racism, 217 n 35. *See also* anti-Semitism
railroads: exploitation of land fever by, 12, 94; domination by, 119, 125, 146
Rasselas (Johnson), 131
Raynal, Abbé Guillaume, 128, 131
Redmond Corners (Parma Corners?), N.Y., 40
replevin laws, 97
"Return of Private Smith" (Garland), 165
Rick, Qua, 62 n 69
Rider, O., 41
Ripley, George, 33 n 20
Robb, John, 135
Robinson, Thomas, 77
Rochester, Minn., 57, 133
Rochester, N.Y., 30, 41
Rölvaag, Ole, 21
Roosevelt, Franklin D., 145, 188, 191
Roosevelt, James I., 34 n 21
Roosevelt, Theodore, 145, 191
Roscoe, Minn., 117
Rosendale, Wisc., 46 n 38, 53, 117
Roughing It (Twain), 169

Sabbatarians, 54 n 56
Sampson, William Thomas, 197, 198
Sandburg, Carl, 137
Sandusky, Ohio, 35
Sawyer, Philetus, 96, 98, 105, 109, 212 n 7
Schlissel, Lillian, 19
"seller sold" device, 153
Shannon, Fred, 11, 13, 100, 123
Sheldon, T., 53, 54-55

Simpson, Elizabeth, 16, 24 n 3, 106, 107
Sioux Indians, 61 n 66
Sister Carrie (Dreiser), 121
Smith, Henry Nash, 4, 5, 12, 125, 129, 180
socialism, 148
"Some Recollections of Thomas Pederson," 121
Song of Myself (Whitman), 7
Son of the Middle Border, A (Garland,) 40 n 30, 121
Spanish-American War, 101, 190, 194, 197, 208
Sparta, Wisc., 55
specie: shortage of, 67 n 80, 75 n 90; circular, 97, 98-99, 100
Specimen Days (Whitman), 126
"speculation fever," 49 n 42, 151, 154, 169
Spoil of Office, A (Garland), 166, 168, 186
"Starving to Death on a Government Claim" (folk song), 8, 136, 141, 167, 175, 185
"State of Arkansas" (folk song), 141
Steinbeck, John, 139
Sterling, Alfredine H. Morse (daughter of Omar Morse), 65, 67, 70
Sterling (or Stirling), Mr., 78, 79
Sterling, Victor W., 70, 174, 177, 201
Sterrand, F.R., 50
Stillwater, Minn., 76, 77
Stinson, Mr., 78
stop and replevin laws, 97
Storer, George, 32
Story of My Boyhood and Youth, The (Muir, 1916), 40 n 30, 121
Stratton, Joanna L., 19
Streaks of Squatter Life (Robb), 135-36
supply and demand, law of, 96, 101, 111, 123
Swierenga, Robert, 93, 180, 212 n 5, 219 n 1
Syracuse, N.Y., 30, 32

Tale of Two Nations (Harvey), 146
Theory of the Leisure Class, The (Veblen), 183
Thomas, C.D., 39
Thomas, Harry, 73, 78 n 95
Thomas, Lydia A. Morse (sister of Omar Morse), 28, 73, 76, 78, 210
Thomas, Sammy (grandson), 194
timber companies, exploitation of land fever by, 12
Titan, The (Dreiser), 155
"To a Person Sitting in Darkness" (Twain), 198
Townsend, C., 66
Townsend, Father, 77
Townsend, Peter, 68
Traverse de Sioux Treaty, 61 n 66
"Trip to the Frontier" (Croffut), 142-43
Turner, Frederick Jackson: image of the frontier, 11, 101-2; and role of nature, 125
Twain, Mark, 8, 43 n 34, 120, 127, 133, 168-71, 175, 183, 198
Twitchell, Mr., 69

"Under the Lion's Paw" (Garland), 121, 139, 165
United States, 1830–1850, The (Turner), 11
"Up the Coulee" (Garland), 163-65, 167
utopian novels, 149

Virgin Land (Smith), 4, 12, 180, 215 n 1

wages: inequality of, 27, 200; advantages of, 201. *See also* specie, shortage of

Wahpekuti tribe of Sioux, 61 n 66
Warner, Charles Dudley, 120, 133, 168
Waseca, Minn., 64, 65
Wasioja, Minn., 195
"Wayfaring Stranger" (folk song), 139–40
Welland Canal, 108
Whitman, Walt, 7, 126, 127
Williams, Roger, 37 n 26
Wilton, Minn. 65
Women's Diaries of the Westward Journey (Schlissel), 19
Wood, Grant, 126
Woodward, C. Vann, 191, 220 n 1
Woodward, James, 146
work ethic, 104

Youngdale, James, 94-95

Zoar, Ohio, 147
Zumbrota, Minn., 193
Zury (Kirkland), 120-21, 154-62